The
Inflammation
Cure

Simple steps for reversing

• Heart Disease • Arthritis • Diabetes • Asthma

• Alzheimer's Disease

• Osteoporosis • Other Diseases of Aging

William Joel Meggs, M.D., Ph.D.
with Carol Svec

McGraw·Hill

New York   Chicago   San Francisco   Lisbon   London   Madrid   Mexico City
Milan   New Delhi   San Juan   Seoul   Singapore   Sydney   Toronto

Library of Congress Cataloging-in-Publication Data

Meggs, William Joel.
    The inflammation cure : how to combat the hidden factor behind heart disease,
arthritis, asthma, diabetes, Alzheimer's disease, osteoporosis, and other diseases
of aging / William Joel Meggs with Carol Svec.
        p.   cm.
    Includes index.
    ISBN 0-07-141320-0 (hardcover) — ISBN 0-07-143871-8 (paperback)
    1. Inflammation—Popular works.   2. Chronic diseases—Etiology—Popular
works.   I. Svec, Carol.   II. Title.

RB131.M384   2003
616'.0473—dc21   2003051528

1 2 3 4 5 6 7 8 9 0   DOC/DOC   3 2 1 0 9 8 7 6 5 4

ISBN 0-07-141320-0 (hardcover)
ISBN 0-07-143871-8 (paperback)

McGraw-Hill books are available at special quantity discounts to use as premiums and
sales promotions, or for use in corporate training programs. For more information, please
write to the Director of Special Sales, Professional Publishing, McGraw-Hill, Two Penn
Plaza, New York, NY 10121-2298. Or contact your local bookstore.

This book is printed on acid-free paper.

○

To the loving memory of Philip B. Meggs
Artist, Writer, Designer, Educator, Humanitarian, Humorist
Who wrote great books that will endure
Who touched everyone who admired our postage stamps
Whose unfinished work is everyone's loss
A great husband to Libby
A great father to Andrew and Elizabeth
A great son to Lib and Wallace
The best friend and twin brother a person could possibly have
—William Joel Meggs

To "Billy Lee,"
who knows that the journey
is too short not to have fun along the way.
—Carol Svec

○

CONTENTS

◉

PART I

INFLAMMATION AND YOUR HEALTH

PART II

INFLAMMATION'S DAMAGE

PART III

THE ANTI-INFLAMMATION GAME PLAN

ACKNOWLEDGMENTS

◉

So many people are involved in taking a book from concept to reality. We are indebted to them all. We wholeheartedly thank our editor, Judith McCarthy. This book would never have existed without her vision and guidance. Special thanks also to Jane Dystel, of Dystel & Goderich Literary Management. She's the type of responsive, enthusiastic, and supportive agent most writers think exists only in their dreams. And thanks to Kathy Dennis for smoothly making the manuscript a book.

W.J.M. wishes to thank the many patients I have had the privilege to treat and help over the past two decades, for all you have shared and taught. Thanks to my many physician colleagues and mentors, most notably Drs. Donald Mitchell, Dean Metcalfe, Robert Hoffman, Lewis Goldfrank, and Theron Randolph. Thanks to my Chief of Service, Dr. Nicholas Benson, for your unending support and tolerance of my multifaceted interests and pursuits. Special thanks to my family, Thomas, Josephine, Jerome, Benjamin, Jason, and most especially my wife, Susan Martin Meggs, for your love and support and for tolerating the insanity of writing a book while also working a demanding and more than full-time job.

C.S. thanks Alan Lee Jones and Joanna Jones for their guidance during the early stages of writing, and Sid Kirchheimer for teaching me everything I know about health writing. Thank you also to everyone who made my life a little easier during the writing of this book through their support and encouragement, including Teresa and Jay Lawrence, Ann Agrawal, Marina and Ted Rudisill, Virginia Svec, Rhonda and Chris Sutton, Doris and George Margosian, Wendy and Gene Potkay, Amy and Joe Pellerito, Peter Guzzardi, and Diana Dell. And heartfelt thanks to Bill Svec, the most patient man in the world.

INTRODUCTION

◉

The most powerful concept in disease prevention and treatment today is *inflammation*. If this is the first you're hearing of it, prepare for more. Soon, we'll all be talking about inflammation as easily as we talk about cholesterol, doctors will recommend blood tests to measure the amount of inflammation in your body, and targeted medications will be developed to control its effects. Inflammation may well turn out to be the elusive Holy Grail of medicine—the single phenomenon that holds the key to sickness and health.

Inflammation touches every aspect of our health. In a series of medical breakthroughs, scientists have discovered that inflammation is a common thread linking heart disease, some forms of cancer, diabetes, osteoarthritis, asthma, migraine headaches, Alzheimer's disease, fibromyalgia, periodontal disease, sinusitis, irritable bowel syndrome, inflammatory bowel disease, and chronic fatigue syndrome. Inflammation is related to aging, obesity, stroke, fatigue, depression, and allergic reactions. Inflammation is also part of the process that damages body tissue in multiple sclerosis, rheumatoid arthritis, systemic lupus erythematosus, and other autoimmune diseases.

As part of immunity, inflammation is one of the most basic human processes. The cardinal signs of inflammation—redness, heat, pain, and swelling—are easily perceptible. Every fever, bump, rash, or bruise is the result of inflammation. On a microscopic level, the inflammatory response involves dozens of different chemicals, each performing a specific action. The purpose of inflammation is to limit damage to the body after injury or invasion by foreign organisms, such as bacteria or viruses. Limiting damage sounds good, but problems arise when the body experiences severe or long-term inflammation. It is this type of uncontrolled inflammation that has become the focus of so much research.

For more than two thousand years, doctors have been treating inflammation, but it took a long time for scientists to understand how the process works. Almost everything we know about inflammation has only been learned in the last forty years, when medical technology finally gave scientists a chance to peek into the inner workings of the human body. What they thought was a relatively simple body function turned out to be massively complex, involving many different types of body cells and occurring in multiple stages. Something as simple as being hit on the arm sets in motion a barrage of physiologic effects. Immediately, the body senses trauma and releases several different body chemicals that signal the start of the inflammation process. Blood vessels dilate, getting wider. Small blood vessels called capillaries become leaky, allowing fluid to seep out of the bloodstream and into the surrounding body tissue. If the hit on the arm is severe, you'll get a bump from the accumulation of this leaked fluid. Immune cells become activated, and more chemical messengers are released, which triggers more cells to become involved. It's a circus of activity at the cellular level. For more serious problems, like when the body is invaded by a virus, the process becomes infinitely more complex.

A Multitude of Connections

Even though we still don't know everything there is to know about inflammation, we are finally at a point where we can begin to make sense of what is known and to apply it in our everyday lives. And we owe it all to doctors who recognized the "inflammation connection." Until recently, most inflammation research has been disease-specific, mainly because research scientists tend to specialize in particular areas of medicine. Dentists and periodontists focus on gum disease, cardiologists focus on heart disease, rheumatologists focus on arthritis, and so on. But in the past several years, some scientists took a step back and looked at the research in its entirety. When the artificial boundaries of specialization are ignored, a pattern emerges: inflammation is not disease-specific. It affects the entire body, not just individual body parts. And research has shown that diseases we thought were unrelated are actually intimately linked. Scientists have discovered that there are connections between heart disease and gum disease, between diabetes and thyroid disease, and among obesity *and* depression *and* insomnia *and* chronic fatigue syndrome. This inflammation connection tells us that caring for our health means more than just caring for individual body parts. The same inflammatory factors that cause heart attacks also are suspected to cause stroke, diabetes, gum disease, premature birth, and many other seemingly unrelated disorders. When we treat inflammation in one part of the body, other parts of the body also become healthier.

This inflammation connection makes sense intuitively. For example, think back to the last time you had a cold. The common cold virus takes hold in your nose and causes a local immune reaction that includes a runny nose and inflammation of the nasal passages. Despite the fact that the virus remains in your nose, your entire body can feel tired, heavy, and lethargic. Those symptoms of overall fatigue are a side effect of the inflammation process; the virus is in your nose, but you feel the effects of inflammation everywhere.

So what do we do with this information about the inflammation connection? For starters, we acknowledge the links and use them to prevent diseases or make earlier diagnoses. Take the case of gum disease and heart disease. Because of the strong connection between the two, dentists are starting to play an important role in the early detection of atherosclerosis and prevention of heart attacks. Imagine going to your dentist and getting a referral to a cardiologist! That is happening every day now, thanks to general recognition of the inflammation connection. Ophthalmologists are also getting into the act. Because certain types of eye inflammation are sometimes signs of a larger, bodywide inflammation disorder, such as rheumatoid arthritis or lupus, ophthalmologists are now helping to detect these diseases in their earliest stages, before inflammation has a chance to ravage the body. Cardiologists are beginning to test for blood levels of a substance called C-reactive protein (CRP). A high CRP level means a high level of inflammation and a high risk for the development of atherosclerosis (another inflammation-related disorder). When the inflammation is treated, CRP levels come down and the risk of having a heart attack due to atherosclerosis is lowered. A class of prescription drugs called statins, which are widely used to treat atherosclerosis, works in part by controlling inflammation. These and other anti-inflammatory drugs may be among the first of a vanguard of medications that do nothing less than change the way we live and die.

A Balancing Act

The big question now is how much our health is affected by this connection. Are just certain body systems affected, or the entire body? No one yet knows the answer, but consider the case of a man who was given a powerful anti-inflammatory medication, a corticosteroid, for two weeks to treat a foot disorder. During those two weeks, the foot disorder was cured. In addition, the medication cleared up a mild rash on his head, helped him breathe better despite allergies, and took away the pain in his knees so he could run with his dog for the first time in two years. He had inflammation everywhere, and the anti-inflammatory corticosteroids zapped it all away. If he had gone to a dermatologist, he would have received treatment for his rash; if he had gone to a rheumatologist, he would have received treatment for his knees. But a single anti-inflammatory drug relieved all his seemingly unrelated symptoms simultaneously. Inflammation was the key to all his health woes.

Unfortunately, corticosteroid medications are only a temporary fix, and they can cause serious side effects if used for a long period of time. Remember that first and foremost, the role of inflammation is to protect the body. Corticosteroids suppress the immune reactions that cause inflammation. If we take away the protective side of inflammation, we can fall prey to all those nasty germs that our immune system usually eliminates. This dual nature is what makes treating inflammation so complicated. The same mechanisms that help protect us against foreign invaders can also harm us and cause pain.

The body must constantly balance inflammation and anti-inflammation. Too much inflammation can result in disease and sometimes death—but too little inflammation means a lowered immune function, which can result in disease and sometimes death. The body can overreact to normal cells, mistaking them for foreign invaders, and develop an inflammatory autoimmune disorder—but the body can also underreact to dangerous cellular changes and allow cancer to take hold. Severe inflammation of the brain (which occurs with encephalitis) can cause coma or death. Long-term inflammation, even if it is mild, can alter cellular functioning and cause the body's greatest threats: heart disease and cancer.

So what determines how well the body keeps its inflammation balance? The answer is frustratingly inclusive. Inflammation is influenced by what we eat, how much exercise we get, the level of pollutants in the air we breathe, the toxins in the cleaning products we use and the insecticides we spray, the amount of sleep we get, how much stress we experience, the intensity of our emotions, and the quality of our social relationships. In short, everything we eat, breathe, think, feel, and do has an effect on inflammation.

Even age affects our body's inflammation responses. Ever wonder why your body seemed to "fall apart" after age forty? (If you are not yet forty, ask someone what this feels like!) Inflammation is a part of the reason. Although inflammation issues are important at every age, they become urgent as we get older. Aging is so intertwined with inflammation that scientists have coined the term *inflamm-aging* to refer to changes occurring in the body as we get older that make inflammation more likely. And when inflammation is more likely, disease is also more likely.

It makes sense, then, to consider inflammation control as part of our overall personal health strategy, the way we do weight control. With weight control, however, we understand the basics of what needs to be done—watch calories, count fat grams, get exercise, et cetera, et cetera. But where do you start when you want to try to control inflammation? You start here.

About This Book

The purpose of this book is to explain what causes inflammation, how it is related to disease in the body, and—most important—what steps you can take to minimize your inflammation risk. It was designed to give you the information you need to start making healthy changes immediately.

There are three parts to the book. In Part I, I discuss what inflammation is and how it works to protect or harm the body. At the end of Part I is the Inflammation Risk Quiz, which will analyze your personal risk factors, and then guide you to other chapters based on your individual answers. Part II talks about the inflammation connection—how various diseases and disorders are related to inflammation, and how they might increase your risk for other inflammation-related disorders. Part III provides advice on things you can do to feel better, now as well as in the future. The recommendations include lifestyle changes, medical tests, new anti-inflammatory medications, and hidden causes of inflammation that can be avoided. The Anti-Inflammation Game Plan in Part III gives recommendations for the best ways to prevent or reduce inflammation.

The inflammation connection encompasses all fields of medicine. As research continues, more connections will be discovered and our understanding of what drives inflammation will become more precise. The potential payoff for all this research is tremendous. Once inflammatory processes can be adequately controlled, many of the big killers—heart disease, autoimmune disorders, asthma, and diabetes—may be as easy to treat as a common headache. Some diseases may become entirely preventable. Until then, there are important steps each of us can take to assure ourselves the longest, healthiest life possible, and that's what this book is all about.

My Personal Connection

Inflammation brought me to medicine and to this book. Years ago, someone very dear to me developed a horrible and mysterious disease. Attacks were characterized by fevers as high as 105 degrees Fahrenheit, which led to after-hours emergency visits with no cause found. A virus, they said. Profound weakness wracked her body, and often she could not get out of bed for several days in a row. Aching muscles and fatigue became disabling. The attacks waxed and waned but came with increasing frequency. A virus, a virus, a virus, we heard over and over again.

It was not until I studied medicine that I realized the diagnosis missed by so many practitioners was polymyositis, meaning "many muscles inflamed." Sooner or later, if the disease had progressed, she would have seen a specialist and the correct diagnosis would have been made. But the disease did not progress because of the timely appearance into our lives of Dr. Donald Mitchell.

Dr. Mitchell was a semiretired dermatologist who came to believe over years of practice that inflamed skin—dermatitis—did not occur without a cause. He broke with his colleagues who treated dermatitis with creams and pills that suppressed inflammation. His approach was to exhaust all avenues to find something that was triggering the inflammation. For each of his patients, he looked for those substances in food, air, and water. He manipulated patients' environments, put them on elimination diets, and had them live in rooms cleansed of air pollutants. Sometimes he hit it big and the dermatitis would go away with some simple change in a person's diet or lifestyle.

Over time, Dr. Mitchell noted that things other than dermatitis could improve with his elimination routines. Chronic sinus congestion would clear, or arthritis would get better, or mood would improve. He was the dermatology consultant at a mental hospital, and once he put a woman with intractable catatonia on an elimination diet for her dermatitis. To his amazement, her mental condition improved. As I followed Dr. Mitchell on his rounds and learned of his practice, it aroused both my scientific curiosity and my desire to help people like he did.

The case of polymyositis mentioned above turned out to be a simple one for Dr. Mitchell. After asking careful questions about dietary habits, his first guess was that some sort of wheat intolerance was triggering the inflammation of muscles. His patient was told to eliminate wheat for five days, then eat a big helping of wheat. Her weakness improved while not eating wheat, then came back with a vengeance after eating the big serving. The polymyositis went into complete remission by avoiding one simple food.

The thought of abandoning a scientific career and pursuing medicine seemed totally impractical until a colleague told me about a special M.D. degree program for Ph.D. scientists at the University of Miami. At that time, conditions for scientific careers were dismal in this country, while there was a shortage of physicians. Dr. Bill Herrington, a renegade hematologist, proposed to solve both problems by designing a very successful special program for Ph.D. scientists to get medical degrees by running twice as hard for half as long as a normal medical student. Soon after hearing of this program, I found myself in Miami trying to dissect a human heart instead of a law of nature.

While I was studying medicine, it became crystal clear that the central theme in almost all diseases was inflammation. Even the names of many diseases—arthritis, vasculitis, sinusitis—carry the *-itis* suffix, which means "inflammation." I could not accept that inflammation just happened, without some cause or trigger, though this was rarely addressed in the medical texts.

After receiving my medical degree, I trained in internal medicine at the University of Rochester and completed a fellowship in allergy and immunology at the National Institutes of Health in Bethesda, Maryland. Subsequently, I was privileged to become certified in emergency medicine and to complete a fellowship in medical toxicology at the New York City Poison Center and Bellevue Hospital in New York, putting me in a unique position to explore the relationships between immunology, toxicology, and inflammation.

It is now over twenty years since I began my study of medicine. At that time many physicians were hostile to the notion that diet, lifestyle, and environmental exposures could cause disease. I heard a pulmonologist teaching residents and medical students to never refer their patients to allergists because environmental factors don't cause asthma attacks. Once a rheumatologist played show-and-tell and brought his patients with various joint diseases to a seminar for medical students. One student in all seriousness asked a patient with gout if there were any foods that made his gout flare. The rheumatologist interrupted to state that if his patients took the pills he prescribed they could eat anything they damn well pleased. He never heard his patient answer that every time he drank red wine or ate steak he got an attack of gout, even while taking his pills.

One evening I did an admission history and physical examination of a farmer with panniculitis, which is inflammation of the fatty tissue beneath the skin, a horribly painful condition. He explained to me that he had finally figured out the cause of his panniculitis. Every spring when he started working with pesticides, the condition appeared and persisted until spraying was completed for the season. When

I reported the patient's thoughts at rounds the next morning, the attending physician scoffed at me that what I was saying was ridiculous. "Some [stupid] people even claim that drugs can cause panniculitis," he chided, as if that was the most ridiculous thought he had ever heard. The farmer became a tractor mechanic and had no further attacks of panniculitis.

In spite of all the money we spend on health care, medications, and medical research, we as a nation are in many respects sicker than we were when I began to study and then practice medicine. In great part, this is due to the successes of medicine. Yesteryear's fatal diseases, such as diabetes, coronary artery disease, and renal failure, have become expensive health maintenance projects. Our population has aged. There are trends toward more and more asthma, obesity, diabetes, depression, osteoarthritis, and Alzheimer's disease. Our knowledge base has greatly expanded, particularly in terms of our knowledge of inflammation and how it cuts across all medical specialties and all diseases.

The eminent rheumatologist Dr. Michelle Hooper and I were residents together in an intensive care unit back in 1979. Our supervisor was a cardiologist who ridiculed us when he heard that Michelle and I had both signed up to do fellowships in immunology. Like two squawky birds, we chided back. "Dave," we ridiculed, "when all is said and done, research will show that your disease, coronary artery disease, is all about immunology and inflammation." Whether clairvoyant or lucky guessers, we hit the nail on the head. Emerging knowledge of the role of inflammation in coronary artery disease, asthma, Alzheimer's disease, and a host of others will be followed by expansion of our knowledge about what causes inflammation and how it can be prevented.

We are on the cusp of a great change in the way medicine is practiced. Diet, lifestyle, and environmental exposures interact with genes and even pure luck to determine health and disease. Though more research is needed and the final answers are not in, I am compelled to write this book now for those who want to know more about inflammation, its role in health and disease, and things that can be done to reduce the risk of inflammatory diseases taking over their bodies, with attendant pain, suffering, and premature death.

DISCLAIMER

◉

The information in this book is not intended to be a substitute for the medical advice of a physician. Readers should consult with their doctors in all matters relating to health and for treatment of their medical problems. Although every effort has been made to ensure that all information is presented accurately in this book, the ultimate responsibility for proper medical treatment rests with the prescribing physician. Neither the publisher nor the authors take any responsibility for errors or for any possible consequences arising from the use of information contained here.

PART I

INFLAMMATION AND YOUR HEALTH

I

THE INFLAMMATION CONNECTION

◉

Inflammation is truly a matter of life and death. Inflammation keeps us alive, and inflammation ultimately kills us. Without inflammation, humans would die shortly after birth, our bodies consumed by a host of bacteria, fungi, and viruses. But inflammation also underlies most diseases that afflict humanity. Just as inflammation destroys germs, it can destroy the organs of our bodies, from blood vessels to hearts to lungs and brains.

Inflammation is a perfect example of yin-yang synergy working at the level of biology. Long-term health depends on keeping pro-inflammatory and anti-inflammatory forces in balance. Yet most people outside of the healing professions know very little about this all-important process. If you ask ten different people to define inflammation, you'll likely get ten different answers. What individuals know depends almost entirely on how they've interpreted comments from their own physicians after receiving a diagnosis of an inflammation-related disease.

Indeed, in the doctor's office, inflammation can look very different in different patients. Common examples of inflammation include a swollen wrist, a sore throat, a burning stomach, an itchy rash, a runny nose, infected cuts, blisters, bunions, bleeding gums, puffy feet, and tender joints. Rheumatoid arthritis, osteoarthritis, systemic lupus erythematosus, multiple sclerosis, inflammatory bowel disease, emphysema, type 1 diabetes mellitus, gingivitis, and ulcers are all primarily inflammatory disorders. Migraine, asthma, allergies, and irritable bowel syndrome are all caused by extreme inflammation reactions by the body. Inflammation is related to depression, lethargy, and fatigue. Some cancers, atherosclerosis, heart disease, stroke, Alzheimer's disease, and type 2 diabetes mellitus have been shown to be caused—at least in part—by inflammation. Recently, inflammation has even been implicated in causing obesity and aging itself.

What this means is that in order to take advantage of everything that medical science has to offer, in order to live the longest, healthiest life possible, we all need to become savvy about inflammation. We need medical specialists to help us treat and manage particular diseases, but we also need to be aware of the pervasive nature of inflammation and strive to keep its effects in our bodies in balance. If we know what causes and reduces inflammation, then we'll also know how to modify those factors. We'll know how to control or manage inflammatory diseases we may already be facing, and we'll know what to do to lower our individual risk for developing inflammation-related disorders.

WHOLE-BODY DISEASE

Although the medical community has long understood the functions of inflammation and its role in causing or sustaining certain diseases, scientists are only now beginning to grasp the devastating impact inflammation can have on the entire body. As individuals, we are not merely a collection of organs held together by skin. Our bodies are complex systems in which every cell interacts and communicates and coordinates activities with every other cell in the body. The oxygen that you inhale into your lungs is carried by the bloodstream to nourish cells in your brain, fingers, toes, stomach, skin, and bones. The music that reaches your ears excites nerve cells in your brain, which in turn trigger the release of body chemicals that can influence your mood. The protein-rich foods you eat are broken down into smaller components that are used to create or repair cells throughout your body. Similarly, the effects of inflammation in one part of the body can have repercussions on other parts of the body.

This whole-body concept of inflammation reaction seems logical, and medical studies are confirming that inflammation indeed has widespread effects in the body. The exact causes and physiologic mechanisms underlying the connections are still unknown, but scientists can no longer think of inflammation strictly as a local phenomenon. Inflammation is global. This means that we can no longer accept that inflammation in one part of the body is somehow isolated from every other part of the body. If you release a drop of ink in a glass of water, the color starts out intensely in one place, but eventually all the water will be lightly tinted. Similarly, if inflammation starts out affecting one part of the body, the associated physiologic chemicals will be present in other parts of the body as well. Which body parts are affected, how much damage is done, and who is most susceptible are questions that still need to be answered.

Solid evidence for the inflammation connection became available in the 1990s, although all the discoveries thus far fall in the realm of correlation. This means that researchers discover that Factor X is somehow related to Factor Y, but the exact relationship isn't known. Does Factor X cause Factor Y, or does Factor Y cause Factor X, or is there some other factor that causes both Factor X and Factor Y to occur simultaneously? For example, one clear discovery is that people with inflammation of the gums (periodontal disease) are at greater risk of having atherosclerosis, a condition in which chronic inflammation causes the walls of the arteries to become thick and stiff from a buildup of plaque. So people with gum inflammation also have inflammation in their arteries. Which came first? Does gum inflammation lead to artery inflammation, or does artery inflammation lead to gum inflammation? Or perhaps there is another as-yet-undiscovered environmental, genetic, or other factor that increases inflammation in both gum and arteries. This is not an idle question. Atherosclerosis increases the risk of heart attack and death. If we understand where the inflammation starts, we have the potential to prevent that inflammation from occurring in the first place, or to interrupt the inflammation before it leads to disease. If it were true that gum inflammation leads to artery inflammation, then oral hygiene would become a greater priority, cardiologists would provide free samples of dental floss, and pharmaceutical companies would race to find a cure for periodontal disease.

WEB OF CONNECTIONS

Chances are that none of the causal connections will be so easily isolated. Inflammation involves hundreds of different biological and chemical processes and has unexpected effects on unexpected organs. Consider that women with periodontal disease have a greater risk of giving birth to a preterm, underweight baby than women without periodontal disease. There are several theories about why this might be. In this case, we know that giving birth to a preterm baby doesn't cause gum disease—but can gum disease lead to some alteration that eventually causes premature labor? Some scientists suggest that perhaps there are toxins released from bacteria in the mouth that affect the production of pregnancy-related hormones. Another hypothesis is that cytokines (body chemicals that are involved in inflammation) move from the mouth to circulate in the bloodstream and may then enter the placenta to affect pregnancy. Another possibility is that there is another factor (or set of factors) causing both gum disease and problems in pregnancy.

Now consider that periodontal disease is also related to diabetes. People with diabetes are more likely to have gum inflammation than people without diabetes. Additionally, people with diabetes who maintain good control of their blood sugar have lower levels of periodontal disease than those who have poor control of their blood sugar. Again, the causal relationship between the two is unknown, but they are related.

So—we know that gum disease is related to heart disease, gum disease is related to preterm delivery, and gum disease is related to diabetes.

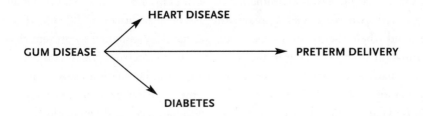

But when we dig a little deeper into the medical literature, we find that even more connections exist. For example, researchers have reported that women who give birth to preterm babies have an increased risk of heart disease later in life (heart disease related to preterm delivery), that women with diabetes are more likely than women without diabetes to give birth to preterm babies (diabetes related to preterm delivery), and that there is a strong relationship between heart disease and diabetes—compared with healthy people, those with heart disease are more likely to develop diabetes, and those with diabetes are more likely to develop heart disease. It becomes clear, then, that the relationships among all four of these health problems are multidirectional and complex.

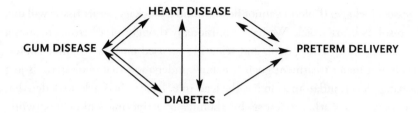

The relationships exist, and inflammation, with all its chemical mediators, is a common factor. Again, medical science does not yet know how one disorder is tied to another. When that information is revealed, it will provide a starting point for the development of targeted treatment plans and medications. But for the average person, the questions of *why* and *how* the connections occur are less important than simply understanding *that* they occur. We all know that there is a connection between cloudy skies and rain. We don't need to understand everything about weather patterns, convections, thermals, and earth rotation to appreciate that it is more likely to rain on a cloudy day than a sunny day. Once we understand that the connection exists, we can take steps to avoid getting wet, such as to carry an umbrella on cloudy days. Similarly, if we understand that the inflammation connection exists without knowing the details of how it works, we can still take steps to reduce dangerous levels of inflammation in our bodies and not allow a chain reaction of illnesses to take hold.

THE INFLAMMATION RISK

So then the question becomes: who needs to worry about inflammation? The easy answer is that we all do. Inflammatory disorders are very common, and we will all eventually experience one or more major inflammation-related disease. But there are groups of people who will benefit most from taking immediate action to control inflammation:

1. **Anyone with high cholesterol, high blood pressure, or any indication of heart disease.** One of the strongest disease connections discovered so far is the relationship of inflammation to heart disease—specifically, atherosclerosis, the disease responsible for more deaths worldwide than any other single cause. People with atherosclerosis have a buildup of plaque in their arteries, which can eventually lead to

blood vessel blockage. If blood cannot flow around a blockage, heart tissue will die, and the result is heart attack. We have traditionally thought of atherosclerosis as a problem of too much cholesterol, and scientists focused on how to lower cholesterol levels as a major treatment goal. It is now understood that cholesterol is just a supporting player; inflammation has the lead role. Researchers acknowledge that inflammation causes atherosclerosis by chemically attracting leukocytes (white blood cells), low-density lipoprotein (LDL) cholesterol, and platelets (cell fragments in the blood that form clots) to the artery walls. The buildup of these substances is called plaque. As the plaque accumulates, it puts more strain on the arteries, creating more damage, which in turn results in more inflammation. Unless the cycle is broken, heart disease is the inevitable end. (The role of inflammation in atherosclerosis and heart disease is discussed further in Chapter 4.)

2. **Anyone with diabetes.** Scientists have long understood that type 1 diabetes is caused by an autoimmune inflammatory reaction that attacks and destroys the insulin producing cells of the pancreas. Recent studies suggest that type 2 diabetes may also be related to inflammation. In a large-scale study in Scotland, researchers found that high levels of an inflammatory marker called C-reactive protein predicted the development of type 2 diabetes within five years. In another study, reported by researchers in North Carolina, people with higher numbers of inflammation-related white blood cells (although still within the normal range) had a higher risk of developing type 2 diabetes than those with lower numbers. It is entirely possible that many cases of type 2 diabetes could be prevented by controlling inflammation processes. (The role of inflammation in diabetes is discussed further in Chapter 4.)

3. **Anyone who is overweight.** It is not entirely surprising that diabetes would be related to inflammation because we know that type 2 diabetes is related to obesity. Fat cells produce inflammatory chemicals, and weight loss reduces the overall amount of inflammation in the body. Excess weight itself, then, creates an additional inflammatory burden on the body. This connection explains why people who are overweight are at higher risk of developing heart disease and type 2 diabetes. (For more information about the relation of weight and inflammation, see Chapter 6.)

4. **Anyone with a family history of heart disease, stroke, diabetes, or Alzheimer's disease.** These disorders have been shown to have a strong hereditary

component. The major current hypothesis is that some people are genetically predisposed to develop these diseases. Being predisposed to a particular disease doesn't mean that you are guaranteed to get sick; some trigger factor is usually also necessary. So, for example, people with a family history of heart disease can greatly reduce their risk of developing heart-related problems by exercising regularly, maintaining a lower body weight, and avoiding smoking—in other words, by following an anti-inflammatory lifestyle. By reducing the number of inflammation triggers in their lives, people with a genetic risk for these diseases may be able to prevent the diseases entirely. (For more information on anti-inflammatory lifestyle changes, see Chapters 9 through 12.)

5. **Anyone with an autoimmune disorder, such as rheumatoid arthritis, lupus, or multiple sclerosis.** Autoimmune disorders arise from out-of-control inflammation reactions. The body mistakenly targets normal body tissue for destruction, the same way it would target and destroy an invading virus or rogue cancer cell. These disorders are marked by long-term, severe inflammation. It is not surprising that people with an autoimmune disorder are at risk for developing other inflammation-related disorders—the inflammation reaction seemingly overflows, affecting different parts of the body. For example, studies have shown that compared with healthy people, those with rheumatoid arthritis or systemic lupus erythematosus have a higher risk of cardiovascular disease, those with multiple sclerosis have a higher risk of also having type 1 diabetes, and those with lupus or Sjogren's syndrome have a higher risk of developing an autoimmune thyroid disease. Although the inflammation-reducing suggestions in this book will not cure an autoimmune disorder, they may help reduce the risk of developing some of the other common inflammatory disorders, such as atherosclerosis. (For more information about autoimmune disorders, see Chapter 7.)

6. **Anyone with inflamed gums or periodontal disease.** So many physical signs of inflammation are hidden from us. Without special medical equipment, we cannot physically see the buildup of plaque in our arteries, inflamed liver cells, or the crowd of inflammation-related chemicals in our blood. We can, however, see our gums. Our gums are the most visible indicator of an inflammation imbalance in our bodies, and we would be wise to pay attention. Something as simple as psychological stress in our lives can affect the progression of gum disease, which, as discussed earlier, is related to heart disease, diabetes, and other inflammatory disorders. (For more information about gum disease, see Chapter 4.)

7. **Anyone who feels tired or fatigued all the time.** Many people are frustrated because they feel tired all the time, but upon medical examination, their doctors cannot find anything wrong with them. Where there is fatigue, there is inflammation. It may be due to a complex, as-yet-undiagnosed condition, or it may be chronic, low-level inflammation that is just beginning to do physical damage. Reducing inflammation factors will increase energy levels and perhaps prevent more serious disease from developing. (The role of inflammation in fatigue is discussed further in Chapter 6.)

8. **Anyone over age forty.** Along with all the familiar changes associated with aging, our bodies' responses to insult and inflammation also change. Chronic whole-body (systemic) inflammation is associated with an increased risk of dying, no matter what the cause. And unfortunately, our bodies become increasingly primed for inflammation as we get older because we tend to produce more pro-inflammatory chemicals and fewer anti-inflammatory chemicals. This means that inflammation becomes more likely as we age. These types of aging changes occur even in people who demonstrate "successful aging"—those who have remained healthy and vital into extreme old age. Scientists believe that the changes in aging are not so much a deterioration of the inflammatory process as a remodeling of a system that learns to adapt to changes required for successful aging. By understanding what changes occur in aging and how to adapt our behavior in response to those changes, we will be better able to maintain optimal health. Further, by controlling inflammation through lifestyle changes or medications, we may be able to delay or avoid many of the factors that make us old before our time. Getting older is inevitable, but physical degradation can be delayed. (Inflammation and aging are discussed in Chapter 8.)

9. **Anyone who lives or works in an inflammatory environment.** Over the past two decades, new knowledge has been gained about how certain environments promote the development of inflammation in our bodies. Sick buildings are unhealthy environments that promote inflammation. These buildings have poor ventilation, allowing complex mixtures of organic chemicals such as solvents, fragrances, cleaning products, and pesticides to build up in the indoor air and promote inflammation. (For more information about environmental causes of inflammation, see Chapter 10.)

10. **Anyone suffering from depression or anxiety.** Systemic lupus erythematosus (also known as SLE, or lupus) is a disease with a particular pattern of

inflammation affecting joints, skin, and other organs. One of the clinical diagnostic criteria of lupus was a prior episode of depression or psychosis. Inflammation of the arteries of the brain, and perhaps even the brain itself, is thought to lead to psychiatric disorders in people with lupus. There is also a strong association between allergy, another inflammation-related disease, and depression. And anti-inflammatory medications are currently being tested in clinical trials as a new treatment for depression. (For more information about the relationships between inflammation and depression, see Chapter 6.)

THE INFLAMMATION CURE

We cannot eradicate inflammation in the body. We wouldn't want to. Inflammation is a key component of the immune system, which protects us from dangerous infections and heals our injuries. But inflammation processes can and do malfunction. Why? Sometimes our genes cause our immune systems to overreact, which is why autoimmune disorders often run in families. Sometimes it is our own behavior. Good health is a blessing that we often take for granted. As human beings, we all sometimes make unhealthy food choices, eat too much, drink too much alcohol, stay out too late, sleep too little, and avoid exercise. The immediate changes in our bodies because of this behavior are barely noticeable. Over the long run, however, we are setting the stage for chronic inflammation, which causes the changes in our bodies that will eventually kill us.

Sometimes the inflammation process short-circuits because of external factors. The environment we live in now is not the same environment of a hundred years ago, let alone the hundreds of thousands of years ago when *Homo sapiens* first evolved. The contaminants in the air we breathe and the water we drink, the additives in the foods we eat, and the atmospheric changes caused by modern technology all have an effect on inflammation in our bodies. In the United States, there is currently an epidemic of childhood asthma (an inflammatory disease of the lungs). Air pollution—including air particulates, diesel exhaust particles, and respiratory irritants such as ozone—is at least one of the causes. There is also an epidemic of childhood obesity, thought to be due to lifestyle factors. You don't have to look too deeply into the medical literature to discover that children who are overweight have a greater risk of developing asthma. Could this be another example of an inflammation connection? Could the low-grade chronic inflammation caused by excess weight make children more susceptible to air pollution, and thereby trigger asthma? What other inflammation-related disorders are these children headed for? The inflammation connection would say that their chronic inflammation due to being overweight would eventually cause our children to develop heart disease and type 2 diabetes. Indeed, today a frightening number of U.S. children are developing type 2 diabetes, a disorder formerly known as adult-onset diabetes because it was rarely seen in children.

We live in an environment that sets us up for inflammation. To live the healthiest life possible, we need to adapt. Forty years ago, almost no one used sunscreen products. Today, many people apply sunscreen daily because we've learned the truth about the damage the sun can do to skin, and because the world is different than it was forty years ago. The ozone layer has deteriorated, so an hour of sun is more dangerous today than it was in the mid-twentieth century. We adapted. In the same way, we need to think differently about inflammation by understanding the connections and applying the inflammation cure.

I am not talking about stopping all inflammation in the body, nor about preventing or curing all diseases. The inflammation cure works on the principle of lowering individual risk of disease by changing the factors that are within our power. It's about modifying the little factors in our lives as a way of offsetting the uncontrollable factors in the environment. It's about being aware of the connections among diseases so that we will know when our bodies are out of balance, and then focusing our attention to reestablish control. It's about acknowledging that the body is an integrated system that sometimes malfunctions. Reducing inflammation may be the single best way you can help to set it right again.

2

THE BODY'S ALARM SYSTEM

⊙

When a fire alarm goes off in a burning building, it sets in motion a sequence of events designed to save lives and prevent damage to the structure. Once the alarm is triggered, residents become aware of the danger and evacuate the building. Firefighters are notified of the location and severity of the blaze and speed to the scene with the appropriate equipment. If the fire is small and contained, a fire extinguisher or hose may be enough to put it out; if the fire is large, multiple engine companies may be called to the scene. Rescues may require battering down doors or breaking windows—damage well worth the cost when the outcome is more lives saved.

The body has a similar alarm system. When the body senses danger from physical trauma or invasion of microbes, it sets in motion a sequence of events designed to contain the danger and protect itself from additional harm. These events make up the inflammatory process. Inflamed tissue has an enhanced ability to kill invading microorganisms (such as bacteria, fungi, viruses, or parasites), and inflammation sets the stage for repair of damaged tissue. When appropriately activated, inflammation acts as a defense against injury or infection.

The key phrase, however, is *when appropriately activated.* To return to the fire alarm example, we understand that a faulty alarm system can create major problems. If a fire is raging but the alarm doesn't sound, the building will burn to the ground. Alternatively, if the alarm sounds even when there is no fire, there are different problems. If firefighters respond to a false alarm with the same energy and determination as if there were a real fire, doors may be battered down, windows may be broken, and hoses may flood the building in an attempt to put out the non-existent fire.

Something similar happens in the human body. If our immune system fails to send a signal for help, viruses or bacteria can create havoc in a defenseless body. And if the immune alarm rings without true cause, the body's defenses against a nonexistent threat can do great harm. This is, in fact, what is believed to happen with autoimmune disorders, such as lupus or rheumatoid arthritis. The body mistakenly identifies normal body tissue as foreign and calls for a full immune defense. In the process of wiping out this imagined enemy, portions of the healthy body are destroyed. The key factor in all these reactions is inflammation.

WHAT IS INFLAMMATION?

Inflammation is an abnormal state of living tissue that occurs in reaction to an insult or injury to the body. It is a body process so basic and obvious to the naked eye that the ancient Egyptians described inflammation in papyrus scrolls. The Greek physician Hippocrates understood and described inflammation in association with infected wounds. But the most complete early writing about inflammation occurred about two thousand years ago. In his book *De Medicina (On Medicine)*, the Roman physician Aulus Cornelius Celsus succinctly described inflammation with his four cardinal signs: *rubor* (redness), *tumor* (swelling), *calore* (heat), and *dolore* (pain). This description holds up today (although we've added quite a few details to this basic knowledge). Inflamed tissue, whether on the surface or internal to the body, is red, swollen, hot, and painful.

Inflammation is set off by insult or injury to the body, and it turns out that the body can be pretty sensitive to insults. Inflammation can occur in reaction to infections, physical injuries, exposure to chemicals and allergens, stretching and manipulation of body tissue, burns, lacerations, and contusions. Sometimes substances occurring naturally in one's own body can trigger inflammation, in what is called autoimmunity. And under the right circumstances, stress or other emotional reactions may trigger inflammation in some people.

Not only can just about any provocation set off inflammation, but virtually any tissue or organ can be inflamed. In medicine, the suffix *-itis* is added to words to denote inflammation of the organ or tissue represented by that word. So anytime

TABLE 2-1: TERMINOLOGY TO DESCRIBE INFLAMMATION OF VARIOUS BODY PARTS

arthro- = joint	*arthritis* = inflamed joints
broncho- = bronchial tubes	*bronchitis* = inflammation of the bronchial tubes
cardiac = heart	*carditis* = inflammation of the heart
cerebro- = brain	*cerebritis* = inflammation of the brain
choleo- = gallbladder	*cholecystitis* = inflamed gallbladder
conjunctiva = outer lining of the eye	*conjunctivitis* = inflammation of the outer lining of the of the eye
dermis = skin	*dermatitis* = inflamed skin
gastric = stomach	*gastritis* = inflammation of the lining of the stomach
hepato- = liver	*hepatitis* = inflamed liver
myo- = muscle	*myositis* = inflamed muscle
nephro- = kidney	*nephritis* = inflamed kidney
neuro- = nerve	*neuritis* = inflamed nerves
osteo- = bone	*osteitis* = inflamed bone
periodontal = gums	*periodontitis* = inflamed gums
pneumo- = lung	*pneumonitis* = inflamed lung
salpingo = fallopian tubes	*salpingitis* = inflamed fallopian tubes
vagina = vagina	*vaginitis* = inflammation of the vagina
vascular = blood vessel	*vasculitis* = inflamed blood vessels

you see a word that ends in *-itis*, the subject is inflammation. For example, the Greek word *rhino* refers to nose, so the word *rhinitis* refers to inflammation (of the inner lining) of the nose. *Arthro-* refers to joints, so *arthritis* refers to inflammation of the joints. A person with arthritis has joints that are painful and swollen, and which can also be red and hot. Table 2-1 lists the medical terms for different body parts, along with the word that describes inflammation of that part.

Pain is closely related to inflammation. Even the lightest touch can cause severe pain in inflamed tissue. This is one of the reasons doctors squeeze and poke and prod at various locations of your body when you are sick. They are trying to locate potential sites of inflammation. In medicine, the suffix *-algia* means "pain." Hence, *arthralgia* means "pain in a joint." A person with *arthritis* (inflammation of the joints) has *arthralgia* (pain in the joints), but there are other causes of arthralgias in addition to inflammation.

TRIGGERING INFLAMMATION

Inflammation can be triggered by both the immune system and the nervous system. The immune system is an organ system that is scattered throughout the body. The various cells of the immune system are on high alert, wandering the body, constantly looking for invading germs, viruses, fungi, or tiny tumors to attack and destroy. The immune system stores a virtual "most-wanted list" of dangerous proteins. When one of these villain proteins is encountered, immune cells release messenger chemicals that lead to inflammation.

Inflammation triggered by the nervous system is called neurogenic inflammation. There are certain types of nerve fibers called sensory nerve C-fibers, which run throughout our bodies, especially in the skin, the linings of the airway, the gastrointestinal tract, and the urogenital tract. When these types of nerves are stimulated, they release chemicals that trigger inflammation in the tissue. Chemicals, physical stress, or mechanical manipulation (pushing or pressing on the nerve) are all capable of causing inflammation this way. So if you were to physically stress a nerve in your hand by applying extreme heat, for example, that part of your hand would become inflamed.

Neurogenic inflammation can also result from central nervous system stimulation. Here, an electrical signal travels from the central nervous system (the brain and spinal cord) to a remote body part to produce inflammation. For example, asthma is a condition in which the bronchial tubes in the lung are inflamed. We recognize that breathing in chemicals or pollen can trigger asthma by activating immune cells in the airway. But emotional stress can also trigger asthma when nerve signals are sent from the brain to the bronchial tubes, causing them to become inflamed. I saw an example of this while I was working as an emergency physician in Washington, D.C. (a town known for its rabid love of the Washington Redskins football team). I had to resuscitate a man with asthma who abruptly went into respiratory failure during the fourth quarter of a hotly contested Redskins–Cowboys game. After he regained the ability to talk, he told me, "I just got too excited."

PHYSICAL CHANGES DURING INFLAMMATION

When inflammation is triggered, certain basic physiologic changes occur, all signaled by the release of chemical messengers. First, the diameter of blood vessels in the area of the inflammation is increased. The walls of blood vessels contain smooth muscle cells that expand and contract to change the size of the blood vessels. When blood vessels expand and get wider, more blood can flow to the inflamed tissue. This increased blood flow is why inflamed tissue appears red and feels warm. Greater blood flow means more immune cells can reach the area to fight infection, and greater amounts of simple sugar (glucose) and oxygen are available to nourish cells of the inflamed tissue.

Inflamed skin blanches, or turns white, when it is touched. This is because a finger can exert enough pressure to block the blood flow to the tissue. Most of us have seen this after a mild sunburn. When you apply firm pressure with your finger and then lift the finger away, you see a white spot where the finger was pressing. This white spot rapidly becomes red again as the pressure is released and blood flow returns to the tissue.

A second inflammation-related change is that blood vessels in the area of inflammation become leaky, and fluid from the bloodstream leaks out into body tissues. Capillaries, the tiniest blood vessels, are made of a single lining of cells called endothelial cells. In normal tissue, these cells are joined together so tightly that they form a tube to carry blood. In response to chemical messengers released during inflammation, endothelial cells contract, or become smaller. As the cells shrink, the junctions between them open wide enough to let fluid escape from the bloodstream into the tissues. The fluid contains proteins, such as clotting factors and antibodies, that can help protect the tissue. Inflamed tissue becomes swollen because of an accumulation of this fluid that leaked from the capillaries, and the pressure of this additional fluid can cause pain.

When this system malfunctions, the results can be horrifying. A few years ago, at the Brody School of Medicine, where I currently teach, we treated a woman who was admitted to the hospital with a rare and unusual disorder called capillary leak syndrome. Every now and then, capillaries all over the woman's body would open up and start leaking for no apparent reason. Fluid would stream from her blood into all the tissues of her body. Her entire body would swell, and her blood pressure would drop into the range of cardiovascular shock. After multiple episodes, the patient noted that the leak occurred whenever she ate pork. In her case, the leak was induced by a strange and unusual inflammation reaction to pork, and by avoiding pork she greatly reduced her number of attacks.

In really bad cases of inflammation—for example, when the blood vessels themselves are inflamed—leakage is so bad that the gaps between endothelial cells become big enough for red blood cells to leak into the tissue. In these cases, pressure from a finger will not be enough to force the red blood cells away, so the inflamed skin will not blanch when pressed. Nonblanching rashes can be a dangerous sign, quite often heralding severe disease, such as vasculitis (inflammation of the blood vessels) or meningococcal sepsis (a severe bacterial infection).

A third effect of inflammation is that fluids can ooze from the inflamed tissues into body cavities. This fluid can be thin and watery, or thick and white. Thin, watery fluid is the liquid part of the blood (serous fluid), without red or white blood cells. This is the type of fluid you might see in a blister. The thick, white fluid is known as pus. Pus is white because it is loaded with white blood cells. These white blood cells, also known as leukocytes, come from the bloodstream and leak out of the capillaries. Their job is to fight infection by killing pathogens (bacteria, viruses, or fungi) and to aid in healing by detoxifying body tissue that has been damaged by injury.

Of course, if this were all there was to inflammation, there would be no need to write this book. It would be a simple case of the body healing itself. But with dozens of cellular and chemical factors, all of which have specific actions that need to be coordinated with all the other body processes, the alarm system is bound to malfunction. And when things go wrong in the human body, somebody suffers.

SYSTEM FAILURE

Immune system failure can be dramatic. Sometimes the system loses the ability to respond to attacks. The most infamous disease that strips away a person's ability to destroy germs is the acquired immunodeficiency syndrome (AIDS). The virus that causes AIDS has an appetite for certain cells that control the immune response. People with AIDS can end up with no immune system to ward off infection, leaving them defenseless while bombarded by a variety of fungi, viruses, and parasites that a healthy person's immune system would easily kill.

Missing even a single tiny piece of the immune response can also lead to a system malfunction. For example, there are a dozen proteins in human blood called complement proteins. Complement proteins exist in the blood, but they sit idle, not really doing much until the system gets turned on by an infection. Then these proteins are activated in sequence to form a large protein structure called the membrane attack complex, which looks like a tube. This tube attaches to the surface of invading cells and punches holes in them. Water rushes into the holes and, just like a balloon that is overinflated, the cells swell up and burst. Missing just one of these complement proteins means that the membrane attack complex can't form properly, and the body can fall victim to serious bacterial infections.

Malfunctions also can occur when the body becomes tricked or confused. Two classic examples are autoimmune disorders and allergies. When foreign proteins and pathogens get into our bodies, the inflammation process signals specialized cells to search out and kill these invaders. As these cells roam through our bodies looking for intruders, they challenge every cell they encounter and ask: are you *self* or *other*, friend or foe? If the challenged cells don't know the passwords, they are considered intruders and destroyed. The passwords are, in fact, proteins on the surface of our cells that are unique to each individual (with the exception of identical twins, identical triplets, et cetera). The reason people with organ transplants have to take powerful drugs to suppress their immune systems is because the transplanted organs have someone else's passwords. When a transplant is rejected, it is because the immune system successfully attacked and destroyed the foreign, transplanted organ—at the expense of the organ recipient.

Sometimes the password system breaks down, and the immune cells mistake body cells for intruders and attempt to destroy them. The term *autoimmune diseases* is used to describe disorders in which the body treats its own tissues as foreign and destroys normal, healthy body cells. Which autoimmune disease develops depends on the type of response and which tissues are attacked. For example, if immune cells attack the lining of the joints, rheumatoid arthritis develops; but if the myelin sheaths that surround nerve cells are attacked, multiple sclerosis develops.

Allergies occur when the immune system overreacts, and chemical sensitivity is an example of the nervous system overreacting. The substances that trigger allergy—pollen, animal dander, mold, and others—are usually harmless. The body of an allergic person doesn't see it that way. A pollen grain is about the same size as a germ, and like germs, pollen has proteins on its surface. Unlike germs, pollen grains cannot grow and multiply in the body, so there is no reason for the body to mount an attack on pollen grains. But in some people, inhaled pollen grains are treated like germs, and the body attempts to destroy them by mounting the same massive immune response as it would in response to a dangerous virus. The result is allergy, with the familiar inflammation of the airway (rhinosinusitis) and asthma. A simple allergy can also cause other inflammatory reactions, including swelling of the skin, tongue, throat, and vocal cords, as well as rash or hives (urticaria), fatigue, malaise, headache, and depression.

Something similar happens with chemical sensitivity, which occurs when people react strongly to chemicals in the environment at doses well below toxic levels. Chemicals interact with receptors on nerve cells to cause them to release chemicals that induce inflammation. Inflammation-related symptoms can include nasal congestion, sinus pain, headaches, skin rashes, gastrointestinal symptoms, muscle and joint aches, fatigue, malaise, and depression.

SITE SWITCHING

One of the most interesting facets of inflammation is how it can have multiple effects all over the body. When a person is punched in the face, it is the face and not the foot that swells. If a person were punched in the face and his foot swelled up, we would think it strange indeed. Inflammation can be just that strange.

Inflammation typically occurs at the site of the insult, but sometimes other locations can also become inflamed. For example, gonorrhea is a sexually transmitted bacterial infection that attacks the genitals, but gonorrhea can also cause inflammation of the joints, even without infection of the joints. Even stranger is the case of a woman who was referred to my hospital for treatment of what was thought to be the bite of the poisonous brown recluse spider. The woman had a big, ugly sore on the knuckle of the index finger of her dominant hand that looked like it had eroded down into the joint. She was also being treated for a boil on her buttocks, which a surgeon had recently lanced. The note from the referring surgeon said the bite was too complicated for him, and he felt the woman needed the care of a plastic surgeon. I looked at the sore with skepticism and asked if she had seen the spider bite her. She couldn't remember having been bitten. I knew then that she needed a dermatologist, not a plastic surgeon. It is possible for an inflammatory disorder at one site to produce one or more sores on the skin in another site. It can occur with infections, tumors, and inflammatory bowel diseases. In this case, the boil on the butt had produced a deep, raging, painful sore on the hand—a classic case of site switching named Sweet's syndrome after a British dermatologist who first described the phenomena.

Site switching is very common in allergy and chemical sensitivity. Systemic anaphylaxis (allergy shock) is a dangerous and life-threatening allergic event that occurs when the entire body simultaneously undergoes an allergic reaction, usually after a bee sting, after eating a food such as peanuts, or after taking a drug to which a person is allergic. In a matter of minutes, the entire skin can be covered with hives. The lungs go into an asthma attack, with production of mucus and spasm of the breathing tubes leading to oxygen starvation. Blood vessels all over the body expand and leak fluid into tissues, and if the vocal cords swell, suffocation is imminent. Blood pressure plummets while the heart races. The victim goes into shock and may even die.

How does the bee venom or the peanut protein spread throughout the body so quickly? It doesn't. What happens in allergic shock is that histamine, one of the chemicals in the immune arsenal, is released by the immune cells and attaches to nerves around the site of the bee sting or wherever peanut proteins touch the gut wall. Those nerves send a signal to the brain, which then sends out an alarm to the entire body. Nerves all over the body fire off and release a chemical messenger called substance P, which binds to other immune cells all over the body and causes them to release their own stores of histamine and other allergy-producing substances. Scientists believe that whenever you have an insult to the body in one location and it produces inflammation in another location, this type of neurogenic switching is involved. Could this be the basis for the inflammation connections among so many different diseases? No doubt scientists will be investigating this possibility in the future.

INFLAMMATION'S TAIL END

Throughout our lives, our bodies sustain insult after insult. We are damaged by infections, cuts, bruises, bumps, and burns. Body tissues can be harmed beyond repair, and vital organ function can be lost. Despite all these insults, our bodies are pretty tough. They are designed to survive, and part of survival is cleaning up the mess and repairing the damage.

Tissue repair is so intimately connected to inflammation that repair can be considered the tail end of inflammation. In wound repair, lymphocytes (a type of white blood cell) and other inflammatory cells travel into damaged tissue and release growth factors to begin the repair process. Other white blood cells called monocytes change into macrophages, which clean up the dead cells and other debris to make way for new, healthy cells to be repaired, grow, and divide.

Two types of cells—endothelial cells and fibroblasts—grow and divide to fill up holes left by damaged tissue. Endothelial cells form the inner lining of blood vessels. These types of cells are important because if a hole is to be filled in with living tissue, it must have a blood supply. Fibroblasts are a specialized type of cell that move into injured areas where they grow and divide and produce strands of a tough material called extracellular matrix to fill up the hole, rather like the way we use caulk or spackle to fill in holes in walls.

The result of the healing process is a scar. Anyone who has had a bad cut or scrape has visible scar tissue on their skin for the rest of their lives. Even though we can't see it, damaged tissues inside our bodies also scar. For example, after a heart attack, the dead heart muscle is replaced with scar tissue; and after a stroke, scar tissue replaces brain tissue. Although the actual wound is healed, scar tissue only takes up space—it does not function like the original tissue. Brain scars can't help us think, and heart scars don't help blood move through the body.

Healing, too, can malfunction—scar tissue can fill a hole, but then continue patching and spackling throughout an organ, or even throughout the body. Sometimes scar tissue simply goes berserk in the body. One example is the disease scleroderma, in which normal body tissue is replaced with scar tissue, seemingly for no reason. The skin, lungs, and other organs become hard. When examined under a microscope, these tissues look just like a scar. Eventually, body organs may fail due to pervasive scarring. Another example is illustrated in the case of an elderly woman who came to the emergency department complaining of severe pain in her arms and legs. She had fallen about two weeks earlier and deeply bruised her left thigh. The deep muscle bruise was healing nicely until she developed severe pain. I was baffled when I examined her—there was a long, rock-hard object in the muscle of her thigh that paralleled her thigh bone. X-rays revealed that the bruised muscle had actually turned to bone. This condition is known as myositis ossificans, which translates as "inflamed muscle turning to bone." In the healing process, the body had become confused and muscle had healed as bone. It is an extremely painful condition that often resolves spontaneously once the body figures out it erred.

MOVING FORWARD

Ideally, inflammation should subside when the pathogens are killed, or when the insult is removed and the body tissue heals. When the virus that causes the common cold dies, the inflammation in your nasal passages goes away. When the cut on your arm heals, the swelling and redness subside. The chemical messengers stop ringing the inflammation alarm, and blood vessels and the lymphatic system carry the excess fluid, dead pathogens, damaged cells, and leaked blood cells away from the site of inflammation. The threat is demolished, damage is controlled, and the body is returned to health.

Unfortunately, that's not always true. When the body becomes unbalanced, the system can overreact, or stop working, or turn against us, or just continue fighting small battles every day so that inflammation continues indefinitely. In any case, the long-term health consequences for us are not good.

Plus, it's hard to get back to normal if the bout of inflammation causes permanent change, and there are changes after every inflammatory episode. Some changes may be too small to notice or to make any difference, but sometimes the changes are large enough to cause disease. For example, people with severe, untreated asthma can experience a phenomenon known as airway remodeling, during which the actual physical structure of the lung changes in response to repeated damage from inflammation. Another example is when inflammation causes the body to begin growing new blood vessels, a process called angiogenesis, which can contribute to the problems of cancer, psoriasis, and other inflammatory diseases.

And as if our bodies didn't have enough to contend with, aging itself changes our inflammatory reactions. As we age, we naturally start making more of certain pro-inflammatory molecules and less of certain anti-inflammatory molecules. In the great balance of inflammation and anti-inflammation, the deck becomes stacked in favor of inflammation. That means that we have to start making concessions to age and work a little harder to keep inflammation at bay.

Inflammation seems to always be with us. Pick almost any body condition, and chances are it will be related to inflammation in some way. The common cold—yes, inflammation of the nasal passages. Mosquito bite—inflammation of the skin. Heart attack—inflammation of the blood vessels leading to blockage. Migraine—inflammation of blood vessels in the brain. Asthma—inflammation of the bronchial tubes in the lungs. Cancer—yes, many types are caused by inflammation. Autoimmune diseases—they are all caused by a malfunction of the body's inflammation alarm system. Arthritis, diabetes, depression, fatigue—yes, yes, yes, yes, all are related to inflammation.

Although it is a natural process, inflammation should not be a constant part of our lives. There is always an underlying risk of disease, based in part on our genetic makeup. If heart disease runs in your family, that means you have a built-in problem with inflammation of your blood vessels. You can't change the genes you were born with, but you can change other things about your life to decrease your total inflammation, which will help protect your heart (as well as many other parts of your body). That's why doctors recommend that we eat right—not because they are sadists, but because fruits and vegetables have known anti-inflammatory properties. So yes, eating right will decrease your risk of inflammation and make you healthier. But there are so many additional things you can also do to decrease your personal health risks from inflammation. The kinds of chemicals you use to clean your house, the type of carpeting you have, how often you dry-clean your clothes, your emotional state, and other lifestyle choices all affect the overall level of inflammation in your body.

The decision about which healthy changes you make is totally up to you. There are lots of options. Make one change, make a dozen changes, make a hundred changes. Every change will make a difference in the way you feel, and some may even save your life.

3

INFLAMMATION-RISK QUIZ

◉

Do you generally feel healthy? Or do you believe that serious disease is lurking right around the corner? Most of us believe that we are relatively healthy and strong. Sure, we have our bad habits, but we also do a lot of things to stay as healthy as possible.

Want to put it to a test?

It's human nature to downplay our personal risk for any disease, especially the serious ones. When we're healthy, it's hard to imagine ever getting sick; and if we already have a disease, we don't think that we could possibly be unlucky enough to get a second one. The truth is that serious illness is lurking around everyone's corner—it's just that for some people, that corner is farther away than it is for other people. Everything you do to lower your level of chronic inflammation will put a little more distance between you and that corner. And if you have already turned that corner and are facing illness head-on, reducing your exposure to factors that increase inflammation may improve your overall strength and help your immune system fight disease more effectively.

Just about everyone who adopts an inflammation-balancing lifestyle will see improvements in overall health. Imagine having more energy, sleeping better, and having more stable moods. Imagine fewer bouts of migraine headaches, allergies, or irritable bowel syndrome. Imagine walking without aches, breathing without coughing. Imagine being less at risk for a heart attack at age fifty-five than you were at age thirty-five.

What is your personal risk of disease? Because inflammation is involved in nearly every disease process, we can get a general idea of overall risk by evaluating the inflammation-causing factors in your life. The Inflammation Risk Quiz was designed to help you see which facets of your life might be contributing to your health problems, now or in the future.

To complete the Inflammation Risk Quiz, read and answer the questions honestly and as accurately as you can. When you have completed the quiz, add the points for all answers to get your Inflammation Risk score. From there, we'll help you prioritize which anti-inflammation solutions to start immediately, and which you might want to consider later.

INFLAMMATION RISK QUIZ

For each question, circle the appropriate response. There is a number value associated with each answer. Write the number for your answer in the separate score column on the right. When you have completed the quiz, add the numbers you wrote in the score column to determine your Inflammation Risk. The chapters listed in the score column may be of particular interest for anyone who scores high for that particular question.

1. **What is your age?**   _____

   20 or younger = 0   *Chapter 8*

   21 to 30 = 1

   31 to 40 = 2

   41 to 50 = 3

   51 to 60 = 4

   61 or older = 5

2. **Have you ever had a heart attack or stroke?**   _____

   Yes = 5   *Chapter 4*

   No = 0

3. **Do you have high blood pressure or high cholesterol?**   _____

   Yes = 5   *Chapter 4*

   No = 0

4. **Do you currently smoke?**   _____

   Yes = 5 (go to question 5)   *Chapter 4*

   No = 0 (skip to question 6)   *Chapter 11*

5. **Do you smoke more than 10 cigarettes per day?**   _____

   Yes = 5 (skip to question 7)

   No = 0 (skip to question 7)

6. **Did you ever smoke regularly?** _____

    No, never smoked = 0

    Yes, but quit more than 10 years ago = 1

    Yes, but quit 5 to 10 years ago = 2

    Yes, but quit within the past 5 years = 3

7. **Do you have type 1 or type 2 diabetes?** _____

    Yes = 5   *Chapter 4*

    No = 0

8. **Do you have periodontitis (severe gum disease)?** _____

    Yes = 3   *Chapter 4*

    No = 0

9. **Do you currently have medical complaints, but doctors can't seem
    to find anything wrong with you?** _____

    Yes = 3   *Chapter 6*

    No = 0

10. **Do you often feel fatigued, even after a good night's sleep?** _____

    Yes = 5   *Chapter 6*

    No = 0

11. **Do you have trouble falling asleep, or do you wake up too early
    without being able to fall back to sleep?** _____

    Yes = 3   *Chapter 6*

    No = 0

12. **Look at the Body Mass Index (BMI) chart on page 65. What is your BMI?** _____

    < 25 = 0   *Chapter 6*

    25 to 29.9 = 3

    30 or higher = 5

13. **Do you feel depressed or sad most of the time?** _____

    Yes = 3   *Chapter 6*

    No = 0

14. **On an average day, how much pain do you experience—from all causes?** _____

    No pain = 0   *Chapter 7*

    Minor aches, nothing serious = 1   *Chapter 8*

Enough pain to be annoyed = 2

Sometimes a lot, depends on the day = 3

Usually a lot of pain = 4

15. **How many servings of fish do you eat each week, or how many times each week do you take omega-3 fatty acid supplements?**

    _____
    Chapter 9

    None = 3

    1 or 2 = 0

    3 or more = −3

16. **How many servings of fruits and vegetables do you eat each day?**

    _____
    Chapter 9

    None = 5

    1 to 3 = 3

    3 to 7 = 0

    $> 7 = -5$

17. **What size city do you live in (by population)?**

    _____
    Chapter 10

    > 1 million = 5

    500,000 to 1 million = 3

    $< 500,000 = 0$

18. **What fuel do you use for home heating?**

    _____
    Chapter 10

    Kerosene heaters or wood stove = 5

    Oil or gas furnace = 3

    Heat pump or other electric = 0

19. **How often do you use heavy-duty cleaning products (bleach, ammonia, bath and shower cleaners, mildew removers, and similar products) in your home?**

    _____
    Chapter 10

    Never, I only use natural cleaners = 0

    Rarely = 1

    Often = 2

    Every day = 4

20. **Do you regularly use air fresheners (spray or plug-in)?**

    _____
    Chapter 10

    Yes = 2

    No = 0

21. **How often do you feel stressed?**

    Rarely = 0   *Chapter 12*
    Probably about average = 1
    Quite often = 3
    Always feel stressed = 5

22. **How often do you exercise?**

    Never = 5   *Chapter 11*
    Rarely, at most once a week = 4
    Sometimes, once or twice a week = 1
    Regularly, 3 or more times a week = −5

23. **Do you regularly take steroids (by prescription or for performance enhancement?)**

    Yes = 5   *Chapter 13*
    No = 0

24. **Do you take aspirin, ibuprofen, other nonsteroidal anti-inflammatory medication, or statin medication regularly, if recommended by your physician?**

    Yes = −5   *Chapter 13*
    No = 0

25. **Are you exposed to pesticides?**

    Frequently = 5   *Chapter 10*
    Occasionally = 3
    Never = 0

TOTAL INFLAMMATION SCORE

Add up the numbers associated with your answers—the numbers you wrote in the scoring column—to get your total Inflammation Score. The highest possible score is 95. The lowest possible score is −18 (points are subtracted for certain activities that reduce inflammation).

What Your Total Inflammation Risk Score Means

This quiz is meant to give you a general idea of your level of susceptibility to inflammation-related disorders by measuring your exposure to the most common sources of inflammation. The higher your score, the greater your potential risk.

If Your Score Was 50 to 100. You have a lot of sources of inflammation in your life. Don't panic. A high score doesn't mean you are guaranteed to become ill, but it does mean that you have a higher than average risk of developing a serious illness sometime in the future. The good news is that there are things you can do to lower your risk. As you read through the book, choose the actions that make the most sense for your life, and begin making changes immediately. Keep making improvements at least until your Inflammation Quiz score goes down below 50. You might want to consider seeing your doctor for a checkup. Talk with your doctor about whether getting a blood test for C-reactive protein (CRP) is right for you. CRP is a good indicator of inflammation, and high levels of CRP have been associated with a risk of early death from heart attack. By knowing your CRP levels, you and your doctor will be better informed about your current health status and can work together to help prevent future disease.

If Your Score Was 20 to 49. You have a moderate number of factors that might be causing inflammation in your life. You may be perfectly healthy now, but scores in this range suggest that there are a few important things you could be doing to lower your risk of developing an inflammation-related disorder. Read over the quiz again and note where your scores were the highest. Then read the recommended chapters listed in the score column for those questions to learn what additional actions you could be taking. Some things, such as a history of heart attack or diabetes, cannot be changed. This means you'll have to work harder to maintain inflammation balance as you age.

If Your Score Was Below 20. Congratulations! This is a great starting point for a lifetime program of disease prevention. Remember, some of the world's great killers—cancer, heart disease, and diabetes—develop very slowly, over decades. The more you can do now to eliminate or reduce the inflammation-causing factors in your life, the healthier you'll be in the long run. Use this book as a guide for the best ways to maintain good inflammation balance.

PART 2

INFLAMMATION'S DAMAGE

4

THE WORST OFFENDERS

HEART DISEASE, STROKE, DIABETES

◉

Heart disease, stroke, and diabetes are very destructive diseases. In the United States, together they kill almost twice as many people each year as all cancers combined. They do their damage by starving our bodies' cells—either by choking off the blood supply (in the case of heart disease or stroke) or by the damaging effects of high blood sugar (in the case of diabetes). Typically these diseases develop slowly, causing no overt symptoms until decades later, after they have progressed to the point of being dangerous.

Many of the physical deficits we think of as part of the normal aging process are really the result of damage to the circulation system. Every cell in our bodies needs oxygen to survive, and oxygen is delivered by blood. If blood can't reach a cell, usually due to blockage in a blood vessel, the cell dies. This looks different depending on where in the body that cell is. If a blockage occurs in a cardiac artery and a significant number of cells in the heart die, we call it a heart attack. If a blockage occurs in a blood vessel in the brain so that brain cells die, we call it a stroke. If blood vessels in the toes are damaged due to the effects of diabetes, toe cells die, and gangrene can set in.

If a blood vessel is only partly blocked, cells don't die, but they stop functioning optimally because they are partially suffocated. Our stamina suffers. Our bodies suffer. Our quality of life suffers. Piece by piece, these diseases rob us of our ability to do the things we love. Simple chores make us puff and pant, we start having memory problems and mental confusion, our vision fades, we begin to experience sexual dysfunction, and we always feel tired. Although we think of these symptoms as typical signs of aging, they are not inevitable. They are only considered normal because so many people suffer from artery disease.

We've known for a long time that our genetic inheritance helps determine our personal risk for disease. If people in your family tend to have heart attacks at young ages, you are also probably at risk for having a heart attack at a young age. But genetics only tells us what *might* be, not what must be. Think of dog breeds. Certain breeds, such as Doberman pinschers and pit bull terriers, have a combination of genes that give them certain characteristics, one of which is the potential to be aggressive. But with proper handling, these animals can be loving and obedient pets. They always have the potential to be more aggressive than genetically more passive breeds, such as the basset hound, but they are not doomed to a future of aggression. Similarly, people with a genetic predisposition for heart disease, stroke, or diabetes are not doomed to develop these diseases, but they must work harder to avoid them than someone who does not carry those genes.

What does "work harder" mean? We've all heard that keeping your arteries healthy and avoiding diabetes means getting plenty of exercise, keeping your weight down, and eating healthy foods. We know, we know. But interestingly, we've never known exactly why these recommendations helped. Now the big picture is becoming clearer. Within the past few years, scientists have discovered that the connection is inflammation.

HEART DISEASE AND STROKE

It is common to think of coronary artery disease and stroke as two separate diseases—after all, one happens in the chest, the other happens in the head. But they are intimately related. Both problems are caused by lack of blood flow due to blockage in a blood vessel. Although a total blockage may occur in a single part of the body (causing a heart attack or stroke), the common element, atherosclerosis, causes arteries to become narrower and more rigid all over the body. If you have atherosclerosis, whether you get a heart attack or stroke is really a matter of chance.

Inflamed Hearts

Coronary artery disease used to be rare. When a patient with blockages in the arteries of his heart was admitted to a hospital around the year 1900, interns and residents would descend upon the hapless victim thinking it might be the only case they would see in a lifetime of practice. But as our society changed, heart disease roared from obscurity to prominence. By the end of the twentieth century, coronary artery disease was the leading cause of death for both men and women in the United States. Today, coronary artery disease remains the number one killer.

The heart beats approximately once per second. With each pump, blood leaves the right side of the heart and goes to the lungs, where it picks up oxygen and unloads carbon dioxide. The blood from the lungs is pumped from the left side of the heart to the rest of the body, where it delivers oxygen and picks up waste products in the form of carbon dioxide. If the heart stops beating even for a few minutes, the cells of the body start dying off from lack of oxygen and nutrients.

If the heart muscle doesn't get enough oxygen, some people experience chest pain called angina. This occurs when arteries of the heart become narrowed by disease or when the arteries become so rigid that they cannot expand the way they normally do when there is increased demand for blood. For example, angina can be stable or unstable. Stable angina occurs in a predictable pattern, such as exercise-induced angina, which comes on during exercise and goes away after resting. Unstable angina occurs unpredictably with increasing frequency and can sometimes be felt even when a person is resting. Unstable angina is a very dangerous condition that often forewarns of a heart attack.

When an artery in the heart becomes totally blocked, a heart attack occurs, and that portion of the heart muscle supplied by the blocked artery dies from lack of oxygen and nutrients. The heart attack is fatal if 40 percent or more of the muscle of the left ventricle (which pumps oxygen-rich blood to the body) dies off, if there is disturbance of the heart rhythm caused by lack of oxygen, if the heart muscle ruptures, or if damage occurs to vital structures.

Brain Attack

There are two types of stroke: one caused by blockage in a blood vessel in the brain (ischemic stroke), and one caused by blood leaking out of a burst blood vessel (hemorrhagic stroke). In both cases, brain damage is done because the flow of blood to brain cells is interrupted. Hemorrhagic strokes cause further damage if the blood leaking from the vessel compresses the brain. Strokes caused by blockage—ischemic strokes—are so similar to heart attacks that physicians have begun calling them brain attacks.

The type of damage done by a stroke depends on which part of the brain was affected by the blockage, and the extent of damage depends on how many brain cells were starved of blood and for how long. For example, there is a portion of the left side of the brain that is responsible for speech. If many cells in that part of the brain die from lack of oxygen, a person can lose the ability to speak. But because a different area of the brain is responsible for understanding speech, that person may understand everything that is said, but still be unable to respond. If enough cells die, however, the brain cannot continue its job of regulating the body, and death occurs.

Just as angina is a warning sign of impending heart problems, people with impending stroke may experience transient ischemic attacks (TIAs), or ministrokes. TIAs are temporary disturbances of blood flow that don't last long enough for permanent damage to be done. The symptoms are exactly the same as symptoms of a stroke and can include numbness or weakness in the face, arm, or leg; mental confusion; difficulty talking or understanding speech; dizziness; trouble seeing; or loss of balance. The only difference is that TIA symptoms disappear relatively quickly, usually within an hour. (Because it is impossible to tell a TIA from a stroke, it is important to treat all symptoms of stroke as an emergency. Never wait to see if the symptoms will go away on their own—go to a hospital immediately.)

It has been estimated that about one-third of people who experience a TIA will experience a full-blown stroke in the future. In the medical world, that is a powerful predictor. It should be a wake-up call for preventive measures. Brain cells that die during a stroke can never be replaced. The only treatments for stroke are medications to unblock the blood vessel (which must be given within three hours of the onset of symptoms) and rehabilitation to try to overcome some of the disability left in the wake of a stroke.

The Role of Inflammation

One of the most frightening aspects of heart disease and stroke is that they can strike suddenly, without warning. Sudden cardiac death strikes several hundred thousand previously healthy people each year in the United States. Typically, this happens to middle-aged men in the prime of life who had previously undiagnosed and unsuspected coronary artery disease.

When diseases like heart disease and stroke come from nowhere to become the leading causes of death, when they creep up on us and kill so suddenly, it becomes imperative to figure out causes and preventive measures. Much of what we know comes from one of the most famous and definitive heart studies, the Framingham study, which has been ongoing for decades in the town of Framingham, Massachusetts. Investigators went to the town, enrolled people of all ages in their study, and began collecting data about their blood pressure, levels of cholesterol and fats in the blood, cigarette smoking, and other health issues. As time rolled on, the investigators were able to see who got heart disease and which factors made them different from people who did not get heart disease. What they found was that people were more likely to develop heart disease if they had high levels of cholesterol in their blood, if they smoked cigarettes or were exposed to secondhand cigarette smoke, or if they had high blood pressure. In addition, being a couch potato (what scientists call a sedentary lifestyle) increases the risk, whereas regular exercise protects against heart disease. Age was also found to be an important risk factor. As people get older, their risk of artery disease increases.

What this and other studies showed was that there was no single change from the year 1900 to the year 2000 that caused the emergence of heart disease and stroke as major killers. Rather, it was all the innovations of the twentieth century that caused a change in lifestyle. Riding in automobiles replaced walking. Half the adult population became addicted to cigarette smoking by 1950. Fast foods with high fat content replaced fruits and vegetables in the diet.

But these types of studies are limited because they tell us nothing about the underlying mechanisms of how the risk factors and the disease are connected. Why does being a couch potato cause heart disease? Why do fats in the diet make us more likely to have hardening of the arteries? Although it was discovered that high cholesterol greatly increases the risk of developing heart problems, many people with heart problems never had high cholesterol. So although high cholesterol is related to heart disease, it cannot be the sole cause. When scientists delved deeper to discover what happened in the body to cause atherosclerosis, they were pretty surprised to discover that inflammation topped the list of possible culprits.

Fragile Plaque and Heart Attack

The early inflammation research involved feeding animals a type of food known to promote atherosclerosis and then studying the changes that occurred in the animals' blood vessel walls. (The biology of humans and other mammals is the same. Just as the heart performs the same function in all mammals, the mechanisms of other basic physiologic functions, including inflammation, are the same in humans and other mammals.) Researchers discovered that atherosclerosis starts when a type of white blood cell called a monocyte sticks to the artery walls and then migrates into the interior of the walls. No one knows exactly why this process starts, but it is thought that some sort of inflammation-promoting insult to the body, some damage to the blood vessels, jump-starts the disease.

Once monocytes enter the wall, the smooth muscle cells release inflammatory chemicals called cytokines that cause monocytes to change into a different type of cell called macrophages. The macrophages devour fat (including cholesterol) and become foamy in appearance, leading to the name *foam cells*. These fat-filled foam cells cluster together and cause fatty streaks in the arteries, the first sign of disease. They also secrete additional chemicals that continue the inflammation process. Over time, a hard substance known as fibrous plaque is created from foam cells, muscle cells, connective tissue, collagen, and other inflammation-related cells.

Interestingly, the body doesn't see plaque as the bad guy it is. As far as the body is concerned, it is simply trying to heal that initial damage done to the blood vessel walls. But the healing process goes out of control, and instead of patching over the damage and then quitting, bigger and bigger deposits of plaque are laid down, spreading outward along the vessel walls.

If enough plaque accumulates in one place, it creates a firm barrier that can impede blood flow and cause a heart attack or stroke. More often, however, clots form when plaque deposits rupture or burst. Like a dam in the river, the clot can block the flow of blood and cause a heart attack or stroke. We see, then, that inflammation packs a double punch because it first initiates the process of plaque development and then makes plaque fragile and more likely to burst and form clots. This is why so many heart attacks strike suddenly, unexpectedly, and with no warning. The arteries don't have to be totally clogged with plaque—all you need is one fragile plaque that bursts at the wrong time.

Once scientists recognized that inflammation was such a major player in artery disease, they could start looking for markers of inflammation, a chemical indicator that signals the presence of inflammation. Currently, the most powerful marker is C-reactive protein (CRP). Blood tests show high levels of CRP whenever there is inflammation in the body, no matter the location or cause. Studies have shown that people with unstable angina, the kind most likely to lead to a heart attack, have very high levels of CRP. Among healthy people, high blood levels of CRP mean an increased risk of future heart attack, stroke, and death. Even mildly elevated CRP levels have been shown to double the risk of future cardiovascular events, such as heart attack. A host of other inflammation markers, including interleukin-6, tumor necrosis factor-alpha, and adhesion molecules, have all been shown to predict future coronary events and stroke.

Study after study has shown that atherosclerosis, regardless of which part of the body it is in, is related to inflammation. And inflammation anywhere in the body is related to atherosclerosis in different parts of the body. There is not a single inflamed spot on the artery corresponding to the location of a plaque. When there is disease, there is widespread inflammation.

Sources of Inflammation

Of course, once we know that inflammation causes hardening of the arteries, the next question is: what causes arteries to become inflamed? Once we know that, then we'll know what we can do to reduce the inflammation and how inflammation can be prevented. The most popular theory of what causes inflammation in general is the response-to-injury hypothesis. This states that inflammation in the arteries, like inflammation anywhere in the body, occurs because of some injury or insult. The inflammation is a result of the body trying to protect itself, but the process goes haywire, and the excessive nature of the inflammation becomes part of the problem. The best guesses as to what can cause this type of injury are infection, smoking, air pollution, and cholesterol.

Infection

A number of germs have been suggested as possibly causing the inflammation of coronary artery disease, but in scientific research, no single virus or bacterium has been shown to be directly related. One study found that the more antibodies found in the blood, the greater the risk of coronary artery disease, but no one knows why or what it means. It may be that a large number of antibodies is a marker of general inflammation, rather than identifying or indicating particular germs as causing the inflammation.

It is also possible that there is an interaction effect: infection alone may not cause inflammation and artery disease, but if infection is teamed with irritation from smoking, inflammation may result. On the other hand, it has been very clearly documented that gum disease—periodontitis—is very closely linked with heart disease. When a dentist sees that a patient has suddenly developed gum disease, it is now standard practice to refer that patient to a primary care physician for a full physical examination. Could whatever germ is causing the periodontitis also be responsible for the heart disease? Or is the chronic inflammation associated with heart disease causing the body's immune system to be less effective and therefore losing its ability to control germs in the gums? Right now, no one knows, but this will be a hot topic for future research.

Smoking

Smoke from cigarettes is a known irritant and contains inflammation-causing substances. Evidence proving that cigarette smoking greatly increases one's risk of coronary artery disease, heart attacks, and stroke is overwhelming. A number of studies have also verified that nonsmokers who are exposed to tobacco smoke have an increased risk of heart attacks. In fact, a Swedish study published in 2001 found that being married to a smoker increases one's risk of a heart attack by approximately 58 percent if exposed to twenty "spousal cigarettes" a day. (For more information about smoking as an inflammation risk, see Chapter 11.)

Air Pollution

Like tobacco smoke, air pollution is a known irritant and has been associated with heart attacks. A 1997 study in London that looked at a total of 373,556 hospital admissions found that when the air was measurably polluted with black smoke, nitrous oxide, carbon monoxide, or sulfur dioxide, there was an increase in heart attacks for that day. It was concluded that one of every fifty heart attacks treated at London hospitals is caused by outdoor air pollution, and that six thousand heart attacks a year could be prevented in the United Kingdom just by cleaning up the air. In the United States, National Resources Defense Council scientists estimated that living in a city with a lot of air pollution shortens lives by an average of one to two years due to air pollution alone. (They reported that the cities with the worst pollution were Los Angeles, New York, Chicago, Philadelphia, and Detroit.) Workers in areas with high levels of air pollution also have an increased risk of heart attack. In some places, so many colleagues die of heart disease that workers call the factories "heart attack alley." Another Swedish study, also published in 2001, found that workers exposed to a high degree of motor vehicle exhaust and other combustion products had more than double the risk of a heart attack as unexposed workers. (For more information about air pollution as an inflammation risk, see Chapter 10.)

Cholesterol

Contrary to what many people believe, cholesterol is not all bad. Cholesterol is used in the body to make certain necessary substances, including vitamin D and some hormones. Problems arise, however, when we have too much of the wrong kind of cholesterol. There are two main types of cholesterol: cholesterol bound to low-density lipoproteins (LDLs) and to high-density lipoproteins (HDLs). The difference is in how they work in the body. LDLs bring cholesterol to all the areas of the body to make it available for use. If there is sufficient cholesterol for the body's needs, the excess is dumped off, frequently in the arteries. So if the body has high levels of LDLs, there will be more cholesterol accumulating where we don't want it—in our blood vessels. HDLs grab excess cholesterol from all over the body and bring it to the liver, where it is broken down. High levels of HDLs are good because it means that cholesterol is being removed from blood vessels and, in a way, taken out to the trash.

High LDL levels play a huge role in starting the whole process of inflammation and probably are one of the major reasons why plaque continues to spread. Cholesterol not only provides "food" for the foam cells, but it is likely to be an inflammation-enhancing irritant. Many scientists now believe that the two best ways of preventing or treating atherosclerosis are to control cholesterol in the arteries by decreasing LDLs and increasing HDLs and to control inflammation. One way of controlling cholesterol is by altering the diet and other lifestyle factors that regulate the amount of cholesterol in the blood. (For more information about the role of diet in controlling inflammation, see Chapter 9. For more information about the role of lifestyle factors, see Chapter 11.)

People who have high LDL cholesterol are often prescribed a class of drugs known as statins, which lower the levels of cholesterol circulating in the blood (brand names include Lipitor, Mevacor, Zocor, and Baycol). But recently, research results have suggested that these drugs may have a double benefit because they also reduce markers of inflammation in the blood. The great success of statins in reducing coronary artery disease may well be due to their anti-inflammatory properties.

For that reason, they may be appropriate for even more people than doctors previously thought. (For more information about statins as anti-inflammatory medications, see Chapter 13.)

An Endless Loop

If air pollution, cigarette smoke, and cholesterol were all there was to atherosclerosis, it would be relatively simple to control. But the process seems to feed on itself. Once inflammation begins, it sets off a series of physiologic reactions that cause additional inflammation. And with each additional layer of inflammation, the body's reactions become more and more difficult to turn off.

For example, aside from cigarette smoking, air pollution, and cholesterol, we know that a person's risk of heart disease and stroke greatly increases if that person is also overweight, or has high blood pressure, or has certain autoimmune diseases (such as systemic lupus erythematosus or rheumatoid arthritis), or has periodontal disease, or has diabetes. We know that being overweight, having gum disease, and having an autoimmune disorder all increase the level of inflammation in the body. We know that losing even a little bit of weight reduces inflammation. We also know that losing even a little weight reduces the risk of heart attack or stroke. It's all connected.

It could very well be that these connections are what keep us unhealthy and eventually kill us. It's like having a metaphorical tapeworm in your gut. The more you eat, the bigger the worm gets, and the bigger the worm, the hungrier you are, and the hungrier you are, the more you eat, ad infinitum. If we have heart disease, we have excess inflammation, which can cause fatigue, which means we aren't as active as we used to be, which means we gain weight, which creates more inflammation in the body, which feeds the heart disease, and so on. Breaking just one little link in the chain of inflammation might be enough to turn your health around. Of course, reducing a lot of inflammation would turn it around sooner.

DIABETES MELLITUS

One of the scariest and yet most misunderstood inflammation promoters is diabetes mellitus. Just as all cells in our bodies need oxygen to survive, they also need energy, which they typically receive in the form of a simple sugar called glucose. Glucose travels throughout the body in the bloodstream. The hormone insulin, which is created in the abdominal organ called the pancreas, binds to receptors on the surfaces of cells to allow glucose to pass from the blood into the cells.

Two main things can go wrong with this system. First, the pancreas may not make enough insulin to keep all the cells supplied with glucose. This is what happens in type 1 diabetes, an autoimmune disease in which the body destroys its own insulin-producing cells in the pancreas. The second thing that can go wrong is that the body's cells can become resistant to insulin. This is what happens in type 2 diabetes. Plenty of insulin is made, but it is powerless.

The whole process is a bit like a lock-and-key mechanism. Imagine that the cell has a lock, and insulin is the key that opens a door for glucose to enter. If there is no insulin key (like in type 1 diabetes), the door cannot be unlocked and opened. Also, if the insulin key doesn't work, the door will not be unlocked or opened. In type 2 diabetes, it's like the lock gets blocked or jammed up. The effects on the body are the same either way. If insulin cannot help cells to pull in glucose, then cells starve.

In addition, if cells cannot pull glucose out of the blood, then the amount of glucose in the blood gets higher and higher. This is what is meant when people with diabetes are said to have high blood sugar. Although high blood sugar doesn't sound dangerous, it is. Excessive glucose damages blood vessels. The smallest blood vessels, the tiny capillaries, are damaged first. If the delicate blood vessels of the eye are damaged, it can lead to blindness. If the blood vessels of the kidneys are damaged, the result can be kidney disease or kidney failure. Nerves can be damaged, leading to numbness or pain wherever the damage occurs, although it is most likely to occur in the areas of the body that are farthest from the heart—namely, the feet. Glucose even damages larger blood vessels. That damage may be enough to trigger an inflammatory reaction in the blood vessels and start us down the road to coronary artery disease, heart attack, and stroke.

In the early stages of type 2 diabetes, the starving cells signal a need for the pancreas to make more insulin. All that new insulin doesn't help the cells (because that lock is jammed), so it stays in the bloodstream. Excess insulin in the blood causes high blood pressure, low HDL cholesterol, and higher levels of a certain kind of fat called triglycerides in the blood. These body reactions are so common that this cluster of disorders is called insulin resistance syndrome, a strong predictor of the development of both type 2 diabetes and heart disease. In fact, one study by researchers at Stanford University found that even people with normal weight who had insulin resistance were at high risk of heart disease. Once diabetes sets in, the risk skyrockets. Overall, studies show that men with diabetes are more than twice as likely to die prematurely of cardiovascular problems than men without diabetes. In women, the effect of diabetes is similar, making them about three times more likely to die prematurely of heart problems than women without diabetes.

No one fully understands what causes insulin resistance and type 2 diabetes, but being overweight is the single greatest risk factor. It is thought that fat in the body can make cells change the way they respond to insulin. Some scientists have suggested that having chronic low-grade inflammation may increase the risk of developing type 2 diabetes. When you consider that being overweight increases inflammation, that may be enough of a low-grade inflammatory state to prime the body for diabetes. Interestingly, having cardiovascular disease often comes first, increasing the risk of developing diabetes. The most likely explanation is that something in the body predisposes a person to both diseases, heart disease and diabetes. Obesity, insulin resistance, and genetics have all been suggested as possible common elements—and now we can add inflammation to that list.

CONNECTIONS

Chronic, low-grade inflammation of blood vessels may be the common link among all the big killers. Obesity, heart disease, stroke, and diabetes are so intricately intertwined that it will be difficult for scientists to separate cause-and-effect body reactions. Which came first, the obesity or the heart disease? The heart disease or the diabetes? The diabetes or the obesity? All these disorders develop very slowly, by tiny increments. It is impossible to monitor their day-to-day development, and therefore impossible to define the moment when a healthy body turns unhealthy.

In addition, there are probably many other as-yet-undiscovered connections. Gum disease is a terrific example. As stated earlier, people with gum disease are known to have a higher risk of cardiovascular disease than those without gum disease. It may be that the infection that causes gum disease is enough to trigger the kind of inflammation that causes heart disease. Or it may be that the low-grade inflammation that is associated with heart disease may mean a change in the body's immune response, which might allow germs in the mouth to do damage to the gums. But consider this: gum disease is also related to both obesity and diabetes. People with diabetes are more likely to have gum disease than people without diabetes—and treating gum disease helps people with diabetes control their blood sugar better, perhaps by improving insulin sensitivity. This would mean that the chronic inflammation in the mouth can affect the whole body. Also, when scientists in Japan studied obesity and gum disease, they found out that people with the greatest amounts of body fat had the highest rates of gum disease. The gum disease connection has only been revealed in the past five years. It is likely that other relationships will be discovered as scientists continue to probe the inflammation connection.

5

Like Gasoline on Fire

Cancer

◉

The world's most common cancers—colon, stomach, esophageal, lung, liver, breast, cervical, ovarian, and pancreatic cancers—have all been linked to inflammation. Not all cases of inflammation cause cancer, and not all cancers are affected by inflammation. But with the right set of circumstances, inflammation can be volatile. Sometimes inflammation directly causes cancer, like the match that starts the fire. In other cases, inflammation causes an already established cancer to grow and spread, which is more like pouring gasoline on cancer's flame. At the same time, the immune system can attack and eliminate small cancers as though they were foreign invaders.

How Cancer Starts

When a person receives a diagnosis of cancer, it is always an unpleasant surprise. It seems to pop up out of the blue, unpredictable, frightening, and devastating. But if it were possible to watch the inner workings of the human body, we would see that cancer develops slowly. It takes many years, possibly decades, before the cancer creates enough symptoms so that the disease cannot be ignored.

Where does cancer come from in the first place? Many people are surprised to learn that cancer starts from normal body cells. Cancer development occurs in three main stages. First, in the initiation stage, something happens to change normal cells into precancerous cells. Actually, many things must happen—there is usually no single event that causes a good cell to turn bad. Scientists generally agree that a cell may undergo ten or more mutations before it becomes capable of progressing to cancer.

Cells can mutate for a number of reasons, including chronic irritation and inflammation, exposure to toxic chemicals, assault by a virus, damage from environmental factors such as the sun's ultraviolet radiation, or simply aging. For example, cells in the lungs can mutate in response both to the chemicals in cigarette smoke and to the irritation and inflammation caused by the presence of the smoke alone. (This is why the so-called herbal cigarettes are not safe. Smoke of any kind is an irritant that can cause cellular changes.) Whether a particular smoker will be one of the unlucky ones to develop lung cancer depends in part on genetics, but also on the number of years and quantity of cigarettes that person smoked. The longer and stronger the assault, the longer the inflammation lasts, the greater the likelihood that cells will mutate.

A mutated cell, however, isn't necessarily dangerous. All of us have mutated cells in our bodies, but we don't all have cancer. Once a cell has mutated enough to become precancerous, it can sit harmlessly in the body for years until a stimulus comes along to push the cell into malignancy. During this second stage of cancer development, called promotion, the cell begins multiplying and starts the process of becoming a tumor. No one knows exactly what causes the cell to become activated in every case of cancer, but scientists do know that additional assault by the same factors that first caused cellular mutation can also cause cancer promotion. So continuing to smoke after cells in the lungs mutate can be enough to turn the cells from passive and harmless to active and cancerous.

Inflammation is often involved in cancer promotion. For example, heartburn is caused when the lining of the esophagus is burned by backed-up stomach acids. For most people, this is a painful but minor inconvenience. But for some people, the damage and inflammation is so severe that they develop precancerous mutations in the cells lining the esophagus, a condition called Barrett's esophagus. At this point, cancer has been initiated (the first stage of cancer development). If irritation continues, the chemicals released by the body during inflammation can push the cells into the second stage, cancer promotion, when the precancerous cells become active and malignant. In this case, inflammation acts as the match that lights the fire of cancer, the actual cause of cancer. If inflammation is avoided, cancer is avoided.

The third stage of cancer development is called progression, when cancer cells begin multiplying and spreading and generally become uncontrollable by normal body defenses. Early in the development of cancer, when a mutated cell is pushed into malignancy and becomes a cancer cell, it is sometimes still possible for the body to control or eliminate the cancer through many of the same immune system and inflammation processes that allow the body to eliminate viruses and bacteria. Unfortunately, the immune system isn't always successful. Remember that the immune system is primarily programmed to destroy foreign invaders. Because cancer starts as a normal body cell, the body often ignores these cells gone bad. After all, they're not foreign, they're part of us!

Once cancer progresses, it becomes even more difficult for the body to defend itself. Most cancers grow in a bed of normal body cells called a stroma, which provides support and nourishment to the cancerous cells. This further protects the cancer from the immune system's defenses by providing a camouflage of normalcy. The malignant cells are harder to find when they are surrounded by normal body cells, and the stroma seems to provide a barrier that keeps the body's immune cells at bay.

The stroma can support a tumor for a relatively short period of time. Soon, the tumor becomes too large and needs its own blood supply to continue to grow and thrive. When a tumor grows to about 1 millimeter in size (roughly the size of the letter *o* on this page), the stroma can no longer support or nourish all the cancer cells. Unless an alternate source of energy and nutrients is found, this baby tumor will simply stop growing and die. Unlucky for us, cancer easily remedies this problem. Once a tumor reaches a certain size, it begins releasing chemicals that create new blood vessels, a process called angiogenesis (from *angio* meaning "blood vessel" and *genesis* meaning "beginning"). These newly created blood vessels attach to the body's existing circulatory system, allowing the tumor to begin to feed like a parasite from the body's nutrients.

During this progressive phase, inflammatory cells and chemicals that are supposed to protect the body can sometimes help a tumor instead. For example, in the early stages of malignant skin cancer (melanoma), a normally protective inflammatory chemical called interleukin-6 (IL-6) can help stop cancer growth. In more established melanoma cells, IL-6 loses its ability to inhibit cancer growth. And very mature melanoma cells produce their own IL-6, at which point it acts as a growth stimulator. IL-6, then, starts out fighting cancer and ends up helping cancer grow faster. Another example concerns macrophages, the inflammatory cells that are responsible for helping to destroy foreign invaders and keep the body healthy. Sometimes, for reasons no one understands, macrophages become part of the stroma. They end up helping the tumor by producing chemicals that promote angiogenesis, providing the tumor with its own blood supply and allowing it to grow indefinitely. In these examples, inflammation doesn't actually start the cancer, but some of the cells and chemicals that are part of the inflammation process help the cancer in its quest for unlimited growth, the cellular equivalent of throwing gasoline on a fire.

How Inflammation Causes Cancer

Any assault on the body that results in long-term inflammation is capable of causing cancer. Most commonly, these types of inflammation are related to chronic viral or bacterial infection, mechanical or chemical irritation, or another disease process. The different cells and chemicals involved in inflammation have been shown to cause cellular mutations that predispose a cell to become cancerous, to cause precancerous cells to become active cancer cells, to cause cells to grow, and to foster angiogenesis so that new blood vessels are formed to nourish larger tumors. In other words, chronic inflammation works to promote cancer at all stages of development. It's important to remember that cancer is related to long-term inflammation. Short-term or acute inflammation, the type that helps wounds heal and destroys most foreign invaders, generally helps protect us from all diseases, including cancer. But when the body is out of balance, when the scales start to tip into a constant state of inflammation, cancer becomes more likely.

Even with all that is known about cancer development, we still can't accurately predict which individual will develop cancer and which individual won't. Genetic differences, the coexistence of other diseases, and multiple risk factors all complicate the picture. One thing we know for certain is that the longer the inflammation lasts, the higher the risk of cancer. Among the factors with the strongest links to cancer are infection, irritation, and inflammation from other body or disease processes.

Infection

Anytime you have an infection, you'll have inflammation. This is normal and desirable. The inflammation process helps rid the body of unwanted intruders. Typically, the invaders—bacteria, viruses, or parasites—create biological havoc for only a couple of weeks before they are killed by the immune system. But some invaders are not so easily killed. They can hang around the body for years, sometimes for a person's entire life, creating a low level of inflammation in a particular portion of the body and increasing the risk of cancer in that body part.

One example is infection by the strain of bacteria known as *Helicobacter pylori*. This bacterium is known to be responsible for stomach ulcers. In recent years, scientists have discovered that people who have this type of infection have a much higher risk of developing stomach cancer than uninfected people. No one is really certain exactly what the role of bacteria is in the cancer chain, but scientists believe that it likely involves two phases. First, the bacteria, as part of their normal life cycle, give off certain chemicals or metabolites. Most of these are harmless, but some may be toxic to body cells and capable of causing cellular mutations.

Second, the presence of the bacteria creates an inflammation reaction. As part of the call to defend the body, macrophages—cells that are part of the body's defense mechanism—are activated. These macrophages may convert bacterial metabolites to a different, more toxic chemical compound, and this new chemical may act as a carcinogen. So the bacteria alone may or may not cause cancer, but when inflammation causes the conversion of harmless metabolites into toxic chemicals, it creates an environment that makes cancer more likely.

H. pylori is a very common bacterium. It has been estimated that at least half of the world's population is currently infected. But most people do not have stomach cancer. Therefore there must be other factors necessary before cancer results. Hereditary factors may play a role, or dietary factors, or something else entirely. But by understanding the link between *H. pylori* (or other bacteria) and cancer, it is possible to break the connection by destroying the germ.

Another example is the link between urinary tract infections (UTIs) and cancer of the bladder. UTIs are the most common bacterial infections in all age groups. Bladder cancer is more common in people who have chronic or recurrent urinary tract infections. One large epidemiologic study published in 1984 found that having three or more UTIs doubles a person's risk of later developing bladder cancer. Although the link is there, we don't really know the specific circumstances that lead to cancer. How long does an infection have to last before it becomes dangerous? Were the original infections treated effectively? Were there other infections that went untreated? Regardless of the specifics, the overall lesson is not to ignore infections, regardless of how harmless they seem.

Cancer is also associated with infection by particular viruses. The hepatitis B virus and hepatitis C virus are linked with liver cancer. The Epstein-Barr virus, which causes mononucleosis, is linked to lymphoma. Certain strains of human papillomaviruses, which cause genital warts, are linked to cervical cancer.

No one knows exactly what happens during or after infection to cause cancerous changes, but we know that viruses can inject copies of their own DNA into normal cells. These changes may alter the way a cell functions, and these changes may be enough to trigger cancerous changes. A cell that has been infected by a virus may react differently to normal inflammatory chemicals so that instead of being destroyed, the cell starts growing in response to the body's immune system. It is likely that these viruses affect all stages of cancer development—the virus itself causes cancer initiation by mutating a normal cell, and then the chronic inflammation works to promote and proliferate the cancer.

Mechanical or Chemical Irritation

Just as mountains are eventually eroded by the pummeling of rain and wind, long-term irritation to our bodies also causes erosion. And where there is erosion in the body, there will be inflammation to try to fix the injury. If the inflammation lasts a long time, it may be enough to change a body cell from normal to malignant. This type of erosion can happen from chemical irritation, such as when the esophagus is burned by digestive chemicals, or from mechanical irritation, such as continual rubbing by an object. An example of mechanical irritation is kidney stones—those small rocks that are formed from crystallized material in urine, usually calcium. It has been shown that people with kidney stones have a greater risk of developing cancer of the kidney, in part because of the mechanical irritation of the rough stones on delicate body tissue. These types of irritations don't cause a cell to mutate, but the chemicals released by chronic inflammation may work to promote cancer development in an already mutated cell.

Disease Inflammation

Certain diseases cause inflammation that, if left untreated or unchecked for a long enough period of time, can result in cancer. Some of the first clues about the role of chronic inflammation in cancer development came from observing people with ulcerative colitis, an inflammatory disease of the colon. People with ulcerative colitis have a risk of colon cancer five to seven times higher than the risk for healthy people. Because not all people with the disease end up with colon cancer, we know that inflammation alone is not the whole story. But just as with heartburn and esophageal cancer, the link between long-term inflammation and cancer of the colon is undeniable.

INFLAMMATION-RELATED CANCERS

Although we know the general processes involved in cancer growth and spread, many of the specifics are still a mystery. In some cases, the role of inflammation is relatively straightforward, cause and effect. In other cases, the link is less obvious, and inflammation is suspected to play a role only because anti-inflammatory medications seem to help. For example, people with rheumatoid arthritis, an inflammatory autoimmune disease, regularly take anti-inflammatory medications. Scientists discovered that women with rheumatoid arthritis developed breast cancer at lower rates than women without rheumatoid arthritis, and they believe it is because of the anti-inflammatory medication. Although breast cancer doesn't seem to have any obvious link to inflammation, if taking an anti-inflammatory medication reduces the risk, then an inflammatory component must be assumed.

Colon Cancer

Inflammation affects the development of colon cancer in a couple of different ways. First, long-term inflammation due to inflammatory bowel disease (IBD) is known to increase the risk of colon cancer by causing cellular mutations that lead to cancer.

Second, bacteria may also play a role. Our colons are filled with many different types of bacteria that normally live peacefully with us. In fact, bacteria are necessary for normal bowel functions, but the population of bacteria is kept in check by the immune system. This means that the colon could be said to be in a constant state of inflammation. The mechanisms leading to colon cancer in people with or without IBD may be similar, but with additional risk for those with IBD because of the severity and duration of the inflammation.

Studies show that people with IBD who take the prescription anti-inflammatory medication mesalamine may reduce their risk of colon cancer by as much as 75 percent. And people without IBD who take aspirin or other over-the-counter nonsteroidal anti-inflammatory drugs (NSAIDs) reduce their risk of colon cancer by about 40 to 50 percent. Although the reasons for this benefit are not clear, researchers believe that these medications act by suppressing a substance called cyclooxygenase-2 (COX-2), which has been known to help promote cancer growth. In one study, taking 300 milligrams of aspirin each day (about one regular aspirin) reduced the risk of colon cancer after about six months of regular usage. If the participants stopped taking the aspirin, the benefits disappeared.

Animal studies have shown that some anti-inflammatory medications—specifically, those that suppress COX-2—may also be a useful treatment once colon cancer has already been diagnosed. Similar exciting results have been reported in people with a disease called familial adenomatous polyposis. People with this disease are prone to developing a large number of polyps in their colons, which greatly increases their risk of colon cancer. Studies have shown that the COX-2 inhibiting medication celecoxib reduced both the size and the number of polyps after six months, reducing the risk of colon cancer. This is the same anti-inflammatory medication being used by thousands of people to treat arthritis. More research will be needed before physicians will start prescribing celecoxib for cancer prevention. (See Chapter 13 for more information about anti-inflammatory medications. Do not start taking any medication without first discussing it with your doctor.)

Stomach Cancer

As discussed earlier, infection with the *H. pylori* bacterium increases the risk of stomach cancer; by some estimates, the risk is nearly six times greater. The bacteria alone are not enough to cause cancer. Many people in the world carry this particular strain of bacteria with no trouble at all. Some people, however, develop severe stomach inflammation (gastritis), which can lead to ulcers or cancer. The stomach inflammation associated with the bacteria is known to cause oxidative stress, which can lead to the creation of carcinogenic chemicals, damage to cellular DNA, and growth of cancer cells.

Although no one knows exactly why some people with an *H. pylori* infection go on to develop cancer while others do not, it seems that inflammation that is more severe is more likely to lead to cancer. And inflammation severity is affected by the particular strain of bacteria involved in the infection, genetics, lifestyle, and even dietary factors. For example, people who smoke while infected with *H. pylori* face a risk of gastric cancer sixteen times greater than uninfected people who don't smoke. And salty foods—whether from processing, pickling, or added salt—also increase inflammation and risk of cancer.

Although studies have not been done to show whether treating the infection will actually reduce the risk of cancer, it seems logical. And since these bacteria are also responsible for ulcers, treatment with antibiotics seems prudent. Most cases of *H. pylori* infection can be successfully treated with antibiotics. In addition, several studies have shown that certain dietary changes may also help reduce the risk of gastric cancer, including drinking green tea and eating lots of green and yellow vegetables. (For more information about inflammation-fighting foods, see Chapter 9.)

Esophageal Cancer

The number of cases of esophageal cancer has been rising, although no one understands why. The disease is caused by long-term inflammation due to gastroesophageal reflux (the backup of stomach acids into the esophagus). These acids burn the unprotected esophagus, creating immediate irritation and inflammation. If the burning and inflammation continue and inflammation becomes chronic, cells of the esophagus can sometimes mutate into precancerous cells, a condition called Barrett's esophagus. At this point, the changes can sometimes be seen by a physician looking down the throat with an endoscope—a narrow lighted tube with a magnifying camera on one end. Typically, however, cells are taken from the esophagus and viewed under a microscope. If the esophagus continues to be irritated and inflammation becomes chronic, the precancerous cells can become cancerous.

The irritation does not have to come from reflux alone. Alcohol and tobacco smoke are also throat irritants that can contribute to the development of esophageal cancer. In fact, people who regularly drink alcohol have more than double the risk, and people who smoke are up to seven times as likely to develop esophageal cancer as people who don't use these substances regularly. Even drinking extremely hot beverages (such as scalding hot tea) may be enough to cause the continual irritation and inflammation that can lead to cancer.

Anything that reduces inflammation will help reduce the risk of esophageal cancer. Talk with your doctor about effective ways to control heartburn and about whether taking an anti-inflammatory medication is right for you. (Do not start taking any medication without first discussing it with your doctor.)

Lung Cancer

Lungs are relatively delicate organs that take quite a lot of abuse in this world. When we breathe, we take in everything that hangs in the air—viruses, toxic chemicals, smoke, dirt, pollution, pollen, and anything else that is light enough to be airborne. All of these things enter the lungs and can cause inflammation. Most of the time, our lungs are able to remove bits of dust and other pollutants naturally. But some of the more troublesome substances that cannot be removed—asbestos, coal dust, silica dust—stay in the lungs and cause permanent inflammation and increase the risk of cancer.

The smoke from cigarettes poses a whole other layer of problems. First, smoke itself is an inflammatory substance simply by being irritating. Smoke in your eyes will cause inflammation. Smoke also irritates and inflames delicate lung tissue. In fact, inflammation of the breathing tubes in the lungs is called bronchitis, and many smokers show signs of chronic bronchitis, defined as coughing with phlegm lasting at least three months. A study published in 2002 found that even nonsmokers exposed to tobacco smoke in the workplace were twice as likely to have chronic bronchitis as nonsmokers who were not inhaling someone else's cigarette smoke.

In addition, tobacco smoke contains hundreds of different chemical compounds, many of which are capable of causing cancerous mutations in lung cells. The combination of carcinogenic compounds and irritated lung tissue is particularly dangerous. In terms of potential damage, imagine pouring toilet bowl cleanser over a raw, bleeding wound on your skin. If lung tissue had sensitive nerve endings like skin does, the pain would be enough to keep anyone from lighting up another cigarette. Unfortunately, the damage done in the lungs is silent.

A large study of more than fourteen thousand women published in 2002 showed that women who took aspirin three or more times each week for at least six months had a decreased risk of lung cancer, even when smoking was taken into account. The researchers suggested that the benefits were probably due to aspirin's anti-inflammatory properties. Although it is always difficult to make conclusions about what individuals should do in response to a broad study such as this one, women who smoke may want to talk with their doctors about taking aspirin. (See Chapter 13 for more information about taking anti-inflammatory medications. Do not start taking any medication without first discussing it with your doctor.)

Breast Cancer

The causes of breast cancer remain a mystery. If you take all of the known risk factors and add them together, they account for less than half of all cases. And those risk factors—including heredity, age at first menstruation, age when your first child was born—cannot be changed. So, although we know that we can prevent lung cancer by not smoking, women cannot choose their parents or delay their menstrual cycle to prevent breast cancer. However, recent studies have shown that taking NSAIDs may reduce the risk of breast cancer by about 20 percent.

Interest in NSAIDs for prevention of breast cancer originally came from the observation that women with rheumatoid arthritis (who take NSAIDs regularly) seem to have a decreased risk of breast cancer. This could be because prostaglandins—hormonelike substances that have been implicated in the development of cancer—are found in higher concentrations in cancerous breast tissue than in normal breast tissue. NSAIDs block the creation of prostaglandins and therefore may block at least one cause of breast cancer. In a 2001 meta-analysis of fourteen high-quality studies, the overall conclusion was that NSAIDs may, indeed, reduce the risk of breast cancer. Nearly all studies found similar results regardless of design, with an average risk reduction of 18 percent. The jury is still out about which type of NSAID is best—ibuprofen and aspirin seemed to have similar effects—and there was not enough information to determine the ideal dosage or duration required to prevent breast cancer. Given these results, it might be worthwhile talking with your physician about taking a low-dose anti-inflammatory medication. (See Chapter 13 for more information about anti-inflammatory medications. Do not start taking any medication without first discussing it with your doctor. All medications have risks, even over-the-counter anti-inflammatory medications such as aspirin or ibuprofen.)

Another interesting inflammation connection is that breast cancer and colon cancer occur in the same patient more often than might be predicted by statistical chance. Is there a connection between the two? Some researchers believe there is. Both cancers seem to be related to a Western lifestyle and/or diet, with immigrants having relatively low levels of these cancers, but quickly assuming the same risks the longer they live in Western countries. Weight gain is also associated with an increased risk for both cancers, and obesity is also associated with increased inflammation. We don't really know the reasons why these two cancers seem to be related, but perhaps if we can control inflammatory factors throughout the body, we may be able to prevent these and other inflammation-related cancers.

Ovarian Cancer

Ovarian cancer is another mysterious disease that seems to defy prediction. Previously, the only risk factors reported were heredity, a high number of lifetime ovulations (which would occur if, for example, a woman was never pregnant and therefore had no "break" from ovulation), or high hormone levels. But in 1999 researchers reported in the *Journal of the National Cancer Institute* that part of the cause of ovarian cancer may be inflammation. Ovulation itself is an inflammatory event, resulting in temporary "damage" to the ovary when the egg is released from the follicle. In addition, other ovarian cancer risk factors also have an inflammation component, such as pelvic inflammatory disease or endometriosis.

Of course, if inflammation is in part responsible for ovarian cancer, then reducing inflammation should reduce the risk. One small study published in 1998 showed that taking at least one aspirin a week for six months or longer reduced the risk of ovarian cancer by about 25 percent. In 2002 the results of a much larger study (the Harvard Nurses' Health Study), looking at 76,821 women over a period of twenty years, showed that aspirin had no effect, but taking other NSAIDs (such as ibuprofen) reduced the risk of ovarian cancer by 40 percent. These conflicting results are confusing. Additional studies will need to be done to clarify the possible benefits of aspirin or NSAIDs in preventing ovarian cancer. But if you have a family history of ovarian cancer, you may want to talk with your doctor about the possibility of taking NSAIDs regularly. (See Chapter 13 for more information about anti-inflammatory medications. Do not start taking any medication without discussing it with your doctor.)

6

WHY AM I
ALWAYS TIRED?

FATIGUE, OBESITY, DEPRESSION,
SLEEP DISORDERS

◉

What does it mean when you just don't have enough energy to get through the day anymore? When you feel tired and run-down, but there doesn't seem to be anything medically wrong—blood tests come back normal, and the doctor can't find anything wrong with you. This problem is more common than you might think. People from all walks of life are sick and tired of being sick and tired, and they are frustrated in their attempts to do anything about it.

It should come as no surprise by now that the answer may lie in the physiology of inflammation.

FATIGUE

Everyone suffers from appropriate fatigue from time to time. Working overnight, something that I'm all too familiar with as a physician, takes a toll. Touring musicians who perform a concert in a different city each night—sometimes for several months on end—will find fatigue creeping up on them, and it gets worse and worse as the tour drags on. By the end of the NBA playoffs, players who make the championship series push hard to get beyond the fatigue of a long season. Parents of newborn infants who wake for feedings several times a night can experience profound fatigue. These types of fatigue are normal and expected.

What we're talking about here is inappropriate fatigue. Unusual fatigue. Overwhelming fatigue. Some people are too fatigued after resting all day in bed to get out of bed and fix dinner. By the next morning, rather than being revived by their day of rest, they are too fatigued to get out of bed again. And on and on it goes, day after day, even year after year. What's worse is that this condition is relatively common. Debilitating chronic fatigue has been estimated to afflict more than one in ten Americans. It can be difficult to understand the enormous impact of this kind of fatigue until you experience it yourself. Think back to the last time you had a bad case of the flu, and how you might have felt that you would never have the strength to get out of bed again. Now imagine waking up to that bone-numbing exhaustion every day, and no amount of rest makes you feel better, and there are no medicines you can take to make it go away.

Fatigue isn't always a mystery—it is a disabling part of many known medical conditions. Cancer patients can suffer extreme fatigue as a result of illness and treatment. Fatigue is also an unavoidable part of daily life for many patients with multiple sclerosis, rheumatoid arthritis, lupus, and other autoimmune diseases. Even more mundane diseases, such as infections and allergies, have fatigue as a common symptom. If the underlying disease can be treated, the accompanying fatigue will usually go away.

The link to all these conditions is, of course, inflammation. No matter what the cause of the inflammation, substances released by the cells involved in inflammation have a profound effect on the brain, resulting in fatigue and sleepiness. It is often said that whenever you have severe fatigue, it is a sign of inflammation somewhere in the body. That's why even simple diseases like the common cold make us feel wiped out—it's not the disease that's making us tired, it's the inflammation.

Unexplained severe fatigue, then, should always lead to a hunt for other undiagnosed inflammation-related disorders in the body. For example, people who live or work in sick buildings (contaminated with air pollutants or environmental toxins) often experience chronic fatigue as their primary symptom. When irritant gasses in sick buildings cause inflammation in the upper airway, pro-inflammatory cytokines are released in the body. Along with some minor airway symptoms, many people also feel the whole-body fatigue that saps their strength and sends them to the doctor. Unfortunately, most doctors do not make the connection between environmental toxins and fatigue, and the patient walks away frustrated, without a diagnosis. Some patients are even told that that their problem is "all in their head." But the fatigue is real, and it takes a real toll on the lives of the people who suffer.

Other "hidden" sources of fatigue are migraine headaches, viruses, and allergies. Migraine headaches, currently thought to be due to neurogenic inflammation, are also characterized by fatigue. More than 80 percent of people with chronic migraine suffer from severe fatigue, and two-thirds actually meet the definition for chronic fatigue syndrome.

Viral illnesses, such as the common cold or influenza, can cause fatigue during the illness. Unfortunately, viral infections can sometimes trigger prolonged and severe fatigue even after the illness has passed. So many people developed chronic fatigue after major influenza epidemics in the early years of the twentieth century that diagnoses like postviral myasthenia (meaning muscle weakness after a viral illness) were created. Recent research has found that people who have severe fatigue after a viral infection have persistently high levels of the pro-inflammatory cytokines interferon-gamma and tumor necrosis factor-alpha in their blood.

At the height of the pollen season, a person with severe pollen allergies can be plagued by inflammation-related problems other than a stuffy nose. Scientists believe that allergic reactions produce chemicals and neurologic stimuli that directly affect the central nervous system, including the brain. Studies have shown that patients with allergic rhinitis (inflammation of the nasal passages) experience fatigue, moodiness, and a mild form of depression called dysphoria, and that these symptoms increase during pollen seasons.

Unexplained fatigue has become so common that it has its own diagnosis—chronic fatigue syndrome (CFS). This disorder is marked by debilitating fatigue for more than six months in the absence of any other disease. People with CFS find their lives ruined by overwhelming fatigue, but scientists don't know how the disease starts or what changes it causes in the body. Some studies have shown an increase in the inflammatory marker C-reactive protein in the blood of people with chronic fatigue and higher levels of a type of immune protein called beta 2-microglobulin; but these results are not found consistently.

Interestingly, people with CFS also often have rhinitis—78 percent of patients with CFS have rhinitis, compared with only 23 percent of the general population. Could the inflammation associated with rhinitis somehow be causing the extreme fatigue of CFS? We know that certain pro-inflammatory cytokines are released during inflammation, so scientists decided to test the effects of one of these cytokines on fatigue. The cytokine interleukin-6 (IL-6) was chosen because it produces symptoms that look like the flu, and high IL-6 levels may be one reason people with the flu get fatigue, malaise, and the other symptoms. In a study conducted at the National Institutes of Health, researchers gave IL-6 to a group of patients with CFS and to a group of healthy people. Both groups were monitored for fatigue, malaise, muscle aches, and difficulties with concentration and memory. Both groups became symptomatic, but the people with CFS had symptoms that came on faster and were much worse, suggesting that they were more sensitive to the effects of the cytokines. It is possible, then, that people who suffer from extreme fatigue actually have some other underlying disorder—perhaps something as mild as an allergy or a sinus infection—but that they have a hyperreaction to the inflammatory chemicals produced in their bodies.

Autoimmune disorders seem to be different. Researchers who looked at patients with multiple sclerosis or lupus found that fatigue was not related to higher levels of cytokines. Eighty percent of patients with lupus reported fatigue, but no cause could be found after searching for a number of possible causes, including sociodemographic variables, medications, disease activity, serum cytokines, autoimmune antibodies, and abnormalities on any routine blood tests. So why do inflammatory cytokines seem to be related to fatigue in viruses and CFS, but not in autoimmune diseases? No one knows, but given the mysterious nature of autoimmune disorders in general, this discovery is not surprising. It is likely that there are different physiologic mechanisms involved. This finding certainly doesn't discount inflammation as a source of fatigue for autoimmune disorders, but it suggests that the relationships are more complex in autoimmune disorders than in other types of diseases.

There are three other possible reasons for fatigue: obesity, depression, and insomnia. Living day to day, we sometimes find it difficult to piece together the puzzle of our health. The relationships don't always seem obvious, and sometimes we may find them embarrassing. Many people who go to the doctor for fatigue are referred to a psychiatrist or psychologist or are given a prescription for an antidepressant. Some people take offense that the doctor doesn't seem to believe in their physical symptoms. Some, but not all, people with CFS are helped by antidepressants. A recent double-blind placebo-controlled trial of the antidepressant medicine named moclobemide found 51 percent of CFS patients improved, with improvement in only 33 percent of CFS patients taking a placebo.

Fatigue, obesity, depression, and insomnia are so closely related that it is impossible to determine their individual effects and relationships. Certainly not all obese people are fatigued or depressed, and many depressed people need to gain rather than lose weight. But we know that a number of diverse diseases (including heart disease, autoimmune diseases, allergies, asthma, and diabetes) are related in some way to obesity, fatigue, depression, and insomnia. It has been suggested that inflammation, no matter what the cause or the source, may be the common link.

OBESITY

Obesity is a severe and growing problem in the United States, Great Britain, and throughout the world. In 2000 a survey found that nearly one-third of American adults were obese, and nearly two-thirds were overweight. (Obesity is defined as being significantly overweight, based on body mass index—see "Are You Overweight?") This large proportion of the population is at risk for serious diseases. Studies have shown that obesity can double the risk of premature death, accounting for three hundred thousand premature deaths each year, primarily from heart attacks and strokes. It is second only to cigarette smoking as a cause of early death.

Scientists are still debating why so many more people are becoming overweight now compared with any other time in history. Certainly it is not because of human genetic changes, because genetic mutations don't occur that quickly in a population. Did we suddenly start watching more television and eating more fast-food burgers and fries? Were some chemicals introduced into our environment that interfered with our bodies' ability to regulate weight? Could it be that our on-again, off-again pattern of dieting has unbalanced our metabolism? No one really knows, and the answers are likely to be complex.

What we do know is that being overweight is an inflammatory condition. It raises the level of some pro-inflammatory chemicals in the body, and it increases the risk of other inflammation-related disorders, including heart disease, some cancers, diabetes, asthma, and arthritis.

Obesity comes in two types: gynoid obesity and android obesity. Gynoid obesity is when the body is shaped like a pear, with a disproportionate amount of fat around the hips relative to the waist. Gynoid obesity is much more common in women than men, particularly prior to menopause. Android obesity is when the body is shaped like an apple, with more fat around the waist than hips. The classic beer gut is an example of the android type. Although most of us can tell our "type" by visual inspection, the physician's measure is the waist-to-hip ratio. To determine your waist-to-hip ratio, measure around the circumference of your waist with a tape measure, then measure around your hips (at the widest point). Divide your waist measurement by your hip measurement. If the number is less than 0.75,

ARE YOU OVERWEIGHT?

The current method physicians use to define who is overweight or obese is the body mass index (BMI), which is a ratio of weight to height. This number is calculated by taking your weight (measured in kilograms) and dividing it by your height squared (measured in meters). (Alternatively, you can take your weight [in pounds] and multiply it by 704.5, then divide that number by your height squared [in inches].) To make things easier for you, we've included a chart of the BMI for each height and weight. Simply find the row for your weight on the vertical axis on the left, then locate the column for your height on the top horizontal bar. Where the row and the column intersect is a number that represents your approximate BMI. The numbers represent standard assessments for all adults:

ADULT VALUES

BMI < 17	anorexic
BMI of 17 to 18	underweight
BMI of 19 to 25	ideal
BMI of 26 to 30	overweight
BMI of 31 to 40	obese
BMI > 40	morbidly obese

you are considered to have a gynoid fat distribution pattern; if the number is greater than 0.85, you are considered to have an android fat distribution pattern.

This simple measurement can tell you a lot about your health risks. Men with a ratio greater than 1.0, and women with a ratio greater than 0.9 have an increased risk of heart disease. There is something about weight carried around the waist or midsection that seems to create an extra health risk. For women, having an apple-shaped (android) body is related to a higher risk for high blood pressure, heart disease, and diabetes. One study found that apple-shaped women have greater levels of inflammation than pear-shaped women, including measures of activity of blood cells called platelets. Greater platelet activation means a greater risk of blood clots, the major cause of stroke and heart disease. When these women lost weight, their inflammation markers decreased.

Body Mass Index (BMI) Chart

HEIGHT → WEIGHT ↓	59 in (1.50 m)	60 in (1.52 m)	61 in (1.55 m)	62 in (1.57 m)	63 in (1.60 m)	64 in (1.63 m)	65 in (1.65 m)	66 in (1.68 m)	67 in (1.70 m)	68 in (1.73 m)	69 in (1.75 m)	70 in (1.78 m)	71 in (1.80 m)	72 in (1.83 m)	73 in (1.85 m)	74 in (1.88 m)	75 in (1.90 m)
90 lb (41 kg)	18	18	17	17	16	15	15	15	14	14	13	13	13	12	12	12	11
95 lb (43 kg)	19	19	18	17	17	16	16	15	15	14	14	14	13	13	13	12	12
100 lb (45 kg)	20	20	19	18	18	17	17	16	16	15	15	14	14	14	13	13	12
110 lb (50 kg)	22	21	21	20	19	19	18	18	17	17	16	16	15	15	15	14	14
120 lb (54 kg)	24	23	23	22	21	21	20	19	19	18	18	17	17	16	16	15	15
130 lb (59 kg)	26	25	25	24	23	22	22	21	20	20	19	19	18	18	17	17	16
140 lb (64 kg)	28	27	26	26	25	24	23	23	22	21	21	20	20	19	18	18	17
150 lb (68 kg)	30	29	28	27	27	26	25	24	23	23	22	22	21	20	20	19	19
160 lb (73 kg)	32	31	30	29	28	27	27	26	25	24	24	23	22	22	21	21	20
170 lb (77 kg)	34	33	32	31	30	29	28	27	27	26	25	24	24	23	22	22	21
180 lb (82 kg)	36	35	34	33	32	31	30	29	28	27	27	26	25	24	24	23	22
190 lb (86 kg)	38	37	36	35	34	33	32	31	30	29	28	27	26	26	25	24	24
200 lb (91 kg)	40	39	38	37	35	34	33	32	31	30	30	29	28	27	26	26	25
210 lb (95 kg)	40+	40+	40	38	37	36	35	34	33	32	31	30	29	28	28	27	26
220 lb (100 kg)	40+	40+	40+	40	39	38	37	36	34	33	32	32	31	30	29	28	27
230 lb (104 kg)	40+	40+	40+	40+	40+	39	38	37	36	35	34	33	32	31	30	30	29
240 lb (109 kg)	40+	40+	40+	40+	40+	40+	40	39	38	36	35	34	33	33	32	31	30
250 lb (113 kg)	40+	40+	40+	40+	40+	40+	40+	40	39	38	37	36	35	34	33	32	31
260 lb (118 kg)	40+	40+	40+	40+	40+	40+	40+	40+	40+	39	39	37	36	35	34	33	33
270 lb (122 kg)	40+	40+	40+	40+	40+	40+	40+	40+	40+	40+	40	38	38	36	36	34	34
280 lb (127 kg)	40+	40+	40+	40+	40+	40+	40+	40+	40+	40+	40+	40	39	38	37	36	35
290 lb (132 kg)	40+	40+	40+	40+	40+	40+	40+	40+	40+	40+	40+	40+	40+	39	39	37	37
300 lb (136 kg)	40+	40+	40+	40+	40+	40+	40+	40+	40+	40+	40+	40+	40+	40	40	38	38

*Shaded area shows range for ideal body mass.

Over the last decade, a number of associations between obesity and inflammation have been discovered. Fat itself excretes pro-inflammatory cytokines. Some research suggests that up to 30 percent of the inflammation-related cytokine IL-6 in blood comes from fat tissue. Another potent inflammatory cytokine, tumor necrosis factor-alpha, is also secreted by fat cells. This means that fat alone is pro-inflammatory and therefore may tip the balance of inflammation in a way that increases the risk of atherosclerosis and other inflammation-related diseases.

Just as significant, weight loss is associated with decreases in inflammatory markers. In one study, blood levels of the inflammation marker C-reactive protein (CRP) fell 23 percent in obese patients who lost weight. Australian investigators found that there was a direct correlation between fat and CRP levels, so that the higher a person's BMI, the higher the level of CRP in the blood. The good news is that as people lose weight, their CRP levels fall. In one study, a weight loss of only about 18 pounds (about 8 kilograms) allowed CRP levels to fall about 26 percent. Even people who lost weight due to surgical intervention had decreases in levels of CRP. These types of relationships are seen over and over again in the literature. Blood levels of the pro-inflammatory cytokine interleukin-18 (IL-18) were much higher in obese women, and those levels fell to normal with weight loss.

Another factor that comes into play is the metabolic syndrome, sometimes called Syndrome X, or the metabolic syndrome. This disorder is a combination of abdominal obesity, high blood pressure, elevated cholesterol, and high blood sugar that puts people at a much higher risk of type 2 diabetes, heart attacks, and strokes. About forty-seven million Americans—nearly one in four adults—have the metabolic syndrome, and virtually all of the ten to fifteen million Americans with type 2 diabetes have the metabolic syndrome.

You have the metabolic syndrome if you have three or more of the following physical characteristics:

- *Abdominal obesity:* waist circumference >102 centimeters (40 inches) in men; >88 centimeters (35 inches) in women

- *Elevated level of triglycerides (fats) in your blood:* ≥150 mg/dL

- *Low HDL cholesterol:* <40 mg/dL in men; <50 mg/dL in women

- *High blood pressure:* ≥130/85 mm Hg

- *High fasting glucose:* (fasting blood sugar ≥110 mg/dL)

People with the metabolic syndrome have been shown to have low-level, chronic inflammation of the type that causes atherosclerosis. Studies have shown that people with high BMI are more likely to have chronic inflammation and to develop the metabolic syndrome. This means people who are overweight put themselves at risk of developing all the major killers—heart disease, stroke, and diabetes—because of the connection to inflammation. Losing weight lowers the levels of inflammation, and therefore automatically lowers the risks for disease.

The studies go on and on. There is no controversy—inflammation and obesity run together. Some research suggests that fat itself increases levels of inflammation in the body. But no one knows about the other option—does inflammation lead to obesity? Although there are no definite answers right now, we can look to studies involving other diseases for clues. A study in Korea found that the higher a person's BMI (that is, the more overweight the person), the greater the probability of developing the inflammation-related diseases asthma, rhinitis, conjunctivitis, or eczema. Breathing in secondhand smoke and living with toxic chemicals in carpets also raised the risk of developing those diseases. We know that secondhand smoke and carpet fumes can cause inflammatory reactions, and in my clinical experience, many people who work in sick buildings (where they breathe in toxic fumes) gain significant amounts of weight. So it is possible that the factors that caused airway inflammation also caused weight gain, and that the weight gain then caused additional inflammation. We see again the downward spiral of inflammation, sucking us down into illness unless we can regain balance and control inflammation-related factors in our lives. (For more information about sick buildings and environmental toxins related to inflammation, see Chapter 10.)

Of course, weight loss is also important. The usual assumption about obesity is that we get fat by eating too much of the wrong kind of food and getting too little exercise. We eat food that contains energy measured as calories. Every calorie is either stored as fat or burned as fuel. If we burn more fuel than we eat, we tap into our fat stores and lose weight. If we eat more than we burn, energy is stored as fat and we gain weight.

This argument seems reasonably simple, but the human body is extremely complicated. Consider all the factors involved in determining how much we eat and how many calories we burn. Our weight is determined partly by genetics, partly by social and environmental factors, and partly by physiology. Obesity runs in families, not solely because we inherit "fat" genes, but because some families prefer to eat more and exercise less. Resting metabolic rates of muscle and other tissues are different for obese and nonobese individuals, so whether we are running, resting, or even sleeping, we burn calories at varying rates. Even the efficiency of absorption of dietary fat and other nutrients can vary from person to person. And perhaps there are other factors, such as that sick building previously mentioned, contributing to weight gain. Weight loss is important as part of controlling our overall inflammation balance, but people who become frustrated in their attempts to lose weight should understand that if other sources of inflammation are eliminated, weight loss might become easier. (See Chapters 9 through 12 for more information about changes you can make to reduce inflammation.)

DEPRESSION

Depression is a brain disorder in which a person is inappropriately sad and unhappy. The pleasures of life vanish, and in extreme cases, victims of depression become suicidal. One of the great triumphs of twentieth-century medicine was the realization that mental diseases such as depression and schizophrenia are not simply "all in the head," but are real, physical disorders in which the brain malfunctions. A person cannot choose to snap out of depression, and advice to cheer up cannot change brain chemistry.

Around the middle of the last century, a drug called reserpine came on the market to treat high blood pressure. This drug, derived from a vine native to India with medicinal uses since ancient times, lowers blood pressure by blocking the action of the neurotransmitter norepinephrine in the brain. About 15 percent of people who took the drug became depressed, some to the point of psychosis and suicide. This suggested a physiologic basis for depression. If drugs that blocked the action of norepinephrine in the brain led to depression, then drugs that enhanced the action of the norepinephrine should be able to treat depression. This is exactly what happened.

Depression is a significant mental health problem in the United States and throughout the world. Interestingly, the number of people who are depressed has risen dramatically in the past few decades. This parallels the rise in environmental pollution, obesity, heart disease, and diabetes. We'll never know why depression has been on the rise. It could be that today there is greater awareness of the disease among physicians and the public, better medications that make people more likely to seek treatment, or more stressful lifestyles. It is possible that depression is increasing because all the other inflammation factors are increasing, and that depression is another inflammation-related disorder.

The evidence for the inflammation connection is everywhere. Depression has been shown to be related to a number of other inflammation-related diseases. We know that inflammation is a major cause of fatigue, and people who are depressed frequently experience devastating fatigue. In fact, fatigue is so common among those diagnosed with depression that it is considered part of the illness. People who are depressed are also more likely to have diabetes and to be overweight. All these problems together are increasingly prevalent and associated with hypertension, heart attack, and increased mortality. And depression alone doubles the risk of heart disease.

Depression is associated with airway inflammation due to allergies or sensitivity to irritants in the air. One study found that all but one of ninety-six people with depression tested positive on allergy skin tests, but only half were aware of symptoms of allergy. Another study found allergic disorders in 33 percent of psychiatric patients with depression, but only 6 percent of patients with schizophrenia. This research suggests that depression and inflammation may be closely related, but schizophrenia is not likely to be related to inflammation.

Several studies found that people with chemical sensitivities (an inflammation-related reaction to environmental irritants) were about three or four times more likely to suffer from depression than nonsensitive people. Autoimmune diseases, inflammatory diseases in which the patient's immune system targets a specific group of tissues, are also related to depression. Lupus is so strongly associated with depression that prior to the development of blood tests for lupus, an episode of major depression was one of the diagnostic criteria. Multiple sclerosis patients have a high incidence of depression that correlates with the severity of the disease. Some would argue that they are depressed because they have multiple sclerosis, but there is most likely a deeper connection, a depression-like fatigue that is part and parcel of the disease rather than an emotional reaction to the disease. Even mice with an experimental form of multiple sclerosis induced by immunization to their myelin demonstrate symptoms of depression. (For more information about depression, see Chapter 12.)

Sleep Disorders

Sleep disorders can be extensions of inflammation-related disorders, including fatigue, depression, and weight issues. Sleep disorders can take a number of different forms, including excessive sleep, an inability to fall asleep, early awakening, frequent wakings during the night, and total insomnia. Sleep disturbances occur in greater frequency in some people with inflammation-related disorders, including people with autoimmune diseases, such as multiple sclerosis and rheumatoid arthritis, and in people with allergies. Sleep apnea, with disordered breathing during sleep and daytime sleepiness, occurs in up to 85 percent of obese individuals.

People with infections are often sleepy, even during the day. This is thought to be due to excess amounts of the cytokine interleukin-1 (IL-1), which is secreted when people are infected. This pro-inflammatory cytokine causes fever, but also sleepiness. Injections of IL-1 into mice actually makes them fall asleep.

In my clinical practice, sleep disturbances are almost universal in sick building sufferers. People with chemical sensitivities often have nighttime insomnia after a daytime chemical exposure. People who suffer from sick building syndrome are often sleepy. In addition to the symptoms related to mucous membrane irritation (such as cough, nasal congestion, and asthma), these people also have difficulties with concentration, memory, and thinking. These cognitive problems may not be due to direct impairment of memory and thinking, but due to drowsiness and fatigue that makes these mental activities difficult.

It is clear that links exist between fatigue, obesity, depression, sleep disorders, and inflammation. These links do not mean that all cases of these disorders are related to inflammation, or that inflammation is the sole cause of depression, fatigue, or obesity. Rather, inflammatory conditions can cause body changes that lead to these disabilities. Some scientists hypothesize that the cytokines released during almost any type of inflammation affect the nervous system, which leads to fatigue, disorders of weight, depression, and sleep disturbance. Certainly, cytokines do play a role, but the situation is much more complex. The whole system is like a giant feedback loop. The nervous system controls inflammation and can even initiate inflammation without activation of the immune system. The immune system, in turn, communicates with the nervous system through its own chemical messengers. With a constant two-way communication between the nervous system and the immune system, inflammation can be escalated unless the endless loop communicating the need for inflammation is broken.

If you are tired, depressed, or having trouble with your weight or with sleep, seek help from your doctor. But at the same time, try everything you can to reduce the inflammation factors in your life (see Chapters 9 through 12). This is the perfect time to take control of your health—while your body is giving you signals that it is not feeling healthy, but before things get worse.

7

MISTAKEN IDENTITIES

AUTOIMMUNE DISEASES, ALLERGIES, ASTHMA

◉

When faced with a threat or an assault, the body's inflammatory response allows us to fight off viruses or bacteria, end infections, and repair damaged tissues. But sometimes the body makes a mistake and identifies harmless things as dangerous, leading to an inappropriate flare of inflammation. This time, instead of helping to heal the body, inflammation causes pain, suffering, damage to vital structures and organs, and even death. This type of inappropriate inflammation might last only a couple of days, or it might persist for months or years. Depending on the type of immune response and where it occurs in the body, a number of diseases can result, from hay fever and asthma, to a simple poison ivy rash, to rheumatoid arthritis and other autoimmune diseases.

ALLERGIES AND SENSITIVITIES

Allergies are so common that almost everyone has experienced them at one time or another. Studies indicate roughly one-third of us have common allergies to pollens, mold spores, pet dander, dust mites, or cockroaches. In a loose sense, having an allergy means getting sick from exposure to something that is harmless to most other people. Technically, having an allergy means that the body makes a specific kind of antibody (immunoglobulin E, or IgE) in reaction to a foreign protein. Reactions that don't involve IgE antibodies can also make a person sick, but they aren't allergies. For example, inflammation reactions that look and feel like allergy attacks can be caused by stimulation of nerves in the airway—reactions called irritant, or chemical, sensitivity. Many people who claim to be allergic to cigarette smoke or perfume, for example, are not actually allergic. Rather, the nerve endings in their noses and airways are responding to those irritants. Between 15 and 30 percent of us have sensitivities to chemicals such as tobacco smoke, fragrances and perfumes, cleaning products, and other solvents at levels that are usually harmless.

When we inhale, the air goes in through the nostrils, up through the nasal passages, down the throat (pharynx) to the windpipe (trachea), and through the tree-like bronchial tubes, to the tiny air sacs of the lungs where oxygen diffuses into the blood. This pathway is collectively called the airway. With each breath, we inhale a lot more than oxygen. Some of the stuff in the air we breathe is alive: bacteria, viruses, fungi, and mold spores. Other things in the air are poisonous, such as the carbon monoxide and sulfur dioxide found in vehicle exhaust, furnace fumes, fireplace smoke, and fumes from gas cook stoves. Other stuff is just plain irritating, including smoke, dust, and many types of fumes.

With each breath, our bodies test everything we inhale. If it is alive or dangerous, we try to fight it off. And of course, anytime we fight off germs, the body produces inflammation. In certain susceptible people, allergens and irritants in the air produce inflammation of the airways.

The first points of contact for irritants, allergens, and germs we inhale are the inner lining of the nose and the sinuses, the air-filled cavities located above, between, and below the eyes. The linings of the nose and sinuses are continuously exposed to the same air, and become inflamed at the same time by the same things, leading to rhinosinusitis (inflammation of the nose and sinuses). This causes all those familiar allergy symptoms: sneezing, runny nose, nasal and sinus congestion, and sinus headaches. Allergies also cause an itchy nose, while irritants are more likely to cause a burning sensation.

Asthma

Along with sinuses and nasal passages, other parts of the airway can also become inflamed, including the bronchial tubes (producing bronchitis). Asthma is a type of bronchitis that is triggered in susceptible people by such diverse things as allergens, pollutants, exercise, cold dry air, and sometimes emotional stress. During an asthma attack, the bronchial tubes become inflamed, narrowing the airway so that less air can pass through. Muscles in the walls of the bronchial tubes constrict to further narrow the airway. Breathing becomes hard work, and the forced airflow through the narrowed tubes causes a whistling sound called a wheeze, although it is possible to have asthma inflammation without wheezing. If a person with asthma can get clean air—free of pollen, dusts, fumes, or whatever is inciting the inflammation for that particular attack—asthma can go away.

From a biological standpoint, narrowing the tubes is a good thing—it reduces the amount of air taken in, reducing the amount of allergens and irritants entering the lungs. So narrowing the bronchial tubes is actually a protective action of the body. That's why medicines that improve wheezing without reducing inflammation can actually lead to death from asthma. By opening up the bronchial tubes to increase airflow and reduce wheezing, more inflammation-causing stuff enters the lungs, inflammation gets worse, and the airways sometimes close entirely from mucus that dries to form thick plugs. Anti-inflammatory medicines need to be given along with medications that open up the airways.

There is currently an epidemic of asthma in the United States, but no one knows exactly why. In 1929 about one in every two hundred people suffered from asthma. Now it is estimated that about one in twenty adults and perhaps as many as one in four children have asthma. Other airway inflammation disorders are also on the rise, including rhinosinusitis and pollen allergies. Inflammation of the eyes is so common in individuals working in sick buildings in which irritant fumes are present (see Chapter 10) that the term *office eye syndrome* has appeared in the medical literature.

Three possible causes for the increase in asthma and rhinosinusitis are being investigated: the chemical hypothesis, which holds that air pollution is responsible; the viral hypothesis, which claims that viral infections might be to blame; and the hygiene hypothesis, which proposes that our high standards of cleanliness are doing us in.

Chemical Hypothesis

Allergies to Japanese cedar tree pollen were rare in Japan before the 1950s but are now very common. The disease first appeared in places where motor vehicles were introduced, and Japanese scientists wondered if this was more than a coincidence. During experiments, they found that allergies to a particular protein developed only when that protein was combined with diesel exhaust. In other words, Japanese people have been breathing in Japanese cedar pollen since the beginning of time, but few of them became allergic to it until they started breathing it in along with diesel exhaust particles and other pollutants, such as ozone, sulfur dioxide, and oxides of nitrogen. These results were confirmed in other studies, so now we know that air pollution contributes to allergies.

Although we tend to think of allergies as a mild case of sniffles, the inflammation can sometimes be extensive. When I was a resident at the University of Rochester, I saw a young man named Hal, who, during ragweed pollen season, had been admitted to the intensive care unit, where he was put on life support. He had previously been in excellent health, had never had an asthma attack, and had a very mild allergy to ragweed pollen that was controlled with over-the-counter antihistamines. One day at the printing factory where he worked, some solvents and ink spilled onto the floor. Hal was near the fumes and soon began wheezing and became short of breath for the first time in his life. From that one exposure, Hal developed chronic asthma that persisted long after the initial exposure ended. Every year, when the ragweed pollen season hit, his previously mild allergy turned into a potentially deadly asthma attack.

Since that time, the medical literature has been swamped with similar reports of chronic asthma and rhinosinusitis that began with an exposure to any of a number of respiratory irritants. Once the inflammation starts, it can persist for months or years. This is because inflammation leads to release of a protein called nerve growth factor, which does just what its name implies—the lining of the airway grows new sensory nerve endings to respond to irritants. Other substances are released that cause the cells lining the airways to slough off and expose the nerve fibers, making the airway hyperresponsive to even tiny insults. It's kind of like scratching an open wound. If the skin were normal, scratching wouldn't hurt. But scrape off a couple layers of skin to expose the nerves, and even the slightest touch will be painful. So air pollution acts as an irritant, which causes inflammation. Over time, we become hypersensitive so that just about anything will provoke additional inflammation, leading to allergy symptoms or asthma.

Viral Hypothesis

Our bodies fight viruses with inflammation, and inflammation of the airway is what asthma is all about. Viral infections of the airway cause inflammation with damage similar to that of chemical exposures. In both cases, damage to the cells lining the airway exposes sensory nerves. Sensory nerves release chemicals called neuropeptides, which produce additional inflammation. Some viruses are more likely to lead to chronic asthma than others, perhaps because different viruses trigger different patterns of inflammation. For people who already have asthma, attacks are often triggered by a viral infection. The rhinovirus, which causes the common cold, can cause asthma flares; and influenza can be enough to send a person with asthma to the hospital. Anyone with asthma should get a flu shot every year.

Hygiene Hypothesis (or Adaptation Hypothesis)

The hygiene hypothesis states that excessive cleanliness leads to allergies and asthma. The theory is that if children are exposed to a large number of different immune stimuli (allergens and irritants) in early childhood, then their immune systems learn not to have allergic reactions to things like pollen and dust. This hypothesis is difficult to study because so many different factors are involved. For example, a recent study comparing farm and non-farm households in Germany, Switzerland, and Austria found higher levels of endotoxin, a component of the cell walls of bacteria, in the farm homes. And children who grew up in farm homes with high levels of endotoxin had less asthma, rhinosinusitis, and allergy. So more bacteria equals less asthma. Although this would seem to support the hygiene hypothesis, there are other factors that weren't part of the study that could have made a difference. For example, maybe farm children have fewer viral infections, less exposure to vehicle exhaust and other city air pollutants, or different kinds of indoor irritants.

If all of this sounds confusing, that's because it is. Even medical investigators can become confused by the deluge of conflicting study reports. So what's causing the epidemics of asthma, rhinosinusitis, and allergies? Is it chemicals, viruses, or hygiene? The current best guess is option number four: all of the above. All the hypotheses are interrelated, and it all comes down to layers of inflammation. For example, the chemical irritants from cigarette smoke can cause airway inflammation in smokers and the nonsmokers around them. Some viruses cause inflammation of the airway. Each alone might cause minor inflammation, but put the two together and you've got a disease.

Another layer of inflammation that may or may not be affecting the rising prevalence of asthma is obesity. The rise in asthma has paralleled the rise in obesity in the United States. Studies that have looked at this relationship have shown that, at least for women, being overweight increases the risk of developing asthma at all ages. In addition, studies have shown that certain foods are related to asthma in teenagers, especially—get ready for it—high-fat, deep-fried foods, the type served by the billions in fast-food restaurants. We know that obesity increases the amount of inflammation in the body. We know that high-fat, deep-fried foods contribute to obesity, and that obesity is related to asthma. In addition, one study has demonstrated that people who are overweight and have asthma improve their lung function, symptoms, and overall health after they lose weight. Could the low-level, chronic inflammation that comes from being overweight be enough to push someone over the precarious health cliff into asthma? Research on this topic is ongoing, but it certainly is a possibility.

VISIBLE INFLAMMATION: THE SKIN

The skin is one place where inflammation can be seen, felt, and, in some cases, even smelled. A standing joke passed to each year's class of medical students learning about skin diseases is that, other than skin cancers, there are two thousand skin diseases but only two treatments: medicines to kill infections and medicines to squelch inflammation. Skin infections trigger inflammation, which shows up as rashes and swelling. Treatment with appropriate antibiotics to kill the germs, whether bacteria, fungal, or virus, removes the source of inflammation, and the rashes usually clear up.

There are two main ways, other than germs, that things can inflame skin. There can be an immune response, in which T cells and other immune cells react to things on the skin, or an irritant response, in which nerve cells react to things on the skin. The most common rash—contact dermatitis—is caused by touching something that is irritating to that person. Poison ivy is a rash caused by exposure to a resin in the leaves of the poison ivy plant. Immune cells react to a chemical on the poison ivy leaf, and an angry rash will appear wherever the leaves touch. Believe it or not, the same chemical that causes poison ivy rash is also found on the skin of mangoes (so be careful not to bite off the fruit stuck to the inside of the skins!) and in cashew shells (but not cashew nuts). Cashew processors have to take great care not to touch the shells.

Hives is a skin rash with itchy bumps caused by the allergy chemical histamine, which is released by mast cells. The rash is a visible indication of some acute inflammatory reaction in the body. Hives can occur if a foreign substance finds its way under your skin, such as venom from a bee sting, or from eating food, ingesting a medicine, or inhaling something. For example, some people with pollen allergies get hives during high-pollen seasons.

People can even get a rash from breathing chemicals in the air, a condition called airborne contact dermatitis. A skin rash pops up even though the chemical never touches the skin. Essentially, the site of the inflammation is shifted from the respiratory tract to the skin. This switching phenomenon occurs in many forms of inflammation. More than four hundred chemicals have been identified that can cause airborne contact dermatitis, including chemicals found in wall paint.

In addition, the inflammation associated with many autoimmune diseases can spill over onto the skin. For example, rashes frequently occur with lupus and are less commonly found with rheumatoid arthritis.

AUTOIMMUNE DISEASES

The ever-vigilant immune system is always looking for invading cells to kill. When a rogue cell or foreign protein is discovered, not only is that invader destroyed, but the immune cells also sound the invasion alarm and call for support. Soon, much of the body's resources are devoted to looking for, attacking, and killing any other cells that look remotely like that invading cell.

Sometimes, more often than we'd like to think, the immune system makes a mistake and starts attacking the body's own healthy tissue. It confuses *self* with *other* and begins attacking the self. Because all body tissue is not alike, not all body tissue is attacked. Immune cells are programmed to attack tissue they identify as foreign because that tissue has a particular protein signature. So the type of disease that results depends on the type of tissue that is targeted for attack. The disease may attack a particular type of skin tissue and give rise to a horrible array of rashes; it may attack a portion of the nervous system and cut off the body's communication system; it may attack the connective tissue of the body and cause horrible pain and debilitation as the body feels as though it is literally falling apart; it may attack specific tissues of the heart, lungs, or liver and cause fatal organ system damage.

Autoimmune diseases are among the great mysteries of medicine. They attack normal, healthy body tissue, but most of the time we don't know why. On average, they strike women three times more often than men, but we don't know why. They often strike people in the prime of life, between ages twenty and fifty, but we don't know why. Many autoimmune disorders flare up and die down, making patients' health an unpredictable roller coaster, but we don't know why they flare up or what makes them go away. What we do know is that autoimmune diseases are incurable, and the longer the period of time the disease is active and causing inflammation reactions, the more damaging it is.

Autoimmune Triggers

In a few cases, scientists have discovered that a variety of environmental factors, including infectious agents, chemicals, and drugs, can trigger an autoimmune disease. For example, autoimmune hemolytic anemia, a disease in which the body starts making antibodies to its own red blood cells, can be caused by an immune response to penicillin (and a handful of other medications). What happens is that the penicillin binds to molecules on the surfaces of the red blood cells, changing their chemical structure. Sometimes the immune system notices this new structure, sounds the alarm, and starts treating the red blood cells as if they were foreign bacteria. The blood cells become coated with antibodies, which trigger mechanisms that burst the cell membranes and kill the cell.

Another trigger is called molecular mimicry. When the body encounters a virus, it goes on the attack. The immune system gears up, creates antibodies against viral proteins, and then destroys the virus. Now suppose that the viral protein looks almost identical to a protein on a normal body cell. What happens? The immune system gears up and destroys the virus, but goes on to destroy all body cells with the nearly identical protein. This is what happens when a person develops type 1 diabetes mellitus. The immune system mistakenly destroys all the insulin-making cells in the pancreas. People who get type 1 diabetes have a gene that codes for a special type of protein on insulin-making cells, *and* they must be exposed to the very particular virus that has a similar protein. So both genetics and the environment play a part in creating the disease.

Collagen Vascular Diseases

We have no idea what causes most autoimmune diseases. But the category of autoimmune diseases known as collagen vascular diseases—which includes systemic lupus erythematosus (known as lupus), rheumatoid arthritis, and scleroderma—is commonly triggered by exposure to chemicals and environmental hazards. In these conditions, the immune system makes antibodies to a variety of normal proteins found in the human body, leading to inflammation of the blood vessels and connective tissues, including the synovial lining of joints. Prognosis is highly variable, and in the worst cases, vital organs become inflamed and fail.

Lupus

Lupus gets its name from the Latin word for wolf, because lupus skin rashes can look as ravaged as wolf bites. People with lupus have immune systems that make antibodies to naturally occurring body chemicals, including DNA and some proteins found in chromosomes. There can be inflammation in multiple organ systems, including the skin, joints, heart, lungs, brain, and kidneys. The disease can start slowly, with vague symptoms like fatigue and poorly defined aches and pains. As lupus progresses, inflammation spreads throughout the body, and at the extreme end it can lead to organ failure.

The percentage of people in the United States with lupus is growing, although no one is exactly sure why. We know that it runs in families and that the risk is higher in people with certain protein markers on the surface of cells. It is also strongly suspected that certain environmental toxins play a role in the development of lupus. We know that some drugs, foods, and air pollutants can induce lupus. For example, the drug procainamide (brand names Procan and Pronestyl), used to treat abnormal heart rhythms, can cause symptoms of lupus in about 25 percent of people who take the drug. Body builders who use anabolic steroids also can sometimes develop drug-related lupus.

It is difficult to pin down the links between environmental chemicals and autoimmune diseases because we don't always know what's in the air around us. We can absorb toxic chemicals into our bodies as complex mixtures, in unknown doses and sometimes from unknown sources. Neither physicians nor the people they treat have a clue about when, what, or how many chemicals the patients were exposed to prior to diagnosis. Still, there are some lupus-causing suspects. A particular chemical in a purported "health food"—raw alfalfa seeds, like the kind attached to the sprouts—is believed to cause lupus in some people and definitely causes lupus in monkeys. Industrial emissions are also associated with an increased risk of lupus. When scientists went to Gainesville, Georgia, a town with long-term exposure to industrial emissions, they discovered that the residents were nine times more likely to get lupus than people not living there.

Another example is malathion, a pesticide used extensively in the United States. Malathion is generally less toxic to humans than other pesticides, so it has been extensively used in situations where human exposure could be high. When medflies are spotted in Florida or California, huge areas are sprayed with malathion from airplanes and helicopters. Although it has never been proven that malathion exposure can cause lupus in people, we know that in mice with a certain genetic predisposition, malathion can cause lupus and cause the disease to progress.

If the environmental factor that triggered the lupus can be identified and removed, some patients go into remission, with all symptoms of the disease disappearing. In most cases, however, the triggers cannot be identified. It becomes important, then, to eliminate any potential source of additional inflammation, regardless of the original cause. For example, anyone with lupus should take tremendous care to avoid inhaling malathion if they live in an area that is sprayed. (Specific tips for protecting yourself against these types of environmental exposures, and for reducing your overall chemical load, are given in Chapter 10.)

Rheumatoid Arthritis

Rheumatoid arthritis is the most common of the collagen vascular diseases, affecting about one in every fifty Americans. It is primarily a disease of the joints. Patients are very stiff when they get up in the morning or if they sit still for a relatively short time, but they loosen up as they move about. Joints are swollen, painful in motion, and tender to touch. As the inflammation of rheumatoid arthritis progresses, joints can be destroyed, sometimes resulting in deformities. These deformities usually strike the hands, but hip and knee joints can also be destroyed. Inflammation can spill over into other organs, including the heart, and blood vessels can become inflamed, causing damage throughout the body.

Studies have looked at the relationship of rheumatoid arthritis to environmental exposures, but no clear pattern developed. Workers in certain industries (such as farm, mining, and forestry) have been shown in some studies to be more likely to get rheumatoid arthritis than workers in other fields. For example, coal miners can be afflicted with a form of rheumatoid arthritis that affects the lungs.

Sometimes rheumatoid arthritis can be related to food intolerance. In 1999 a review of the published medical literature found that some—but not all—people with rheumatoid arthritis benefited from changes in their diets. Since then, two important scientific studies have appeared in support. First, Dr. M. A. Haugen and his collaborators in Oslo, Norway, placed a group of people with rheumatoid arthritis on an "elemental diet," which is a synthetic, protein-free diet consisting of laboratory-assembled collections of amino acids, sugars, fats, and vitamins and minerals. A comparison group of people with rheumatoid arthritis ate normal foods. Because it's generally assumed that food proteins cause inflammatory food reactions, this protein-free elemental diet was a way to wipe the food slate clean of proteins while still keeping all other important nutrients in the diet. If it was a food-related inflammation, then being on the elemental diet should reduce symptoms. In fact, the patients who ate the elemental diet, eliminating all proteins, had a significant improvement in joint tenderness compared with the group that ate proteins.

In another study, researchers compared the effects of a vegan diet (vegetarian diet with no milk, eggs, or other animal products whatsoever) to a healthy but non-vegetarian diet in people with rheumatoid arthritis. After a year on the diets, 40 percent of the people on the vegan diet improved, compared with only 4 percent of the people on the nonvegan diet. A third, multi-center study of rheumatiod arthritis patients conducted in environmental control units with pristine air and dietary elimination found an improvement in objective markers of the disease. These studies suggest that people with rheumatoid arthritis might significantly decrease pain and reduce the risk of additional joint damage by eliminating animal proteins from their diets. (For more information about dietary changes and what a vegan diet looks like, see Chapter 9.)

So what does this mean for the average person with rheumatoid arthritis? It is clear that some people with rheumatoid arthritis have a remarkable recovery after eliminating one or more common foods from their diets. Others, unfortunately, do not. One possible reason is that all patients with rheumatoid arthritis may have hypersensitivity, but to different things. One person may be sensitive to foods, another to chemicals, or drugs, or a common bacteria or fungus that colonizes humans, or just about anything else in the world. Eliminating that particular thing should help improve symptoms, but the problem is discovering what the triggers are for each individual patient. This can be done by reducing your overall chemical load, controlling the chemicals you allow into your home, and experimenting with food allergies by systematically eliminating various possible food triggers. (Environmental controls and chemicals are discussed further in Chapter 10, and elimination diets are discussed in Chapter 9.)

Scleroderma

Scleroderma is the most devastating of the collagen vascular diseases. Scleroderma gets its name from the Greek words for hard (*skleros*) and skin (*derma*). Scleroderma can be thought of as the healing process gone wild. After an injury, immune cells called lymphocytes initiate a series of molecular events that cause special cells (fibroblasts) to start making collagen and other proteins, the same proteins that hold the cells of our bodies together. Fibroblasts are responsible for healing cuts and forming scars. Scleroderma is like an assembly line with no off switch. Excessive amounts of collagen and connective tissue proteins are made and deposited, leading to a progressive hardening and thickening of the skin. A person's fingers become stiff and unusable, and because skin hardens around the mouth, it becomes difficult to eat or speak. As the disease progresses, this hardening spreads throughout the body. When the heart, lungs, or kidneys harden, those organs eventually fail.

A number of environmental factors have been suggested as potential causes of hardening and thickening of the skin, similar or identical to the effects of scleroderma. Of these, the stongest evidence exists for silica dust and vinyl chloride. Workers can be exposed to silica dust from sandblasting, mining, tunnel digging, and glassmaking. Vinyl chloride is used to make polyvinyl chloride, which is used in PVC pipe, furniture, toys, automobile upholstery, floor mats, and a variety of other products. Workers at PVC factories have been known to develop scleroderma-like symptoms. (There have been no documented cases of vinyl chloride disease associated with use of consumer products; the problem is restricted to factory workers.)

Can Symptoms Be Relieved?

Many people with autoimmune diseases either accidentally or intentionally have discovered one or more chemical substances found in foods, air, or water that they believe trigger their symptoms. When they avoid those substances, the disease sometimes goes into remission. Other people are not helped at all by these types of environmental approaches. There is no simple test that can tell who will benefit from an environmental approach, nor a test that can screen for possible environmental causes. Sometimes possible environmental causes are known, and these can be investigated in a particular case. Most of the time, however, it is simply a process of trial and error.

For anyone suffering from an autoimmune disorder, the question becomes: why *not* try an environmental approach to disease management? Although the process of sorting out possible environmental causes can be time-consuming and frustrating, the chance of having an autoimmune disease go into remission by avoiding a food, a medicine, or an inhalant is more than worth the risk for most people. (To discover what major and minor things you can do to limit your exposure to potentially toxic chemicals, see Chapter 10; and to learn more about specific dietary changes that might be helpful, see Chapter 9.)

CONNECTIONS

So what does all this mean in the context of other inflammatory disorders? As you might expect, there are connections, but we're not really sure what they mean yet.

It is not uncommon for people with one autoimmune disease to develop a different autoimmune disease—another factor that lends credence to the idea that inflammation has far-reaching connections. For example, people with autoimmune thyroid disease seem to have an increased risk of developing lupus, and scientists have reported an association between multiple sclerosis and type 1 diabetes.

In addition, researchers have discovered that people with lupus and rheumatoid arthritis seem to have a faster rate of development of atherosclerosis, potentially leading to premature heart attack. And people with periodontal disease seem to be at high risk of developing both rheumatoid arthritis and heart disease. Another study has shown that people with lupus have a high rate of migraine, another inflammatory disease.

There might also be a deeper connection that taps into the systemic nature of inflammation. Consider psychological stress, for example. We know that stress can cause an asthma attack—it also worsens heart disease, can bring on an episode of IBS, worsens a rash, and can cause flares of inflammatory autoimmune disorders. And what does stress do to the body? It increases inflammation.

The lesson is that when the inflammation dominoes start to tumble, everything in their way can be affected. Fortunately, there are many things that we can do to protect ourselves from the various sources of inflammation (see Chapters 9 through 12).

8

Inflamm-Aging

Aging, Arthritis, Alzheimer's Disease

◉

A person's life is divided into three stages: growth and development, reproductive years, and aging with decline. From the standpoint of biology, the primary function of an organism is to reproduce so that the species will evolve and develop over time. At the end of reproductive years, biological function has ended and a person enters the period of decline programmed in the genetic code. Changes in the nervous, endocrine, and immune systems take place during aging. Ultimately these changes lead to a biological end, the death of the person. The wheel of birth and death cycles and recycles.

Aging

Just as our growth and development are programmed into our DNA, so is our maximum life span. For human beings, the absolute maximum life span has been estimated to be about 120 years. After that time, the body system falls apart, a virtual disintegration. This means that if everything goes right, if our genes don't force us into early decline, if environmental toxins don't warp our DNA, if we don't allow inflammation-related diseases to take hold and degenerate our bodies, we would all live to be about 120 and then simply expire of old age.

Although more and more people are living to be 100 or older, the vast majority of us never make it to extreme old age. And those of us who do find that our quality of life tends to decline quickly. Even if we avoid the big killers—heart disease, cancer, stroke, diabetes—old age still bombards us with arthritis, osteoporosis, failing vision, and senility. When you think of a person who is 100 years old or older, what do you see? Many people imagine a person who tires easily, who is frail, weak, sick, and faltering.

But the physical declines we think of as normal aging are not "normal" at all. Yes, they happen more frequently in old age, but now scientists understand that most diseases of old age are due in large part to inflammation. Even frailty. Frailty is a medical condition defined as having at least three of the following conditions: muscle weakness, slow or unsteady walking gait, unintentional weight loss of 10 pounds or more in the past year, fatigue, and a decline in activity. In a remarkable study published in 2002 in the *Archives of Internal Medicine*, researchers found that older people who were frail had higher levels of the inflammation marker C-reactive protein (CRP) in their blood compared with nonfrail people of the same ages. These higher levels of CRP remained even when heart disease and diabetes (also known to raise CRP levels) were taken out of the equation. This suggests that even when a person doesn't suffer from any other major diseases, frailty in old age is related to inflammation. It could be that there are as-yet-undiagnosed illnesses causing the inflammation, or it could be that the general low levels of inflammation that occur due to aging are enough to cause the changes that lead to frailty.

Changes in Aging

Inflammation is one of the mechanisms by which the body self-destructs on a planned timetable. Researchers have discovered that people who age most successfully, staying healthy well into old age, are those who are best able to keep inflammation, immune reaction, stress responses, and other factors in balance. Healthy aging is all about adaptability. The person who is hardiest in old age was not necessarily the hardiest in youth. People who are very healthy when they are young tend to have vigorous, extremely reactive immune systems. But this extreme responsiveness puts the body in a near-continuous state of inflammation, which damages the body along the way and creates illness as we age. This pro-inflammatory state is linked to the aging process so closely that Dr. C. Franceschi and his colleagues from Italy coined the term *inflamm-aging* to describe this phenomenon.

Our immune systems change as we age. We know, for example, that as people age, the production or response of certain inflammation-related chemicals decrease, which means that they are less able to fight off infection and tumors. The body's ability to distinguish between *self* and *non-self* malfunctions, leading to an increase in autoimmune disorders. Production of inflammatory cytokines (such as interleukin-1 [IL-1], IL-6, interferon-gamma, and tumor necrosis factor-alpha) tends to increase, and production of anti-inflammatory cytokines (such as interferon-alpha and interferon-beta) tends to decrease with age.

These chemicals, found in minute quantities in the body, can have far-reaching effects. Consider just one inflammatory chemical, IL-6, which plays such a major role in many diseases of aging that it has been called "a cytokine for gerontologists." In a healthy person, levels of IL-6 can barely be detected. But as we age, levels of IL-6 increase to the point where it can be measured in blood. It is thought that IL-6 adds to overall inflammation and may contribute to heart disease, osteoporosis, and Alzheimer's disease. In one study, women with cardiovascular disease who had the highest levels of IL-6 were four times more likely to die in the next three years than those with low levels of IL-6. Elderly people with the highest levels of IL-6 have also been found to have an increased risk of cognitive decline compared with those with lower levels of IL-6.

So just the fact of aging, with the natural change in inflammatory chemicals, is enough additional inflammation to trigger heart attack or other inflammation-related health events. Other studies found that even in healthy older men and women, high levels of IL-6 were related to a loss of muscle mass and strength, and they predicted onset of disability. IL-6 has also been found to be higher in people who smoke than in nonsmokers, once again highlighting the inflammatory nature of smoking. The lesson is that as we age, we've got to do even more to balance inflammatory factors because the natural balancing chemicals in our bodies aren't working the way they used to.

Older and Wiser

Although all these changes sound bad, there's hope. Scientists used to believe that all changes that accompanied aging were for the worse, but that belief turned out not to be true. Instead of a gradual decline in immune function leading to total body chaos, the aging body is more evolutionary. It remodels itself, changing and adapting over the years. So instead of thinking of our aging bodies as stone sculptures that erode over time, we should think of them as sandy beaches that adjust to time, tide, and the wind. Yes, the changes make us less proficient at fighting off disease when we are older, but there is a reason. Throughout our lives, we are bombarded with a variety of factors—infections, radiation, free radicals—that put us in a constant state of low-level inflammation. We age more successfully if we are able to moderate our responses. This is what many scientists believe happens to our physiology as we get older. It's not that our immune system breaks down, but that it learns that it isn't so important to call in all the forces of inflammation every time there's a little problem in the body. The defenses don't weaken, they simply become less responsive because they've learned that it is often healthier to be less responsive. Now this works well for the generally healthy person because it gives the body a way to short-circuit low-level inflammation; but it can be harmful in the face of an unusual pathogen that might easily overwhelm the system. This is why the elderly have a greater risk of dying from the West Nile virus than younger people do.

So aging successfully depends on how our bodies respond to physical stressors, which is determined partly by genetics and partly by how well we take care of ourselves. Genes are powerful. They program the strength of our immune response throughout our lives and influence our life span. For example, it's been shown that a single gene mutation in animals may be enough to lengthen or shorten life span. Unfortunately, we don't yet have control over our genes.

Among the things we have control over, the only proven way of increasing life span is by calorie restriction—a scientific way of saying "eating less." In rodents, calorie restriction improves insulin sensitivity and leads to more efficient regulation of blood sugar, which counterbalances some effects of aging. In people, we know that insulin resistance leads to the kind of oxidative stress that causes inflammation, so it is theorized that calorie restriction should help counterbalance some of that damage. In addition, calorie restriction lowers the metabolic rate, which means that the body becomes less sensitive to oxidative stress and creates fewer free radicals. In one study that looked at the components of aging, it was shown that healthy people age 100 or older ate less than unhealthy older people and had less body fat. Although this was not an experiment in calorie restriction, it suggests that eating less to maintain a lower body weight keeps people healthier longer. Even blood levels of the inflammatory cytokine IL-6 can be reduced by calorie restriction. (To learn more about calorie restriction, see Chapter 9.)

Many of the diseases mentioned in this book are, in fact, diseases of aging. As inflammation increases as we age, our risks of inflammation-related diseases increase. Our inflammatory cytokines increase as we age so that inflammatory diseases can take a foothold. Our anti-inflammatory cytokines decrease so that we lose their counterbalance. Even the diseases we typically think of as diseases of aging—osteoarthritis, osteoporosis, Alzheimer's disease, and macular degeneration—are, in fact, diseases of inflammation.

OSTEOARTHRITIS

Arthritis takes many forms, but the "arthritis" most people think of—the aches, pains, and stiffness that besiege the elderly—is osteoarthritis. As the population of the United States gets older, the number of people suffering with osteoarthritis is also increasing. But osteoarthritis is not a natural part of aging. Rather, it is a sign that there is something wrong in the body. We know, for example, that arthritis symptoms typically get better with weight loss. Given that the number of people who are overweight is blossoming, it should not be surprising that more osteoarthritis cases are also popping up.

The symptoms of osteoarthritis are caused when the cartilage that lines the joints wears down. The big question is why cartilage begins to break down in the first place. Joints are not just bone and cartilage. Surrounding many joints is a synovial capsule, a membrane that secretes a lubricating fluid into the joint space. If the synovial membrane becomes inflamed, it produces enzymes and inflammatory chemicals (including interleukin-1, interleukin-17, and tumor necrosis factor-alpha), which can cause the erosion of cartilage. So it is not just the wear and tear of years of use that cause the joints to get painful. Rather, there is an inflammatory reaction that causes the repair process to break down so that joints are not maintained by the body the way they are supposed to be. The connection between obesity and osteoarthritis, then, makes even more sense when you consider that being overweight generally increases inflammation in the body while at the same time increasing mechanical forces on the large weight-bearing joints. It is possible that this general inflammatory process is enough to set off inflammation damage in the joints. And indeed, losing weight helps reduce arthritis symptoms.

In previous generations, having arthritis was an excuse to rest and take it easy. After all, if the joints are already wearing thin, why stress them further? No one wanted to risk further damage. Those days are over. Now it is well recognized that just about any kind of exercise helps relieve osteoarthritis symptoms. (For more information about exercise, see Chapter 11.)

Of course, nonsteroidal anti-inflammatory drugs (NSAIDs) are the main treatment for osteoarthritis. Although we typically think of NSAIDs (which include ibuprofen, naproxen, and ketoprofen) as pain-killers, their effectiveness is based on their ability to fight inflammation. (For more information about NSAIDs, see Chapter 13.)

Three other substances may be worth trying if you are worried about arthritis: green tea, omega-3 fatty acids, and glucosamine sulfate. Although eating well will generally improve health, a recent article in the *Journal of Nutrition* reported that the phytochemicals in green tea helped protect cartilage against damage and breakdown in the laboratory. No one knows whether green tea will also help protect cartilage in people, but it can't hurt to try.

Omega-3 fatty acids are found in fish and fish oil. Although eating fish or fish oil supplements has been shown to help reduce arthritis pain, one recent study looked at the mechanisms involved. Researchers took cartilage from people with osteoarthritis and then added omega-3s for twenty-four hours. They discovered that omega-3s stopped inflammation and stopped the production of chemicals known to cause joint destruction. Although clinical trials using actual people taking omega-3 supplements are still going on, this research suggests that including more fish oil in your diet may help delay or stop the process of osteoarthritis. (For more information about fish oil, see Chapter 9.)

Glucosamine stimulates production of glycosaminoglycan, an important component of cartilage in joints. Dozens of studies have shown that taking supplements of glucosamine sulfate delays the progress of osteoarthritis. For example, one study looked at the effects of taking 1,500 milligrams of glucosamine sulfate daily for three years to treat arthritis in the knee, the joint most often affected by osteoarthritis. Glucosamine users reported a significant improvement in pain and did not experience any narrowing in the joint space (a physical measurement of the progression of arthritis). People who did not take glucosamine supplements had a narrowing of the joint space every year of the study. (For more information about tea and glucosamine, see Chapter 9.)

OSTEOPOROSIS

Osteoporosis is a condition that causes bone to become brittle and fragile, making fractures more likely. In extreme cases, the bone may crumble and collapse.

Although most of us think of bone as hard and unchanging, bone is living tissue. Throughout our lives, our bones are continually being remodeled. Bone is sometimes broken down and absorbed into the body (a process called resorption), and sometimes new bone is formed. As we get older, more bone is resorbed and less is added, so bones become thinner. It is normal for men and women both to lose about 1 percent of their bone mass per year after about age fifty. If too much bone is lost, its structure is compromised. On cross section, the inside of the bone begins to look like Swiss cheese, with the holes getting bigger and bigger every year. Eventually, the delicate structure breaks under pressure.

Osteoporosis is said to occur if the amount of bone lost every year is greater than about 2 percent per year. Although the amount sounds small, it adds up quickly. An eighty-year-old person will naturally have lost about 30 percent of bone mass since age fifty (thirty years, 1 percent loss per year), but an eighty-year-old person with osteoporosis may have lost 60 percent of bone mass. The most common location for loss of bone is in the hip area, which is why older people are at high risk of breaking a hip even if the fall itself is minor.

As of now, we only know some of the causes of osteoporosis. We know that decreasing levels of estrogen that occur after menopause lead to an increase in some of the inflammation-related cytokines—specifically interleukin-1 (IL-1) and IL-6—which changes the balance of bone resorption and bone formation so that more bone is lost than formed. Unfortunately, this explanation doesn't explain osteoporosis in men. Men with osteoporosis have been shown to have large decreases in testosterone, but scientists are not sure what significance that has on bone.

Although the causes of osteoporosis are still being investigated, what we need to do to prevent it is clear. Calcium supplements for women have been a popular recommendation, and it is true that without enough calcium, the body cannot create new bone. The current calcium recommendations are 1,000 milligrams per day for adults up to age fifty, and then 1,200 milligrams per day for people older than fifty. However, calcium isn't the whole answer. If it were just a question of taking a supplement, no one would need to suffer with this disease. Calcium does not address the inflammatory component of osteoporosis, and bone density may not define the problem entirely. For example, several studies have shown that taking one of the statin medications (usually prescribed after a heart attack to reduce inflammation and to lower cholesterol) can prevent fractures by about 60 percent. This tremendous difference was seen even though bone mineral density increased only slightly—about 3 percent at the hip, and even less in other parts of the body. So although bone density is important, it isn't the whole story. Inflammatory factors have to be added in. (See Chapter 13 for more information about statins.)

For women, hormone replacement therapy (HRT) after menopause has been recommended for years to reduce bone loss. The good news is that taking HRT continuously from the time of menopause does seem to help increase bone density and prevent fractures. The bad news is that HRT does not entirely prevent osteoporosis and fractures. Many women who take HRT have osteoporosis or are at risk of developing the disease, and fractures are still common among these women. Hormones also seem to be important to men's bones. One study found that men who were deprived of androgen (the main male hormone) because of treatment for prostate cancer had a high risk of bone density loss and fractures. (For more information about hormones, see Chapter 13.)

Lifestyle changes that reduce inflammation seem to be the most valuable ways men and women alike can protect their bones. The most powerful bone-protecting actions are stopping smoking, getting plenty of exercise, and eating lots of fruits and vegetables. Smoking is a major risk factor for osteoporosis. Smoking interferes with bone formation, increasing the risk of losing bone density. (For more information about the relationship between smoking and inflammation, see Chapter 11.)

Exercise, on the other hand, is one of the best preventive strategies for osteoporosis. The best kinds of exercises to help protect bones are known as weight-bearing exercises. Putting weight on a bone helps the bone-building process, so the best exercises for osteoporosis prevention are those that require lifting weights or any kind of stress on a body part, such as walking or running, which stress the leg and hip bones. A subset of the large-scale Nurses' Health Study followed more than sixty-one thousand postmenopausal women for twelve years and found that even moderate levels of walking reduced the risk of hip fracture. Every hour of walking per week at an average pace reduced the risk of hip fracture by 6 percent.

Non-weight-bearing exercises, such as swimming or bicycling, are good for general physical conditioning but don't add the extra bone-building oomph of exercises in which your feet hit the ground. This does not mean that you should avoid bicycling or swimming. There are benefits to all kinds of exercise. Bones, like every other part of the body, depend on healthy blood circulation, so any exercise that gets your body moving will improve health—even the daily exercise of housework, yard work, and running after children or grandchildren. All kinds of exercise also help improve balance and flexibility, which are critical for preventing the kinds of falls that can lead to broken bones and hospitalization. Slow-motion tai chi exercises are known to help improve strength and balance, and a recent study also found that postmenopausal women who regularly practiced tai chi for at least four years had less bone loss than nonexercisers. (For more information about the relationship between exercise and inflammation, see Chapter 11.)

Although getting plenty of calcium is critical to building bones, other dietary factors are also important. For example, a large-scale study found that potassium, magnesium, and fruits and vegetables protect against osteoporosis. Men and women who ate the least amount of these nutrients had the lowest levels of bone mineral density. (Potassium is found in high quantities in potatoes, skim milk, orange juice, bananas, and tomatoes. Magnesium is found in high quantities in whole wheat bread, skim milk, cold cereal, bananas, orange juice, and fish. For more information about the relationship between diet and inflammation, see Chapter 9.)

ALZHEIMER'S DISEASE

Alzheimer's disease is unfortunately common. It has been estimated that about 40 percent of people age eighty-five or older are affected. In Alzheimer's disease, brain cells degenerate, leading to memory loss, difficulty thinking, dementia, and, ultimately, death. The hallmarks of Alzheimer's disease are the plaques (patches of beta-amyloid proteins and deteriorating brain cells) and neurofibrillary tangles (deformed remnants of proteins inside brain cells) that develop in the brain. Although some people have a higher risk of developing Alzheimer's disease due to their genetic makeup, scientists believe that everyone becomes more vulnerable to Alzheimer's disease with age. Beta-amyloid deposits are found in the brains of healthy older people, and it may be that the long-term accumulation of these deposits is what eventually causes symptoms.

That means that prevention of plaques and tangles is critical. We can't control the genes we inherit, so we have to look for other factors that contribute to Alzheimer's disease. It is only recently that scientists have had a chance to study the mechanisms of this disease. What they've found is that the initial changes that start us down the road to developing plaques occur twenty to thirty years before any symptoms are revealed. In that time, a series of events takes place. First, a type of brain cell called glial cells becomes activated (for reasons no one really understands), which causes them to change their shape and become macrophages. These macrophages start producing proteins, enzymes, and inflammatory cytokines (chemical messengers). The inflammatory cytokines have a direct effect on the production of the beta-amyloid proteins that accumulate in and ultimately destroy nerve cells in Alzheimer's disease.

No one knows exactly what causes plaques and tangles to develop, but inflammation is heavily involved. Once the plaques and tangles develop, they seem to act as irritants, causing local inflammation, which causes release of chemicals (neurotoxins) that can kill brain cells. This initial inflammation sets into action an avalanche of inflammatory mechanisms not only in the brain but throughout the body. For example, when blood measures of an inflammatory chemical called antichymotrypsin are taken, the levels are much higher in people with Alzheimer's disease than in healthy people.

Inflammation is so integral to the development of Alzheimer's disease that scientists began looking at anti-inflammatory substances as possible preventives. Several long-term studies have looked at the value of NSAIDs, such as ibuprofen or naproxen, in preventing or delaying the onset of Alzheimer's disease. In general, these types of studies have shown that NSAIDs seem to delay the onset or slow the progression of Alzheimer's disease. The most intriguing of these studies looked at identical twins, where one twin had developed Alzheimer's disease three or more years earlier than the other twin. Because Alzheimer's disease is believed to run in families, and because identical twins share the exact same genes, any difference in the onset of the disease must be due to something in the environment. The researchers found that if one of the twins had arthritis—which meant that NSAIDs would be part of the treatment and taken regularly—that twin developed Alzheimer's disease much later than the twin not diagnosed with arthritis.

Studies have also suggested that statins, those inflammation- and cholesterol-fighting drugs that are often prescribed after a heart attack, may help prevent Alzheimer's disease. Taking statins may reduce the risk of Alzheimer's disease by as much as 70 percent. There are two main reasons why statins might work. First, statins reduce inflammation, and cell death in Alzheimer's disease is directly related to an increased production of certain inflammatory chemicals. Second, cholesterol itself raises beta-amyloid production, so reducing cholesterol might reduce the production of these plaque-causing proteins. (For more information about statins, see Chapter 13.)

Whether hormones are a protective factor is still being studied. It has long been believed that estrogen helps protect women's brains, and that the decline in estrogen after menopause can hasten the onset of Alzheimer's disease. For a long time, HRT was recommended to menopausal women as a way of protecting brain function—along with protecting the heart and preventing osteoporosis. Recent research, however, has been conflicting. When scientists review the literature, there seems to be some support for the theory that estrogen helps protect the brain from Alzheimer's disease. The strongest support came from a study reported in 2002 in the *Journal of the American Medical Association*. This study followed more than three thousand men and women (with average ages in their seventies) for three to five years. The participants were asked about their use of calcium and multivitamins, and women were additionally asked about their use of hormone replacement therapy. They found that multivitamins and calcium had no effect on the likelihood of developing Alzheimer's disease. But women who used HRT in the past were much less likely to develop Alzheimer's disease, cutting their risk by more than half. Interestingly, current use of HRT didn't matter unless HRT had been used for more than ten years. The latest theory is that estrogen may help prevent Alzheimer's disease as long as it is taken before Alzheimer's disease sets in. But once the process is under way, adding estrogen may have no effect or may even make memory worse. With the revelation in 2002 that a particular HRT regimen actually increased the risk of heart disease and breast cancer for some women, the decision of whether to receive HRT has become even more complex. Every woman's risk of heart disease, osteoporosis, and Alzheimer's disease is different. In some cases, the benefits of HRT might outweigh the risks, but these decisions must be made by each woman individually after consulting with her physician or health care practitioner.

Because some of the damage done to brain tissue is believed to be caused by free radical oxidation, antioxidants have been studied as a potential preventive measure. One landmark study looked at 341 people with Alzheimer's disease. They were divided into four groups, each receiving a different treatment for two years: 1) 10 milligrams per day of a medication called selegiline, which is a prescription drug; 2) 2,000 IU of vitamin E daily; 3) both selegiline and vitamin E; 4) a placebo, which looks like a medication but has no physiologic effect. The study found that receiving treatment with either the medication or vitamin E delayed the progression of symptoms.

More recent studies, however, have cast doubt on the value of supplements. Different studies show different results. Some find that the antioxidant vitamin C can lower the risk of Alzheimer's disease, but others show no effect for vitamin C and vitamin E. However, one finding that has held up in recent studies is that eating lots of fruits and vegetables that contain high levels of vitamin C and vitamin E— but not antioxidant supplements—reduces the risk of Alzheimer's disease. One study found that people who ate the highest amounts of foods containing vitamin

E had a 70 percent lower risk of developing Alzheimer's disease than people who ate the least amount of vitamin E–rich foods.

Why are foods helpful while supplements are not? Some scientists believe that foods represent a long-term investment in health, and that maintaining a healthy diet over decades may help stave off Alzheimer's disease while a few years of supplements may be a case of too little, too late. Plus, foods contain many more nutrients than just vitamin C and vitamin E. It may be that the antioxidants interact in some way with these other nutrients to boost their activity. Foods high in vitamin C include citrus fruits (oranges, grapefruit, lemons), kiwi fruit, and broccoli. Foods high in vitamin E include olive oil, whole grains, nuts, and egg yolks. (For more information about the value of foods for fighting inflammation, see Chapter 9.)

Ginkgo biloba has also been studied as an Alzheimer's disease preventive. The leaf extract of the ginkgo biloba tree has been used in Chinese medicine for thousands of years. It is believed to be a potent antioxidant and to contain beneficial phytochemicals called flavonoids (see Chapter 9 for more information about phytochemicals). In a review of studies, it was shown that 120 to 240 milligrams of ginkgo biloba extract daily for three to six months had a positive effect on cognitive functioning in patients with Alzheimer's disease. Although ginkgo biloba is generally safe, there have been reports of bleeding problems. (Consult with a physician before trying ginkgo biloba extract.)

Another study that will be of interest to anyone who starts the day with a cup of coffee (or two or three) found that people who drank at least two cups of coffee per day over the course of their lifetimes lowered their risk of Alzheimer's disease by about 60 percent. This was true even when all other possible contributing factors were accounted for. This is not entirely surprising. In low doses, caffeine has been shown to help protect brain cells. Although this is not a prescription for going out and indulging in Starbucks on a daily basis, there's no reason to give up that morning cup of coffee, and it might even protect your brain.

Some of the most important research reported at the 2002 International Conference on Alzheimer's Disease and Related Disorders revealed that many of the same factors that keep heart disease at bay may also help reduce the risk of Alzheimer's disease. This is especially true since there may be an inflammation connection between the two disorders. We know that high levels of the inflammatory marker C-reactive protein (CRP) is a sign that a person is at high risk for heart disease. In a study that spanned twenty-five years, the Honolulu-Asia Aging Study, scientists found that men with the highest levels of CRP had a risk of dementia (including Alzheimer's disease) that was three times higher than people with the lowest levels of CRP. Although no one knows exactly how heart disease and Alzheimer's disease might be connected, there may be a general inflammatory reaction that causes both. So it makes sense that the same lifestyle changes that help reduce the risk of heart attack also seem to reduce the risk of Alzheimer's disease. For example, scientists reported for the first time that lifestyle choices—including eating a low-fat diet rich in fruits and vegetables, lowering the amount of red meat in the diet, exercising, keeping blood pressure and body weight under control, and challenging the brain with intellectual pursuits—have the potential to prevent Alzheimer's disease.

PART 3

THE ANTI-INFLAMMATION GAME PLAN

9

What We Eat

Dietary Solutions

◉

By tinkering with our diets, it is often possible to reduce aches and pains, regain energy and vitality, increase mental clarity, and lower the risk for inflammation-related diseases. Although most of us rarely think about food's purpose (other than to taste good and fill our hungry stomachs), what we eat has powerful effects on our bodies. In fact, food is one of our most valuable tools for maintaining inflammation balance.

Scientists have discovered that some types of foods are pro-inflammatory (able to increase inflammation), and other types of foods are anti-inflammatory. Once we know whether a food causes or reduces inflammation in the body, then we can make educated assumptions about which foods to eat more of and which foods to avoid. The sad truth is that most people in the United States and other Western countries eat a diet that puts them in a constant pro-inflammatory state. With every meal, we have the option of increasing inflammation or decreasing inflammation, increasing or decreasing our risk of heart attacks and cancer, increasing or decreasing the amount of pain in our lives. The typical Western diet tends toward the inflammation side more often than not. This means the balance is lost until we change the types of foods we eat.

For many people, a particular food that is healthy for most people may cause health problems. Many individuals have well-defined reactions to foods, such as allergy, lactose intolerance, and a form of gluten (wheat protein) intolerance known as celiac sprue. Others have ill-defined or poorly understood food intolerances that cause inflammatory reactions. Individuals who know what foods trigger their inflammation can simply avoid those foods and feel better almost immediately.

SIMPLE GUIDELINES FOR

ANTI-INFLAMMATORY EATING

In theory, eating to reduce inflammation is very simple. Making changes that involve breaking habits we've developed over a lifetime is always difficult, but the actual recommendations are simple. Hundreds of medical studies have been conducted, scientists have devoted their lives to studying a single vitamin or mineral or disease, and the media have breathlessly reported on the latest food fads for decades. But anti-inflammatory eating can be boiled down to seven simple guidelines:

Seven Inflammation-Fighting Guidelines
1. Eat lots of fruits and vegetables—at least five servings each day.
2. Eat fish three to five times each week.
3. Add olive oil to your diet.
4. Eat very little meat, poultry, cheese, butter, and other animal products—or become a vegetarian.
5. Take recommended supplements daily.
6. Eat less.
7. Identify and avoid personal problem foods.

Photocopy this list. Cut it out. Tape it to your refrigerator. Make a bookmark out of it. Do anything you need to do to keep it in your awareness because simple guidelines are easy to forget and easy to discount.

The seven guidelines encompass everything you need to know about anti-inflammatory eating. A special diet program to fight inflammation is actually counterproductive for most people. Anyone who has ever tried to follow a particular diet for any period of time knows that it is nearly impossible to stick with it. It is human nature to want to break those rules, to reassert one's independence and sense of control. To cheat. That's a perfectly normal response. If Americans could stick to a diet, we might not be facing an epidemic of obesity.

So I'm not going to burden you with a lot of rules and special menus and disease-specific suggestions. The seven simple guidelines work well for preventing heart disease and cancer, for lowering overall inflammation load, for combating fatigue and obesity and arthritis and Alzheimer's disease, and for generally keeping our bodies in the best possible shape as we age. I'll explain the research that supports them, tell you why each rule is important, and then treat you like an adult by letting you decide for yourself how to use the information. You cannot cheat on this diet because you are the one making the choices, you are the one choosing the solutions to the problem of inflammation. If you follow all seven guidelines, you'll be healthier than if you only follow four. But if you follow four guidelines, you'll still be healthier than if you only follow two. Do what you can!

If you are currently suffering from an inflammation-related disease, you might want to dive right in and make drastic changes to your diet. The sooner you start to reduce the amount of inflammation anywhere in your body, the quicker you'll start to see the health benefits reflected in how you feel. If you are thinking about disease prevention, or if you've had bad luck making dietary changes in the past, start slowly. Change can be hard, especially if you're not under the immediate threat of a disease. Pick one of the guidelines as the change you'll make this month. Then add a new guideline each month after that. Remember, these guidelines are there to help you make the best choices for your health. Every time you follow one of these guidelines—with every day, every meal, every mouthful—your body gets just a little bit healthier.

Guideline 1: Eat lots of fruits and vegetables—at least five servings each day.

A mountain of research has made it clear that eating lots of fruits and vegetables reduces the risk of heart disease and many types of cancers and may play a role in fending off most diseases of aging, including diabetes and arthritis. Although the American Dietetic Association recommends that everyone try to eat five servings of fruits and vegetables each day to stay healthy, the reality is that less than 20 percent of us actually do it. And the inside scoop is that dietitians would like to recommend nine or more servings of fruits and vegetables daily, but they know that people would find that goal impossible and perhaps give up trying at all.

But how easy it would be to make ourselves healthier simply by eating more fruits and vegetables! One study published in the journal *Lancet* in 2002 showed that when people ate an additional one and one-half servings of fruits or vegetables every day for six months, their blood pressure dropped and the amounts of disease-fighting antioxidants in their blood increased. An extra one and one-half servings means about one salad, *or* an apple and a handful of raisins, *or* one large grapefruit, *or* a tall glass of orange juice.

The Power of Phytochemicals

When the body digests food, it breaks everything down into individual components. All food is made up of three basic substances known collectively as macronutrients: carbohydrates, fats, and protein. These nutrients supply the body with the basic material needed to keep building and repairing cells and to give us energy in the form of calories. Food also contains smaller amounts of vitamins and minerals (such as calcium, magnesium, and potassium), which we also need to stay healthy.

In addition, there is a more recently discovered class of compounds known as phytochemicals. Found only in plant foods, phytochemicals are powerful molecules that have been shown to reduce the risks of age-related diseases, including cancer. These go by tongue-twister names such as sulphoraphane (pronounced "suhl-FOR-a-fane"), found in high quantities in broccoli, cauliflower, and other cruciferous vegetables; β-cryptoxanthin ("beta-crip-toe-ZAN-thin"), found in some orange-colored fruits, such as mangoes, oranges, and papaya; and glycyrrhizin ("gly-SEER-rih-zin"), found in licorice root. Thousands of phytochemicals have been discovered, but only a handful have been studied for their contributions to health. Plus, scientists believe that there may be many more of these powerhouse chemicals yet to be discovered.

How powerful are phytochemicals? They have been shown to be valuable as antioxidant, anti-inflammatory, antiallergic, antiviral, and anticancer agents. Some research suggests that they may be among the most effective cancer treatments on earth. Drinking green tea, which contains high quantities of phytochemicals called flavonoids, can decrease the risk of stomach cancer by as much as 30 percent. Brassica vegetables—broccoli, cabbage, mustard greens, collard greens, and bok choy—have been shown to reduce the risk of prostate cancer. For just about any cancer, some phytochemical has been shown to suppress cancer development in laboratory animals.

The focus has been on cancer, but that's only because cancer is easily diagnosed and the cure is easy to measure. Ongoing research is defining the role of phytochemicals in fighting other disorders, including heart disease, diabetes, arthritis, and Alzheimer's disease. For example, a Finnish study looked at blood levels of lycopene—a phytochemical found in high quantities in tomato products and watermelon—and discovered that middle-aged men with the lowest levels of lycopene were more than three times as likely to have a heart attack or stroke compared with men with higher lycopene levels. In animal studies, feeding rats with extracts of strawberry, blueberry, or spinach (all high in phytochemicals and antioxidants) not only prevented many age-related learning and memory deficits, but actually *reversed* documented deficits. That is, all those extra phytochemicals improved the memories and learning abilities of senile rats!

The first question people typically ask after hearing these kinds of results is: where can I buy phytochemicals? We have been trained as a society to look for the quick fix, the pill we can take to make ourselves feel better. For better or for worse, phytochemicals are currently only available in their original packaging—contained in fruits, vegetables, nuts, grains, and seeds. And truly, this is the preferred form. Although research can tell us some of the actions of individual phytochemicals, scientists generally agree that it is likely that the healthful benefits of eating lots of fruits and vegetables come from the full collection of phytochemicals. This means that even if we were able to isolate and package individual phytochemicals, we might be doing ourselves a disservice because we'll miss out on all the other phytochemicals—and many of the healthful effects may depend on the interactions of several different phytochemicals working together. So by taking only an isolated phytochemical supplement, we could very likely miss out on any benefit whatsoever.

An example of a whole vegetable being better than just a component is seen in beta-carotene, a phytochemical found in large quantities in carrots, mangoes, and other orange fruits and vegetables. Several studies have shown that eating lots of fruits and vegetables decreases the risk of lung cancer in people who smoke, and beta-carotene was thought to be the main cancer fighter. But when scientists gave beta-carotene supplements to smokers, they found that lung cancer risk actually increased. No one knows how to explain these results, but it is thought that there is some extra bit of something—extra phytochemicals, extra vitamins, extra fiber, extra something—in fruits and vegetables that make them effective where supplements alone are not. As I'll talk about a little later, there is a place for supplements when it is difficult or impossible to get all the nutrients we need from food alone. But food itself should be the primary source.

Top Inflammation-Fighting Foods

All fruits and vegetables contain healthful phytochemicals, but scientific research has just begun to investigate exactly what each phytochemical does and which foods provide the greatest amounts. From what is known right now, here are some of the top inflammation-fighting foods. Try to eat at least one food from each category at least once each week.

CRUCIFEROUS VEGETABLES

bok choy	cabbage	kale
broccoli	cauliflower	watercress
brussels sprouts		

LEAFY GREEN VEGETABLES

chard	lettuce (the greener, the better)	spinach
collards	mustard greens	

LEGUMES

black beans	navy beans	pinto beans
chickpeas (garbanzo beans)	peas	soybeans
kidney beans		

CITRUS FRUITS

(do not eat if citrus is one of your trigger foods!)

grapefruit	lime
lemon	oranges

BERRIES

blackberries	raspberries
blueberries	strawberries

BETA-CAROTENE–RICH FOODS

(usually dark orange in color)

apricots	carrots	pumpkin
cantaloupe	mango	sweet potato

Inflammation Fighters

• The best way to make sure you get as many different phytochemicals in your diet as possible is by eating a variety of fruits and vegetables. Every fruit, vegetable, herb, nut, seed, and grain has its own set of phytochemicals, and all contribute to good health. So don't fixate on just apples and oranges. Branch out to other types of produce whenever possible.

• Don't be drawn in by media reports of certain foods that are better for certain types of illnesses. All fruits and vegetables have something to offer for health. If you eat a variety of foods, you'll be protecting yourself against all possible diseases. If you focus on the popular food of the day, you could be missing out on an as-yet-undiscovered health secret.

• Phytochemicals give color to foods, so strive to eat a variety of different colors throughout the day—and the darker the color, the more concentrated the amounts of phytochemicals. Blueberries, raspberries, broccoli, cauliflower, red cabbage, papaya, red bell pepper, and kiwi all have different sets of phytochemicals, any or all of which will help stave off cancer, heart disease, and other disorders of aging.

• Don't forget the importance of grains. Whole grain foods have higher levels of phytochemicals than foods that have had their nutrition processed away. The darker color of whole wheat bread (compared with white bread) is due to the nutritious outer shell of the grain. Eating whole grain products—such as whole wheat bread, brown rice, bulgur wheat, wheat berries, and oats—has been shown to be associated with lower risks of digestive cancers, breast cancer, and prostate cancer. And in a twelve-year study of about forty-three thousand men, those who rarely ate whole grain foods were about 60 percent more likely to develop type 2 diabetes than men who ate about three servings of whole grain foods daily.

• Don't worry too much about what constitutes "a serving" of any particular food—just keep adding fruits and vegetables to your diet. Most people don't get nearly enough fruits and vegetables, so chances are you couldn't eat too many if you tried. Remember, the optimum would be about nine or ten servings, which would mean three servings at each meal. If you would like to count, however, a serving is usually one item (one apple, one banana, one carrot, et cetera), a half cup of cooked vegetables (about the amount you could scoop up in the palm of your hand), or a cup of uncooked leafy greens (such as spinach or lettuce).

Guideline 2: Eat fish three to five times each week (choose low-mercury varieties).

There are three main kinds of fats: unhealthy saturated fats found in animal products, healthy monounsaturated fats found in olive oil, and polyunsaturated fats. There are two kinds of polyunsaturated fats: omega-6 fatty acids and omega-3 fatty acids. Omega-6 fatty acids are found in vegetable oils and are pro-inflammatory. Omega-3 fatty acids are found primarily in fish oils (they are also present in flaxseed oil, borage oil, black currant oil, and evening primrose oil) and have been shown to be anti-inflammatory. Although everyone would benefit from eating more fish, eating less vegetable oil is also part of the equation.

When you are trying to get inflammation in balance, you have to consider both sides: the pro-inflammatory fats in relation to the anti-inflammatory fats. To truly balance dietary inflammation, we should be eating omega-6 fatty acids and omega-3 fatty acids in a 1:1 ratio—that is, equal amounts. In Western society, however, we tend to have a ratio that is about 10:1 or greater, because we eat a whole lot more vegetable oil (in fried foods and store-bought baked goods) than fish oil. The best way to get the ratio down to 1:1 (or at least closer) is to simultaneously reduce the amount of vegetable oil and increase the amount of fish oil in your diet. And your reward for this kind of change? Consider Eskimo populations, which eat a large number of fish as part of their daily diets. Scientists who study diet and disease patterns have discovered that typically Western diseases—heart disease, cancer, and diabetes—are virtually unknown among Eskimos. Their anti-inflammatory, high fish oil diets protect them from these inflammation-related diseases.

Medical research backs up those population studies. Just like statins, fish oils work by reducing inflammation. Fish oil has been shown to suppress the production of inflammatory cytokines, those proteins immune cells use to communicate with each other. Fish oil has been shown to help reduce the pain and stiffness of rheumatoid arthritis and to reduce the risks of heart attacks and strokes. An Italian study looked at more than eleven thousand people who had suffered a heart attack. Half received 1,000 milligrams of fish oil daily (in supplement form), the other half received a placebo (a substance that looked like fish oil but really had no physiologic effect). Patients who took fish oil had both short- and long-term benefits. At the end of three months, the patients who took fish oil were more likely to be alive than patients who didn't take fish oil, with a 41 percent reduction in sudden death. At the end of three and a half years, the group taking fish oil had 45 percent fewer fatalities.

SNEAKING FRUITS AND VEGETABLES INTO YOUR DIET

Getting five or more servings of fruits and vegetables daily can feel like a chore. In addition to your usual portions of vegetables, look for ways to add them in as flavor enhancers. For extra zest, dietitians recommend adding:

- On sandwiches (experiment with which tastes go best together): spinach leaves, roasted red peppers (available in jars), sliced hot pepper rings, tomato slices, sautéed zucchini rounds, cranberry sauce, avocado slices, cucumbers
- In tuna or chicken salad: grape halves, chopped celery, olives, diced apples, raisins, diced green or yellow onion, white beans
- In green salads (be creative!): apple or pear wedges, raisins, chickpeas, jicama, red cabbage leaves, corn kernels, walnuts, sunflower seeds, cooked peas, orange slices (without the white membranes), spinach leaves, broccoli flowers
- In cereals (hot or cold): a handful of berries, diced apples lightly coated with cinnamon, sliced banana, diced dates, raisins
- As snacks: baby carrots, raw sweet potato sticks, berry "milkshakes" made with nonfat milk or soy milk, a glass of orange or grapefruit juice (pure juice, not "juice drinks"), dried apricots or prunes, pineapple wedges, any other fruit
- Other tricks: mix pureed cauliflower in with mashed potatoes; sauté portobello mushrooms as a side dish or sandwich filler; make a "salad-to-go" by putting lettuce and other vegetables in a large pita; add sautéed zucchini rounds to chili recipes; add peas, corn, or sautéed onions and mushrooms to rice dishes; add additional vegetables, such as olives, sautéed eggplant, chopped cooked spinach, onions, or bell peppers, to canned or jarred tomato sauce

Inflammation Fighters

• You can choose to take fish oil supplements or add fish to your diet—both methods have been shown to reduce inflammation.

• Although all types of seafood, including shellfish, contain omega-3 fatty acids, some have greater amounts than others. The highest concentrations can be found in mackerel, salmon, tuna, bluefish, sturgeon, anchovy, herring, trout, sardines, and mullet.

• Because of water pollution, many fish now contain unhealthy amounts of methylmercury, which can be toxic in large doses. For this reason, it is not wise to eat fish more than five times per week, and certain types of fish should be avoided because they tend to have higher quantities of methylmercury, including shark, swordfish, king mackerel, tilefish, bass, pike, muskellunge, and walleye. Fish with some of the lowest levels of methylmercury are shrimp, salmon, Alaska pollock, canned tuna, mussels, scallops, and sole.

• There are no definitive amounts of omega-3 fatty acids that can be recommended based on scientific evidence. The goal is to get the omega-6:omega-3 ratio as close to 1:1 as possible, so any extra fish you can eat, the better off you'll be. One study found that eating fish just once per week decreased the risk of dementia. Eating three servings of fish each week will go a long way to improving your ratio. The best recommendation for supplements is to take about 1,000 milligrams of fish oil supplements each day to prevent disease.

• People with rheumatoid arthritis might want to consider taking 3,000 milligrams of fish oil supplements each day. After about twelve weeks, this should improve pain and morning stiffness.

• Be warned, however, that fish oil supplements may make your perspiration and breath smell slightly fishy. People who want to avoid the smell, avoid the possibility of methylmercury toxicity, or avoid all animal products should consider taking flaxseed oil instead. About one teaspoon daily is recommended for good health. People with inflammatory diseases might want to consider taking up to one tablespoon of flaxseed oil each day.

• As with all bioactive substances, you should consult with your physician before taking fish oil capsules or flaxseed oil.

Guideline 3: Add olive oil to your diet.

People in Mediterranean populations tend to have diets rich in vegetables, fish, legumes, whole grains, and olive oil. They also tend to have much lower rates of heart attack and longer life expectancies than people living in the United States, who eat a diet with large quantities of meat products, cheese, and butter. Scientists started to look at the different components of the Mediterranean diet and discovered that olive oil seems to have important health-promoting qualities, including lowering total cholesterol and lowering low-density lipoprotein (LDL) cholesterol, the "bad" cholesterol. In fact, one study found that when healthy men added 50 grams of olive oil (about 1.5 tablespoons) a day to their diets, they reduced some of the bad effects of LDL cholesterol on their arteries within one week. No one is exactly certain how olive oil exerts its benefits. We know that olive oil contains the phytochemicals oleuropein and hydroxytyrosol, which are powerful antioxidants. Plus, in Mediterranean countries, olive oil (which is a healthier monounsaturated fat) often replaces the saturated fat of butter. So we don't know how much of olive oil's positive effects in Mediterranean countries is due to the oil itself, the reduced amount of animal products in their diets, or other factors specific to that population. Still, when olive oil alone is tested, it comes out as a healthful choice.

In addition, a few studies have suggested that olive oil influences inflammation, may be important in fighting inflammatory diseases, and may improve immune functioning over time.

Inflammation Fighters

• Start by using olive oil instead of vegetable oil, safflower oil, lard, or butter when sautéing or frying foods. Substitute equal amounts of olive oil for any type of oil you are currently using. Because olive oil burns at a lower heat than other oils, watch it carefully until you learn the best cooking temperatures and times.

• All brands and types of olive oil are pretty much the same in terms of health benefits, so choose the one that tastes best to you. The cold-pressed, extra-virgin varieties taste lighter and have more subtlety than other varieties.

• Cut down on the amount of fried foods you eat outside the house. None are cooked with olive oil. Fried foods are anything cooked in butter, oil, or lard, including anything deep-fried (such as French fries, potato chips, funnel cakes, and anything "batter-dipped") or pan-fried with butter (such as French toast or grilled cheese sandwiches).

• Eventually, move toward substituting olive oil for butter or margarine. Try using olive oil as a bread dip. You can use it plain or with garlic, herbs, vinegar, or spices.

• Once you've made the transition to olive oil, start cutting back on the amount of frying you do in the home, and stop eating fried foods outside the home. As healthful as olive oil is, it is still a fat, which means that it adds a lot of calories to your diet. Extra calories mean extra pounds on the body. The health effects of olive oil have been seen with as little as 1.5 tablespoons, so there's no reason to think that more is better.

Guideline 4: Eat very little meat, poultry, cheese, butter, milk, and other animal products—or become a vegetarian.

Here's what we know about meat and other animal products:

1. They are not necessary for a healthful life. Many people in the world survive perfectly well as vegetarians.
2. They are the sole outside source of cholesterol. The body makes its own cholesterol, but only foods from animals contain cholesterol.
3. They are among the top inflammation triggers.

Vegetarian diets are great at fighting inflammation. Study after study has shown that eating a vegetarian diet is associated with a lower risk of cancer, heart disease, obesity, and diabetes. There are several reasons why a no-meat diet might be so beneficial. People who eat vegetarian tend to weigh less than most people who eat meat, have lower blood pressure, and have lower cholesterol levels—all of which are healthful changes that lead to less inflammation. A vegetarian diet also seems to make the blood vessels more flexible, better able to dilate, which means that the blood vessels themselves are healthier.

For some disorders, the anti-inflammatory action of a vegan diet may be as good as medication. One study followed people with moderate to severe rheumatoid arthritis who switched to a low-fat vegan diet. After four weeks, the patients reported less pain. In addition, they had lower levels of the inflammatory marker C-reactive protein and lower blood levels of RA factor (a marker for rheumatoid arthritis).

Inflammation Fighters

• Don't try to "go veggie" overnight. The change to a vegetarian lifestyle means a significant change in the way you'll cook, eat out, and shop. Start slowly, perhaps by cutting down on portion size. Another option is to eliminate one type of meat, so that you'll give up beef the first month, then give up pork the second month, then give up chicken the third month, and so on. Alternatively, if you eat meat every day of the week, start by becoming vegetarian for one day each week. Gradually increase your vegetarian days as you feel comfortable.

• Don't give up fish right away—eating fish is one of the seven inflammation-fighting guidelines. The inflammation-fighting fish oils are critical to good health. If you decide you'd like to give up all animal products, make sure you take plant-based supplements to get your omega-3 fatty acids. Look for flaxseed oil, borage oil, black currant oil, or evening primrose oil in a health food store. Follow directions for use on the bottle.

• Consult your doctor before becoming a vegetarian if you have diabetes or other disorders that have dietary restrictions.

Guideline 5: Take recommended supplements daily.

Our diets are haphazard, at best and many times we don't get the minimum daily requirements of vitamins and minerals necessary to prevent deficiency diseases. Unfortunately, we don't know exactly what dosages are optimal for fighting diseases and ensuring good health. The multi-billion dollar nutritional supplement industry would have you believe that more is always better, but high levels of some vitamins and minerals can be toxic. Scientific studies to determine the benefits of supplements give conflicting results. Vitamins seem to be more complex than we originally thought. For example, each vitamin can have several different but closely related chemical structures, and one vitamin may have a benefit when taken alone but not when taken with another vitamin. This is why it is difficult to make blanket recommendations for any particular vitamin. Most scientists agree, however, that at the present time, there is no convincing evidence that taking high doses of vitamins can prevent any disease, and high doses of some vitamins, A, B_6 , D, and C in particular, may be harmful. *Always talk with your physician before taking any supplement.*

• **Multivitamin.** There are so many different trace minerals that are difficult to get from the average diet that some people might want to consider taking a multi-

WHAT'S IN A NAME

There is more than one type of vegetarian, depending on how strict your definition is.

Vegans eat no animal products whatsoever—no meat, fish, poultry, pork, milk, cheese, yogurt, butter, eggs, or anything else that comes from an animal.

Lactovegetarians are like vegans, except they will eat milk products, including milk, cheese, yogurt, and butter.

Ovo-lactovegetarians are like vegans, except they will eat milk products and eggs.

Semi-vegetarians generally eat like a vegetarian, but once in a while eat meat, fish, or fowl, though much less frequently than the average person.

vitamin. There is no need to look for megadoses or special types of multivitamins. Any brand will do, and you should look for tablets that provide no more than 100 percent of the daily requirement for most vitamins. People who eat a diet high in foods fortified with vitamins, such as cereals, granola bars, milk, and bread, probably should not take a multivitamin.

• **Vitamin E.** The research involving vitamin E has been contradictory and confusing. Research that looked at dietary habits and health found that vitamin E seems to protect against heart disease and atherosclerosis. But most clinical trials testing vitamin E directly have shown that vitamin E has no effect on heart health. One study that looked at the effects of high doses of vitamin E in people with type 2 diabetes found that vitamin E reduced the inflammatory marker C-reactive protein and the inflammatory monocyte interleukin-6. The conflicting nature of these results is surprising—the anti-inflammatory effects of vitamin E have been well documented. In June 2002 the *Journal of the American Medical Association* published two separate articles by researchers who looked at the effects of vitamin E on the risk of Alzheimer's disease. One found that vitamin E did, indeed, lower the risk for Alzheimer's disease; the other found that only vitamin E from foods (not in supplement form) reduced the risk. Unfortunately, vitamin E is difficult to get from food alone (it is found most abundantly in fruits and vegetables). *Recommen-*

dation: Take 400 IU vitamin E (also known as tocopherol or alpha-tocopherol) daily. Excessively high doses may be harmful.

• **B vitamins.** A team of American and Chinese researchers found that high folic acid intake reduces breast cancer rate. Another team found that high folic acid intake (greater than 373 micrograms each day) reduces the rate of pancreatic cancer. Folic acid aids in removal of artery-damaging homocysteine from the blood. A study found that people with low folic acid levels were 2.64 times more likely to die of coronary artery disease than those with higher levels. Low folic acid levels have also been linked to an increased risk of dementia and Alzheimer's disease. Vitamin B$_6$ (pralidoxine) and B$_{12}$ work in concert with folic acid to reduce homocysteine levels. We used to think that it was impossible to get too much of the water-soluble B vitamins. It is now known that as little as 200 milligrams of vitamin B$_6$ per day, can cause permanent nerve damage. *Recommendation:* There is no need to take supplements for vitamins B$_6$ and B$_{12}$. People with high levels of homocysteine in their blood might consider talking with their doctors about taking 800 to 1,000 micrograms of folic acid a day to reduce the risk of heart disease. Whether folic acid supplementation benefits people with normal homocysetein levels is unknown.

• **Glucosamine sulfate.** Glycosaminoglycans are important components of cartilage in joints. With age, production of these important structural molecules falls behind the wear and tear on joints so that osteoarthritis occurs. Glucosamine stimulates glycosaminoglycan production and has been shown to reduce the risk of osteoarthritis in more than a hundred studies. There are no dietary sources of glucosamine, and commercial preparations are manufactured from chitin in shrimp, lobster, and crab shells. Glucosamine sulfate is the preferred form because sulfur is needed in cartilage. *Recommendation:* Take 500 milligrams of glucosamine sulfate three times a day.

Guideline 6: Eat less.

Eating less actually has a scientific name: *calorie restriction*. In scientific literature, calorie restriction has been shown to increase life span, slow the progression of atherosclerosis, prevent tumor growth, reduce the amount of brain dysfunction, and retard aging—but all the research has been done with rodents. Very few studies have been done using people because people are not usually willing to submit to strict dietary control for several years (or perhaps a lifetime).

But the data from rats and mice should not be dismissed without consideration. Calorie restriction has impressive antiaging effects on animals, due to its anti-inflammatory action. As we age, certain body chemicals that are associated with inflammation, such as some prostaglandins, increase. It just naturally happens. In rodents that have had their calories restricted, the production of these pro-inflam-matory chemicals is greatly reduced. Calorie restriction also limits the damage done by free radicals (or reactive oxygen species), which are created as by-products of normal body functions or which occur due to environmental stress on the body. This damage is called oxidative stress. Oxidative stress is the single greatest cause of aging and age-related diseases. It is countered by antioxidants (which we can think of as antioxidative stress molecules) and by calorie restriction. How big a deal is calorie restriction? In rodents raised with calorie restriction all their lives, life span can be increased by about 50 percent, with less cancer, better immune function, and less atherosclerosis.

Although most studies follow the rodents throughout their lifetimes, a few researchers have investigated health and longevity in rodents that start calorie restriction in middle age. These studies suggest that it's never too late to start calo-rie restriction for better health. In one study, everyday calorie restriction or a one-day-per-week fast significantly reduced the risk of cancer in cancer-prone mice. Another study found that calorie restriction in middle-aged mice increased their life span by 15 percent and reduced the incidence of cancer.

Calorie restriction also is likely to have beneficial effects on the brain. We've known for a long time that restricting calories improves memory and mental and motor performance (again, in rodents), but scientists have only recently begun to figure out why. There are rodents that are predisposed to get the animal equivalents of Alzheimer's disease and Parkinson's disease. When these mice are studied with and without calorie restriction, scientists have discovered that the degeneration of nerves in the brain seem to be caused, in part, by oxidative stress—and that oxi-dation can be countered by a low-calorie diet. The result of all this research is that scientists are now able to prevent Alzheimer's and Parkinson's diseases *in mice* by cutting back on the calories the animals are fed.

Because there are some people in the world who choose to eat less, scientists have been able to compare their rates of disease with the rates of people who eat their full allotment of daily calories. The results show that anytime people eat less, there is a lower incidence of Alzheimer's disease. For example, people in some Asian countries typically eat what would be considered calorie-restricted diets, and their rate of Alzheimer's disease is about half the rate found in Western countries.

In some small groups of people who voluntarily undergo short-term calorie restriction, we see the beginnings of a real health difference. For example, eight people lived in the enclosed Biosphere 2 for two years during the early 1990s. Their diet was calorie restricted by an average of 30 percent most of the time they lived in the enclosure. Similar to rodent studies, the participants not only lost weight (as would be expected from a low-calorie diet), but they also lowered blood pressure by an average of 23 percent, lowered cholesterol by about 30 percent, and lowered their insulin levels by 42 percent. Of course, no one knows what the long-term outcomes would be, but these are similar to the changes seen in rodents, and they are definitely the types of changes that would lower anyone's risk of atherosclerosis and heart attack.

Inflammation Fighters

• If you would like to try calorie restriction, aim to gradually cut down your food intake by 25 percent. That means eating only three-quarters of what you usually eat.

• Start by eliminating sugary snack foods. Sugary foods tend to be high in calories and unhealthy fats, which undermines your attempts at calorie control. These should be the first foods you eliminate: pure sugar, sweet foods (such as candy, cakes, cookies), and baked foods made with white flour.

• Fried foods not only will unbalance your omega-6:omega-3 fatty acid ratio and lead to inflammation, but they are full of calories. You'll be able to cut out a lot of unnecessary calories by avoiding fried foods, including snack chips and French fries.

• Vow to leave a little bit of food on your plate at each meal. This will be difficult for anyone raised with the "clean plate club" style of parenting, but leave something behind. Don't think of it as wasted food—think of it as less atherosclerosis building in your arteries.

• Don't go for seconds or thirds. Only very active people (athletes, construction workers, furniture movers—you get the picture) actually need more than one helping of food per meal.

Guideline 7: Identify and avoid personal problem foods.

Foods that are healthy for most of us can be problems for some individuals. Sometimes people with inflammatory conditions can see remarkable improvements in their symptoms if common foods are eliminated from their diet.

Once I was stuck in a long reception line and struck up a conversation with the couple ahead of me. When they learned I was a physician, they felt compelled to tell me their latest medical story. The woman had developed severe and progressive rheumatoid arthritis and was told by her rheumatologist that she could be wheelchair-bound within two years. The husband went to the medical library to see if he could find anything that might be of benefit. He read a chapter on rheumatoid arthritis in Bristoff's food allergy book and recommended that his wife eliminate milk from her diet. Her rheumatoid arthritis completely resolved and now only returns when she cheats and eats a little cheese or other milk-based product.

Does this mean that everyone with rheumatoid arthritis can be cured by eliminating milk? Unfortunately not. Intolerances are highly individualized, and one must adopt a systematic approach to find which, if any, foods are triggering their illness. Some illnesses are particularly associated with food intolerance in some individuals, including arthritis, asthma, many skin rashes, heart arrhythmias, celiac disease, Crohn's disease, irritable bowel syndrome, migraine headache, rhinitis, and sinusitis.

How can you determine foods that may be causing your inflammatory reactions? With the help of your doctor, you might want to try one of the following:

- Allergy skin testing, which might reveal intolerances leading to urticaria, rhinosinusitis, asthma, and some cases of migraine headache.

- An elemental diet, which consists of liquid nutrition containing a balance of fats, sugars, amino acids, vitamins, minerals, but no proteins. This is a way to test for protein as a trigger

- Fasting, which is recommended as a definitive method to see if food intolerances are causing a problem. If symptoms do not improve in five to seven days on a water fast, it is unlikely that food allergies or intolerances are causing the illness. Such prolonged fasting should only be undertaken with medical supervision, because electrolyte imbalances and dehydration can occur.

On your own (or with the help of a physician), you can try to identify your triggers by going on an elimination diet, in which you avoid a particular food or foods for a period of time to see if symptoms improve or go away. It can be difficult to identify trigger foods because they differ from person to person, even if the people have the same disease. Plus, the food effects may not show up for several hours or several days, so it can become difficult to track down exactly which food caused the problems.

One time-tested method for finding trigger foods is by starting with an elimination diet. (If you have diabetes or other nutrition-related health concerns, or if you simply want additional guidance, see your doctor before starting an elimination diet.) Here's how it works:

1. For one week, stop eating all foods on the "trigger" list below—they are the most common trigger foods for most disorders. Try to eat only foods on the "safe" list—they typically do not cause intolerance reactions. (Foods that are not on either list are not common triggers, but they may be triggers for some people. Unless you know a food is safe for you, don't eat it during this test period.) By eating only safe foods for a week, you are basically wiping your pain slate clean and starting fresh.

2. Keep a journal daily. List all the foods you eat each day, and keep track of how you feel. Rate each of your most problematic symptoms on a scale of 0 to 10 (0 equals no pain or symptoms, 10 equals the worst possible pain or very severe symptoms).

3. At the end of the week, look back over the journal. Did your pain and symptoms ratings get better? If not, then chances are your symptoms are not made worse by trigger foods. But if you feel better at the end of the week, then you know that one of the eliminated foods was contributing to your pain.

4. To figure out exactly which food or foods are causing your symptoms, add foods back into your diet one at a time, no more than one each day. Eat a large helping so that any reaction to the food will be obvious. Continue to track your symptoms in the journal. If you see that your symptoms get worse within twenty-four hours of adding a new food, that food is a trigger for you. Eliminate it from your diet forever.

5. You may have more than one trigger food, so continue the process of slowly adding foods back into your diet. Continue to keep the journal of foods and symptoms until you are eating a relatively normal diet.

An elimination diet requires a considerable investment of time and can be somewhat uncomfortable and inconvenient, so choose a time when you will be able to follow through on the diet (as opposed to starting the elimination diet a week before your daughter's wedding, for example). Rotation diets, in which only one food is eaten per meal on a five- to seven-day rotation, can be useful.

Common Trigger Foods

Sometimes avoiding trigger foods can be difficult because products might go by different names on food labels. For example, not many people realize that whey is a milk product. Anyone with milk as a trigger food may also need to avoid any product that contains whey. Here are common trigger foods, and some of the places they may hide (in parentheses):

- milk (whey, casein, anything that begins with *lacto-*)

- other dairy products, such as cheese, yogurt, butter, and cream

- eggs (albumen)

- corn (corn starch, corn flour, corn syrup, hominy, grits, caramel coloring, and many sweeteners, such as dextrose and sorbitol)

- wheat (wheat flour, "white" all-purpose flour, any kind of bread product that doesn't specifically say it is made with a different kind of flour, food starch, couscous, bulgur, semolina, monosodium glutamate [MSG])

- beef, chicken, pork, and all other meats and fowl (chicken and beef broths, lard, gelatin)

- nuts and peanuts

- tomatoes

- onions

- apples, citrus fruits, and bananas

- chocolate (cocoa)

- alcohol (wine, beer, spirits)

- caffeinated beverages (coffee, tea, colas)

Common Safe Foods

These foods generally do not cause pain or symptoms:

- brown rice and rice products (including rice crackers, rice milk, rice pasta, rice cereal)

- vegetables: broccoli, spinach, lettuce, chard, collards, squash, sweet potatoes, string beans, carrots, white potatoes, brussels sprouts, asparagus

- fruit: dried fruits (excluding apples and bananas), pears, berries, pineapple, cherries, grapes, kiwi, mangoes, papaya, plums, melons, fruit preserves (not apple butter or orange or grapefruit marmalade)

- water, with or without bubbles (many herbal teas and juices have hidden trigger foods and should be avoided—they can be added back into the diet as one of the eliminated foods)

ADDITIONAL
INFLAMMATION-FIGHTING FOODS

If you've managed to follow the seven guidelines and would like to add a few more anti-inflammatory substances to your diet, curry spice, tea (especially green tea), soy, and ginkgo biloba are others to consider.

Curry Spice

Turmeric, the yellow spice used in curry dishes, has been shown to have potent anti-inflammatory properties. The active substance in turmeric is the phytochemical curcumin, which seems to suppress inflammation-related cytokines and the enzyme cyclooxygenase-2 (COX-2) and is a more potent antioxidant than vitamin E. Curcumin has been shown in laboratory studies to prevent memory deficits in rats, which sets the stage for testing curcumin as a possible agent for preventing Alzheimer's disease.

Indeed, when scientists looked at rates of disease, people in India, who tend to eat larger quantities of turmeric than people in Western countries, were found to have only about one-fourth the prevalence of Alzheimer's disease as people in the United States. In one astonishing study, aged rats with a known propensity for Alzheimer-like deficits were fed one of three different types of chow: normal rat chow, chow with curcumin, or chow with ibuprofen (the same anti-inflammatory medicine found in Advil). Both curcumin and ibuprofen reduced the development of brain plaques (which are associated with Alzheimer's disease)—but curcumin also controlled oxidative damage. This means that eating foods with turmeric may actually help prevent Alzheimer's disease. Another study published in the journal *Cancer* found that curcumin may prevent tumor growth by inhibiting some inflammatory chemicals (specifically, interleukin-8).

Inflammation Fighter

• If curcumin could stop cancer growth in the laboratory, why not add curry dishes to your weekly menus? The amounts found in Indian cooking are safe and high enough to reduce inflammation.

Tea/Green Tea

Drinking tea—especially green tea—has been shown to reduce the risk of some cancers and reduce the risk of heart attack. Tea contains a large number of phytochemicals, especially catechins, which act as antioxidants and can modify inflammatory processes that lead to disease. Drinking green tea has been shown to reduce the risk of stomach cancer and colorectal cancer. Black tea (typically drunk in Western countries) and green tea have been shown to reduce the risk of skin cancer. In a study of 450 older adults in Arizona, scientists discovered that drinking hot, strong, brewed black tea (but not iced tea or instant tea) was associated with lower rates of squamous cell skin cancer.

Tea also seems to reduce the risk of heart attack. Although some studies have used the equivalents of very large amounts of tea (upwards of about ten cups per day), you don't actually need to drink that much tea. A large study of nearly 3,500 adults over age fifty-five found that drinking one to two cups of tea each day reduced the risk of atherosclerosis by more than 40 percent.

Inflammation Fighter

• If caffeine is not a problem for you, try to add tea to your diet by drinking at least one cup of strong, hot (but not scalding) tea daily.

Soy

Soy products—such as soy milk, soy flour, and tofu—contain various phytochemicals, including genistein and daidzein. These phytochemicals have been linked to a decreased risk of prostate and breast cancers. One reason may be that diets high in soy proteins affect inflammatory cytokines. In a laboratory study, rats that were fed a diet high in soy protein had less swelling (edema) and pain than rats fed a diet high in milk protein. If you already have cancer, consult your doctor before adding soy to your diet.

Inflammation Fighter

• Experiment with different soy products to see how they taste and how they can be used. For example, it might take a little while to acquire a taste for soy milk in cereal or straight from the glass, but it can be used as a one-to-one substitute for cow's milk in baking with no discernible taste difference.

Ginkgo Biloba

Ginkgo biloba has several actions that make it a valuable inflammation fighter. It acts as an antioxidant, relaxes blood vessel walls to improve blood flow, and stimulates certain neurotransmitters. Ginkgo seems to improve memory and daily living abilities in people with dementia. A recent review found no side effects beyond those also experienced with placebo, so ginkgo appears to be safe. Although it is sold as a supplement in the United States, ginkgo biloba is a registered treatment in Europe for age-related mental deterioration.

Inflammation Fighter

• If you want to try ginkgo biloba, talk with your physician to make sure that it is safe for you. All studies have used standardized extract EGb761, so that is the preferred form. There is no standard recommended dosage in the United States, but many studies have shown success using as little as 120 milligrams per day.

IO

WHERE WE LIVE

HOME AND WORKPLACE SOLUTIONS

◉

They don't make buildings the way they used to, and we're getting sick because of it. In the first half of the twentieth century, office buildings had windows that opened. Once air-conditioning became popular, buildings were sealed up, and the amount of fresh air that entered a building was regulated by the building manager. At the same time, new materials and products based on synthetic chemicals came on the market. Synthetic materials enjoy many advantages over traditional materials, including lower cost, strength, and durability. They will not rust, rot, or be eaten by moths or termites. They can be engineered not to soil or wrinkle. Upholstery, carpets, carpet pads, wallboard, draperies, and furniture are all made from synthetics. Add in glues and adhesives, paints, pesticides, cleaning products, synthetic fragrances, and air fresheners, and it is easy to see that we have surrounded ourselves with chemicals. Our living and working spaces have been transformed into alien environments.

In the 1970s, in an effort to reduce energy consumption, buildings were insulated and sealed even more tightly to maintain air temperature. Almost immediately, there were widespread reports of illness associated with working in tightly sealed office buildings. A World Health Organization committee coined a new term, *sick building syndrome*, to describe this problem—and the primary health consequence of sick buildings is inflammation.

The respiratory tract is the most common site of inflammation reported in sick buildings. Symptoms of respiratory inflammation—including cough, shortness of breath, nasal congestion, abnormal sputum and phlegm, and wheezing—are found in about 30 percent of people who work in sick buildings. The typical inflammation-related symptoms of fatigue and malaise were reported, along with headaches, difficulties with concentration and memory, and difficulty thinking. To a lesser extent, some people also suffered from skin rashes, itching, and muscle and joint aches.

Do You Know What's Coming out of Your Carpet?

In an effort to understand the problem of sick buildings, the U.S. Environmental Protection Agency (EPA) measured the amount of volatile organic chemicals (VOCs) in the air of sick buildings. (VOCs are known to be toxic in high amounts.) Then Dr. Lance Wallace, an EPA scientist, and his team of researchers conducted experiments to see what people are exposed to. Groups of people were asked to wear a small battery-operated pump that sucked air from an inlet near their noses and mouths into an activated charcoal cartridge, which would absorb VOCs. The study showed that Americans are exposed daily to a host of VOCs, including benzene, xylenes, formaldehyde, and trichloroethylene—the names may be unfamiliar, but trust me, they are all nasty.

Dr. Wallace's research revealed the uncomfortable fact that, for most of us, there is more air pollution indoors than outdoors. The air in our homes, schools, and offices contains more than one hundred organic chemicals, including several carcinogens. These chemicals come into the air by a process called outgassing. When a wall is painted, the paint dries as the solvents evaporate into the air. The same process occurs with a variety of synthetic materials. Pressboard evaporates formaldehyde and solvents from the glue. Synthetic carpets outgas many different substances, including an infamous chemical known as 4-MP. (When the EPA wanted to study 4-MP, a custom chemical manufacturer was contracted to make up a 2-kilogram batch for testing. When the scientists received the order of 4-MP and opened the container, the product was so noxious and irritating that the entire building emptied as people took to the streets to avoid its effects.) Glues used to attach carpet to the floors outgas. Plastics and fabrics outgas for variable periods of time as they harden. Photocopy machines and computers outgas as their inner components are heated.

Even bringing home the dry cleaning can add to the chemical soup in the air at home. Researchers have discovered that measurable levels of carcinogenic dry-cleaning solvent lingered in the air throughout the home for several days after freshly dry-cleaned clothes were hung in the closet. The more tightly sealed the home, the longer the dry-cleaning fumes remain in the home.

The researchers also discovered many different pesticides in the indoor air of the homes sampled. Some pesticides banned as too toxic to be used in human habitats can remain in our homes for decades. Even the biodegradable pesticides that readily break down outdoors can persist for months in well-sealed buildings.

SICK BUILDINGS, SICK PEOPLE

After identifying the chemicals, the next step was to determine if the chemical soup in the air of our buildings could cause inflammation. Dr. Hillel Koren of the EPA and his collaborators built a big chamber and contaminated its air with a mixture of chemicals that matched those found in sick buildings. Healthy students were recruited as volunteers to hang out in the chamber to see what happened. The students had their nasal passages washed out with a saline solution before and after being exposed to sick building gasses in the chamber. The nasal washings were analyzed for white blood cells that migrate from the bloodstream into regions of inflammation. The results were conclusive: even in previously healthy people, sick building gasses cause respiratory inflammation!

If sick buildings only caused a little runny nose, no one would be too worried. But long-term inflammation can wreak havoc on many parts of our bodies, sometimes with unexpected results. Two women came to my clinic because of problems they developed while working in a certified sick building. Before being employed there, they were in perfect health. Their jobs as 9-1-1 dispatchers required that they spend their workdays sitting in a small, windowless building. As time passed, they became sicker and sicker with respiratory problems that got worse at work. One of the women had multiple hospital admissions for asthma. After months of ignoring their complaints, their employer finally hired an industrial hygienist to assess the building. The building was found to have absolutely no ventilation except when the door to the outside was opened, and as a result, it was filled with chemicals.

During one of my examinations, the women revealed that, although they had been plump before working in the sick building, they became obese while working there. Both women were short and weighed over 200 pounds.

"Everyone who came there to work gained weight," they told me. "When new employees started to work, we warned them that they would gain weight. We would joke, look at us, we weighed 110 pounds when we started."

Later I evaluated forty people from a single sick building that was determined to have no fresh air intake at all and a host of pollution problems. In addition to the usual sick building problems, this building was sprayed routinely with toxic pesticides, and synthetic chemicals were added to the ventilation system to add various fragrances to the air. This is done because some studies claimed the fragrances enhanced worker productivity. The workers were crammed together in small booths with a computer and a telephone. There was water damage with heavy growths of mold. The final blow came when an area with absolutely no fresh air was remodeled, with fresh paint, new carpets, glues, adhesives, new wallboard, and new fabrics. A group of individuals moved into the new quarters and became ill. Of those people evaluated in my clinic, 100 percent developed airway inflammation, with bronchitis, asthma, and rhinosinusitis. Fatigue was a major complaint by 97 percent of the workers, 94 percent had headaches at work, 79 percent had memory problems, and 48 percent had mental confusion. Unexpectedly, 64 percent of the women younger than age forty-five developed difficulty with menstruation (including premenstrual syndrome, cramping, and pain) while working in the building, which resolved when they left. Also, we were surprised to learn that 61 percent reported weight gain during their employment. The cause of the weight gain is unknown, but it may be related to the heavy doses of steroids, which are known to increase appetite and cause weight gain, prescribed to squelch their inflammation. Another possibility is that there are toxic chemicals called endocrine disrupters present in sick buildings that can cause hormonal aberrations. Clearly, more research is needed in this area.

When the people got out of the sick building, many of their health problems cleared up. Rashes, joint aches, and muscle pains resolved. Difficult menses went away. What did not go away was the chronic airway inflammation. They continued to have respiratory difficulties with asthma, bronchitis, and rhinosinusitis. Their airways became hyperresponsive, which caused them difficulties in various other settings. Fatigue and headaches continued to be a problem for many.

Scientists currently believe that sick building syndrome is caused by the complex mixture of air pollutants found in the indoor air of buildings. In addition to outgassing from synthetic materials, there can be allergens in the indoor air, endotoxins from bacteria, cleaning products, air fresheners, pesticides, and fragrances. Products of combustion from furnace fumes, gas cook stoves, wood stoves, fireplaces, and tobacco products also pollute the air and can cause health problems. Beloved pets can cause problems for people allergic to cats or dogs. Even natural products such as pine and cedar wood can outgas VOCs into the indoor air. Mold spores can be a serious problem for people with allergies. Heavy growths of mold can release VOCs in the air, which affect everyone. These VOCs give damp basements their characteristic moldy odor. Although no studies have proved a connection, the fact that many VOCs are carcinogens suggests that the long-term consequences of indoor air pollution may be dire.

If Your Building Is Sick

Five years before the phrase *sick building syndrome* was coined, I took a job teaching mathematics and physics at a public college, which had one building to house all of the sciences. It was immediately apparent to me that something was wrong with the building. I had headaches and sinus congestion every time I entered the building. As I looked around, many problems were obvious. A storeroom for volatile organic chemicals, many of which were carcinogens, had a ventilation fan that blew out into the hallway instead of out of the building. The building was laced with decaying and leaky gas pipes for hundreds of laboratory Bunsen burners. There was a print shop that used highly toxic solvents, including methylene chloride. Radioactive materials for research were improperly stored. The building had sealed windows and no ventilation.

Being naive and stupid, I drafted a well-written and reasoned letter to the president of the college that listed twelve hazardous situations in the building and petitioned redress. The response was swift. A bailiff arrived at my home at dinnertime to inform me that a kangaroo court was to be assembled to hear my case and fire me. I argued before the court that the science building was filled with poisonous gas, that I was being fired for pointing out the deficiencies, and that I would stake my job on an objective evaluation of the problems of the building by an environmental expert.

Though my evaluations and job performance were excellent, the court voted to deny my contract for the next academic year, though no cause was ever given. A strong faculty union was negotiating a contract for the entire system, and a grievance on my behalf was filed. My case and letter received wide attention. Other people came forth with complaints related to the building. Abruptly, my contract was renewed.

By the start of the next academic year, I had resigned to begin medical school. Shortly thereafter, an environmental team arrived to evaluate the building. My list of twelve problems paled next to their list, which led to the building being condemned and abandoned. The college lost 25 percent of its classroom space and had to hold classes until 10 P.M. in other buildings. The next year the president of the college was gone and never heard from again.

Inflammation Fighters

• Do not allow yourself to be isolated. If you are having building-related health problems, other people undoubtedly will be also. Ask others if they have any symptoms. Compare notes about symptoms and when they started.

• Keep a journal of "funny" smells, illnesses, headaches, runny noses, and other symptoms. Note dates and severity of your symptoms.

• If possible, take a symptom holiday by taking an extended vacation or changing your work area. If symptoms disappear when you are away from your workplace, but reappear when you go back, you may be working in a sick building.

• Have a group of workers, perhaps through an employee association or union, request an objective evaluation by an independent industrial hygienist experienced in problem buildings. An individual request may have no effect and could even lead to recriminations, but there is strength in numbers.

• Some companies and institutions are responsible and want the best for their workers. Others may think the easy way out is to shoot the messenger, as I found out. Legal advice at this stage can be very helpful.

• A professional who comes in will walk through the building to try to identify obvious problems. Carbon dioxide levels are easily obtained. If carbon dioxide levels are high, there is insufficient ventilation and toxins can build up.

• If sources of pollution are identified, they should be eliminated by a professional.

• Help can be obtained from federal, state, and local governments. The federal Occupational Safety and Health Administration (OSHA) has a toll-free number for inquiries and requests for help: 800-321-OSHA (800-321-6742). You can also visit OSHA's website for more information: osha.gov. Your state department of the environment or health department (either of which can be found under the government listings in your telephone directory) can also provide evaluations and direct you to resources. A number of qualified experts and consultants are available and can be found in the yellow pages under industrial hygienists and at the websites of the American Industrial Hygiene Association (aiha.org) and the Association of Professional Industrial Hygienists (industrial.hygienist.com).

• Until help is found (an innovative approach to pumping fresh air to individual work spaces is being developed in Sweden), do what you can to breathe fresh air. If possible, open windows in the building. Take frequent breaks to walk outside for fresh air. Request to be moved to a different part of the building, or find out if your employer will allow you to work remotely from your home.

• Not all cases of inflammation are related to sick buildings. If you are the only one experiencing problems, or if the expert testing comes back clean, see your doctor. There may be sources of inflammation in your home or in the foods you eat that could be causing your problems.

POLLUTION SOLUTIONS

Reducing the pollution in your home may require a little effort and monetary investment, but it is key to good health. People living in clean air feel better, have more energy, and have fewer illnesses. Some polluted places are hopeless and are best abandoned, while others can be resuscitated without too much effort. With a judicious choice of furnishings, ventilation, pest control, heating and cooling systems, and building materials, clean air can be enjoyed for the life of the structure.

There are a number of references that can be consulted to aid in obtaining clean indoor air. Organizations and consultants are available who can also help, but be prepared to open a checkbook for some consultant companies. For more information, contact either the American Indoor Air Quality Council (800-942-0832;

indoor-air-quality.org) or the American Lung Association (212-315-8700; www.lung usa.org/air/air_indoor_index.html).

Cleaning Products

When you see the warning "Use in a well-ventilated area," take it seriously. You'll see this in the small print on the labels of a number of products, including cleaning products, glues and adhesives, paints, pesticides, and solvents. The most common toxic effect of these products is irritation and inflammation of the eyes, nose, throat, and lungs. Skin contact can lead to allergic reactions and irritations, including rashes from a condition known as defatting dermatitis, which occurs when the chemicals dissolve the fats in skin. Most often, the products contain respiratory irritants that can exacerbate or even induce asthma and rhinosinusitis. Headaches, lethargy, and mental confusion can result from breathing solvents. With heavy exposures, the heart can become abnormally sensitive to the body's own adrenaline-type hormones, and the heartbeat can race out of control and even fibrillate.

Cleaning products are of particular concern because we tend to think of them as "good" products. They clean our homes, kill bacteria, and make everything smell fresh and flowery. But everything that makes cleaning products "good" also makes them pro-inflammatory. The grease-cutting, germ-fighting, soap scum–removing, polishing, and shining chemicals are irritating to nasal passages, lungs, and skin. Even the flowery or fruity fragrances added to cleaning products (to cover the chemical smells) can produce inflammation of mucous membranes.

Where one cleaning product can cause inflammation, two or more might cause permanent damage. Mixing bleach and ammonia can produce an extremely irritating gas called chloramine, which causes inflammation of the respiratory tract, with the possibility of permanent damage. Toilet bowl cleaners often contain hydrochloric acid, which can burn skin and cause respiratory inflammation and damage. Mixing hydrochloric acid with bleach can liberate chlorine gas, which was used in World War I as a chemical warfare agent. Many exposed soldiers developed chronic bronchitis and emphysema, and no toilet bowl is worth that agony.

We are surrounded by dangerous chemicals in our homes, but we never seem to consider that they might be the cause of many of our more difficult-to-diagnose illnesses. For example, fibromyalgia (a disorder that causes pain in the ligaments, tendons, and muscles) and chronic fatigue syndrome are disorders that do not have distinct symptoms, which makes diagnosis difficult. Many people suffer for years, undergoing test after test until all testing is done, nothing is found, and the disorders are diagnosed by default. What if, as some scientists suggest, fibromyalgia and chronic fatigue syndrome are related to chemicals in our environment? Because of the long lag-time between common chemical exposure, first feeling symptoms, and then finally having the disease diagnosed, it is an enormous challenge to researchers to follow the threads of connection back to a cause.

Environmental medicine specialists have suggested that chemical sensitivity, caused by acute or chronic exposure to chemicals, can cause immune system and nervous system problems, headache, chronic fatigue, muscle aches, respiratory inflammation, attention deficit, hyperactivity (in children), and perhaps even tremors and seizures. All chemicals contribute to the increasing incidence of inflammation-related disorders.

Inflammation Fighters

• Check labels on all cleaning products, pesticides, glues, adhesives, paints, and solvents. Follow directions carefully and to the letter. The warnings are not there just to protect the company from lawsuits, but to protect you from becoming sick.

• Consider changing products. Check health food stores for nontoxic cleaners. Some supermarkets are also starting to carry these more environmentally friendly products, too. Look for products without bleach, ammonia, perfumes, or fragrances.

• If you must use these dangerous products, open all windows near where the products are being used. Turn on fans to circulate the air. Ideally, there should be a cross flow, with a fan blowing fresh air into the structure while another fan flushes contaminated air away.

• Never mix cleaning products. Even if you read the label carefully, you may miss some of the chemicals that might interact with other chemicals to form a dangerous gas. If you try one cleaning product and it doesn't do the job, rinse it well and then wait at least a day before trying another cleaning product on the same area.

• Consider cleaning less often. Embrace environmental safety in your home by letting dirt accumulate for just a little longer. Every time you use products with VOCs, you expose yourself and your family to health risks. Take a break.

Air Fresheners

The concept of chemical air fresheners is highly flawed. It doesn't make sense that one can freshen air polluted with irritant chemicals by adding additional irritant chemicals. Plus, many of us are sensitive to the irritating effects of the artificial smells. One study found that 10 percent of the population has inflammatory reactions to air fresheners.

Once I treated an elderly woman who had been healthy except for some minor sinus problems. She had gone on an overnight trip with her church group. When she and her roommate entered the motel room, they noticed a harsh chemical odor in the room. Almost immediately, they began to cough and have tearing of the eyes and nasal symptoms. They complained, and the motel manager tried to fix the problem by saturating the room with an industrial strength air freshener. The women returned to the room, but only got sicker and sicker. My patient developed asthma and bronchitis that would not go away, and her previously minor sinus disease became much more severe. We later learned that the motel room had been soaked with a very harsh and irritating insecticide. Despite label warnings, the pesticide had been sprayed in the motel room, which had then been sealed and locked tight. When the manager sprayed the air freshener, he was only adding additional irritating chemicals to the toxic mixture that was already in the room. Instead, the windows should have been opened and air flushed through to rid the air of the pesticide and its carrier solvents, all of which can be damaging and produce inflammation. Air fresheners might smell pretty, but they are not worth the possibility of short-term irritation or permanent damage.

Inflammation Fighters

• Avoid air fresheners. This includes spray air fresheners, diffusing air fresheners (the solid kind in plastic casings), plug-in air fresheners, and even scented candles.

• Use ventilation to rid a room of smells. More simply put, open a window. Open two or three or more windows throughout the house, turn on fans, and let in the fresh air. If possible, install ceiling fans in most rooms and venting fans in bathrooms or other enclosed spaces.

• If you cannot open your windows, get an air purifier. HEPA filters and electrostatic filters can rid the air of particulate pollution, including pollen and mold spores. Activated charcoal filters can reduce levels of VOCs, but eliminating the sources works best.

• Even potpourri is irritating to some people, so stick with fresh air instead of artificially adding smells to a room.

Perfumes and Fragrances

Perfumes and fragrances can cause inflammation of the skin and airway. One study found that more than 10 percent of health care workers suffer from fragrance allergy, and the sensitivity increases with age. One study found that nearly 15 percent of retired women have fragrance allergy. (For retired men, about 12 percent had fragrance allergy. Could the difference be in the amount of perfumes and scented cleaning products women use?) In another study, more than one-third of people with severe asthma had an asthma attack when exposed to perfumes and fragrances. A whopping 98 percent of people with asthma and 67 percent of people with rhinitis were found to have respiratory inflammation when exposed to irritants, with tobacco smoke, perfumes, and fragrances being the most common offenders.

Some people might have even stronger reactions to fragrances. A physician I knew who wore a rather pungent perfume developed lupus and pulmonary fibrosis. Upon my suggestion, she quit wearing perfumes and had a remarkable improvement in her symptoms. Whether or not this product was the cause of her illness was difficult to determine, but she got considerable relief after discontinuing the product, so it is fair to say it contributed in some way.

Inflammation Fighters

• Stop wearing perfumes. If you feel that you must wear a fragrance, do so only occasionally, and with a light touch.

• Be courteous of others. With 5 to 10 percent of the population suffering from asthma, and more than 30 percent suffering from chronic rhinosinusitis, we all need to be aware of the impact of our choices of personal fragrance products. If you wear fragrances to work, you may be unknowingly making the person working next to you sick. Ask the people who work near you if your fragrance is causing any health problems and then vow to discontinue using them if the answer is yes.

• Fragrances in soaps, fabric softeners, detergents, deodorants, makeup, body powders, shampoos, and other grooming products also cause problems. Consider switching to fragrance-free lines.

Carpets, Flooring, and Paint

Solid floor coverings—such as hardwood floors, parquet tiles, and linoleum—are best for minimizing inflammatory reactions because they don't harbor dusts, allergens, and endotoxins like carpets do. Also, some carpets outgas VOCs. The Carpet and Rug Institute (CRI) has an indoor air quality testing program that certifies carpets, padding, and adhesives that meet low VOC admission criteria. An emerald green CRI label can be found on carpets that meet low emission criteria. Your choice of floor covering can affect your health for as long as you live in the house.

Paint outgasses VOCs as it cures. Water-based paints are preferred over oil-based paints, but both outgas VOCs. Many manufacturers have risen to the challenge of minimizing VOCs and offer special products for indoor use. These are marketed for hospitals and other facilities that can't close for painting but should be considered by everyone with an interest in good health and preventing illness.

Inflammation Fighters

• Use low VOC water-based paints in well-ventilated areas. Ventilate the area until the paint cures so that there is no chemical odor. This is particularly important for small children and people with asthma and other disorders that can be made worse by fumes.

• When possible, choose a solid floor covering. This can be difficult, however, because hardwood floors tend to be expensive, and linoleum flooring doesn't have the same aesthetic appeal and comfort as carpeting.

• If you must choose carpeting, carpets made of natural fibers—such as cotton or wool—should be your first choice. Among synthetics (which, because they are often less expensive and easier to keep clean, may be necessary for some people), choose nylon carpeting. Acrylic carpets are more likely to cause problems. Acrylic is made of acrylamide molecules, which have been shown to cause respiratory difficulties in some people.

• New carpets should be treated like fresh paint. Don't immediately start living in the freshly carpeted room—leave sufficient time to air out the toxic chemicals. After installation, fresh air should be flushed through the room until the initial wave of intense outgassing is over. If the carpet is installed in a room without good ventilation, consider borrowing or purchasing fans to blow the gasses out of the room. Again, cross ventilation, with one fan blowing in fresh air while another fan blows out stale air, works best.

• Look for carpets that bear the Carpet and Rug Institute Indoor Air Quality Carpet Testing Program label, certifying that the carpet meets low VOC emission criteria.

Dry Cleaning

The chemical found in dry-cleaning fluid is called by several different names, including perchloroethylene (perc), tetrachloroethylene, PCE, perclene, or perchlor. Tetrachloroethylene is a fluid, and it evaporates into the air, giving off that typical dry-cleaning smell. This chemical has been shown to be highly irritating, and at high levels it can lead to headache, dizziness, confusion, nausea, and other nervous system problems. Tetrachloroethylene is also considered to be a possible carcinogen by the U.S. Department of Health and Human Services. Although no one knows what effects dry-cleaning fluid has at levels that enter the home, there's no reason to take chances.

Inflammation Fighters

• Freshly dry-cleaned clothes should be aired out before being brought into the house. Take the plastic covering off the clothes, then hang them in a garage or attic for three or four days to let the bulk of the irritant and carcinogenic fumes outgas from the clothes without polluting the indoor air.

• Alternatively, the clothes can be tossed in a drier on the lowest temperature setting, which can quickly lead to outgassing of the solvents without harming the clothes.

• If you can find one near your home, consider taking your clothes to one of the specialty dry cleaners that use only nonsolvent fluids, such as liquid carbon dioxide. These establishments typically advertise their methods, so you can usually find them simply by scanning the ads in the telephone book.

Cooking Stoves

Chefs value gas cook stoves for the fine control of heat and quick responsiveness to cooking temperature adjustments. Unfortunately, gas cook stoves are notorious sources of indoor air pollution. More than twenty years ago, a study of the indoor air pollution associated with natural gas cook stoves found levels of sulfur dioxide and oxides of nitrogen in homes using gas cook stoves to be above the levels allowed in factories. There are no indoor air standards in the United States, but the gas industry reacted to fears of future regulation by developing catalytic burners for gas cook stoves that limited combustion products to acceptable levels. Since indoor air standards were never enacted, catalytic burners were never marketed.

Inflammation Fighters

• Consider replacing your gas cook stove with an electric stove. Indoor air pollution will be greatly reduced, and most cooks find that they can get used to controlling temperature and cooking time with practice.

• Install a hood. Restaurants have fume hoods with a strong fan that ventilates to the outdoors. Depending on the structure of your home, you may be able to install a similar hood over your home stove.

Furnaces, Smoke, and Fumes

When we burn organic matter, whether indoors or out, smoke and fumes are always produced. Although those by-products of burning might be invisible, they can cause inflammation, and they have been associated with heart attacks, cancer, asthma, and rhinosinusitis. Unfortunately, we can't simply avoid these fumes, because our society and our lives depend upon burning many of these products, such as gasoline, diesel fuel, fuel oil, coal, and natural gas. As a society, we need to seek out a long-term solution in the form of alternative, nonpolluting sources of energy, such as wind and solar. As individuals, we need to limit our exposure to pollutants, which can come from unexpected sources.

Furnaces typically burn fuel oil or natural gas, and their fumes contain soot, sulfur dioxide, oxides of nitrogen, carbon dioxide, carbon monoxide, and many VOCs. The way they work is that oxygen is sucked from the air in the house and flows through air intakes into the combustion chamber where burning takes place. Ideally, the smoke and fumes from combustion flow up the chimney and out of the house. But this doesn't always happen. This ideal flow of air can sometimes be reversed, with cold air flowing down the chimney and fumes flowing out into the house. A thermostat controls a furnace, switching it on and off as the house gets too cool then too hot. When the furnace is off, cold outside air flows down the chimney and out into our homes. When the furnace initially comes on, oxygen is obtained from air flowing down the chimney and the exhaust goes out into the room. The indoor air is contaminated with furnace fumes until the furnace becomes hot enough to reverse the flow, and the fumes and smoke go up the chimney. In addition, the sheet metal separating the combustion chamber of a forced air furnace from the hot air chamber is stressed by high temperatures and constant heating and cooling. If cracks and holes develop between the two chambers, the furnace fumes circulate throughout the house. When cold fronts move through and furnaces run full blast, heart attack rates increase, in part due to the extra indoor air pollution. People in colder climates report the "winter blahs," with respiratory congestion, rashes and dry skin, headaches, fatigue, malaise, and poor sleep. All these symptoms can also be caused by furnace fumes.

Inflammation Fighters

• Check for leaks in the furnace. You can see if the sheet metal of the combustion chamber has cracks or holes simply by wiping the inside of the hot air ducts with a paper towel and looking for soot and oily residues. If there is a buildup in the ducts, there is a leak. All leaks should be repaired. If repairs are too extensive, you may need to replace the furnace.

• Contain the furnace. The air in the furnace room should be isolated from the rest of the house by installing airtight doors and ventilation to the outside air. Even a tiny fan blowing air from a sealed furnace room to the outdoors can create enough negative pressure to prevent fumes from escaping into the living spaces.

• Try a heat pump. Heat pumps heat in winter by using electricity to pump heat from the outdoor air into the house, and they cool in summer by pumping heat to the outdoor air. They don't pollute the air indoors or outdoors, and they are the most economical system in warmer climates. Installation cost is reasonable, particularly since one unit serves the role of furnace and air-conditioning. In colder climates, heat has to be pumped from the ground, requiring greater expense, or backup furnaces are needed.

• Fireplaces and wood stoves produce high levels of pollution in the indoor and outdoor air. If they must be used, well-sealed units that are isolated from the indoor air should be used.

Molds

Molds grow in dark, damp areas and hate bright sunlight and dryness. Molds release spores in the air that can cause allergic respiratory inflammation to an increasing number of us who have allergies. In addition, molds produce special toxins called mycotoxins, which can produce respiratory inflammation via irritation, even in people who don't have allergies. Less commonly, mold exposures may be associated with hypersensitivity pneumonitis and skin rashes.

The mold species *Stachybotrys* has produced a lot of concern of late. The problems with *Stachybotrys* first came to my attention over a decade ago, when I took a poison center call from a concerned woman who had been feeling rotten in her home. She hired a consultant to assess her home. Mold plates were put out, and spores from *Stachybotrys* and other molds were identified as living in her home. The consultant told her and her family to abandon their home immediately because they were in grave danger of a horrendous toxin produced by *Stachybotrys* called "yellow rain," which has been used as a chemical warfare agent.

That advice was misguided. The situation is similar to penicillin, which is produced by the mold genus *Penicillium*. Penicillin is an effective antibiotic for human bacterial infections, but in order to get biological activity in humans from penicillin, the mold has to be grown in large fermentation tanks. No one ever had a case of strep throat cured by *Penicillium* spores in the air. Penicillin must be purified from the tanks. The *Stachybotrys* toxin has to be produced and purified to be an effective warfare agent, and finding a few spores on a mold plate should not be cause to abandon one's home.

Every structure in the world, except perhaps for a few igloos, has mold spores floating in the air. All one has to do to prove this is to place a slice of moist bread on a plate in the open air and watch the colorful colonies of mold that grow wherever a spore in the air lands on the bread. Only in extreme situations, where sheets of *Stachybotrys* are found growing over hundreds of square feet of damp sheet rock or in subbasements with moisture-saturated walls, is there even the possibility of problems from the *Stachybotrys* toxin. Still, every kind of mold spore can cause major inflammation problems for susceptible people, and minor irritations to everyone else.

Just as the solution to VOCs in the air is good ventilation, the solution to molds is sunlight and dryness.

Inflammation Fighters

• Patch or replace leaky roofs and pipes and fix any other structural problems that allow moisture to enter or condense anywhere in your home.

• Put a dehumidifier in particularly damp rooms to pull the moisture out of the air. The air in any given room should be maintained at 40 to 60 percent relative humidity.

Dust Mites and Dander

Allergy-causing proteins abound in the air of our homes, causing inflammation that primarily affects the eyes and respiratory system. The most common offenders are proteins from the feces of dust mites, proteins from cat saliva, and proteins from cockroaches. Dust mites are microscopically tiny eight-legged creatures. Their scientific name, *Dermatophagoides*, translates as "skin eaters." Humans shed their skin in tiny flakes every few days, and dust mites feed on these flakes. They are found in our bedding, carpets, draperies, and furniture.

More than thirty million Americans are allergic to dust mites and have positive skin tests to dust collected in their homes. Although these tiny bugs don't seem dangerous, they can start a person down the road to a lifetime of asthma. One experiment conducted in Europe followed 566 children for one year. Half the families were told to conduct their lives normally. The other half were given instructions on how to reduce their child's dust mite exposure, including taking up carpeting, encasing mattresses and pillows in plastic, washing curtains in hot water, and storing books someplace where they wouldn't gather dust. At the end of the year, only 3 percent of children who were protected from dust mite exposure were found to be sensitized to dust mites, compared with 6.5 percent of children who lived their lives normally. These sensitized children were more likely to have allergy symptoms and to have been diagnosed with asthma.

Inflammation Fighters

• For people allergic to dust mites, encase box springs, mattresses, and pillows with solid barriers, such as specially designed thick plastic covers sold in bedding stores.

• If you cannot find these covers, or if you cannot tolerate the odor or crunching sound of the pillowcase when you move your head, then get very fine weave cases. The more thread count per inch, the finer the weave, so a 200-count pillowcase is a better choice for dust mite control than a 100-count case.

• Wash sheets and pillowcases at least once per week in hot water (at least 130 degrees Fahrenheit).

• Store books where they cannot easily collect dust. Children's stuffed toys can also harbor dust mites and it is best for children allergic to dust mites to avoid sleeping with the toy.

• If you have carpeting, vacuum frequently—as often as you can stand, but at least once a week. If you are allergic to dust mites, ask a family member who is not allergic to take over this chore. Vacuuming itself can raise dust so it is more easily inhaled. If you must vacuum, wear a simple filtering mask. Leave the room after vacuuming for at least twenty minutes to allow the dust to settle.

• If your allergies are severe, consider ripping up the carpeting and putting down hard surfaces, such as hardwoods or linoleum. They don't harbor reservoirs of dust the way carpeting does and are easier to clean.

• When you buy new furniture, choose wood or leather or nonwoven coverings for upholstered pieces, since fabric also harbors mites.

• For window coverings, choose washable curtains or blinds instead of heavy draperies.

Cat allergies can be heartbreaking. A woman with worsening asthma and rhinosinusitis came to the allergy clinic to be tested. Her skin tests were negative except for one big red welt where a tiny drop of cat allergen had been placed. She was allergic to her cat. The woman immediately burst into tears and sobbed uncontrollably. She told me that her husband had recently left her and that her daughter had left for college. Her cat was her only companion in the world, and she could not part with it.

Inflammation Fighters

• The harsh solution to severe cat allergy is to get rid of the cat. This can be a difficult prescription for some people, but it is the only guaranteed solution.

• If you live in a climate that is generally warm throughout the year, another option is to train the cat to live outdoors. Some cats readily adapt to being restricted to the yard.

• Wash your cat weekly. This will not be a pleasant experience for you or the cat, but many veterinarians and allergists claim that it will reduce cat allergens in the home. (Ask your veterinarian for the safest way to do this.)

• Purified cat allergens are now available for desensitization shots. Ask your allergist if shots are a good option for you.

• After cats are removed from a home, it can take three or four months before levels of cat antigen fall to safe levels. People with cat allergies moving to a home or an apartment previously occupied by a cat owner can be symptomatic for a few months, even though the cat has moved away. In that time, be sure to take allergy or asthma medications to reduce symptoms and prevent inflammation from getting out of control.

Cockroaches are insects that have adapted to human homes. These bugs particularly love kitchens, where food is found. They are adept at hiding under counters and cabinets until we are sleeping at night. Like dust mites and cats, these creatures contaminate our air with their proteins and can cause severe respiratory problems in allergic children and adults. Elimination of cockroaches, survivors of more than 280 million years of terrestrial upheaval, can be very difficult.

Inflammation Fighters

• Pesticides, preferably in solid form rather than a spray, can temporarily beat back the population. Unfortunately, cockroaches are great at surviving chemical onslaughts.

• Starve them out by restricting food and water. Clean counters and floors meticulously after each meal, and keep food and garbage in sealed containers.

• Seal cracks that provide migratory routes from other apartments or the outdoors. This may require moving the refrigerator, stove, and other appliances and clearing out the cabinets to check for cracks.

Pesticides

Pest control was revolutionized with a variety of sprays and powders. Persistent pesticides were coveted, and products came on the market that would protect a home for its lifetime with one application. Unfortunately, that meant that anyone living in that home was sentenced to a lifetime of breathing the chemical vapors. Pest control services offer maintenance contracts so that homes, schools, and businesses are subjected to monthly visits from exterminators who spray pesticides inside sealed habitats.

Organochlorine pesticides (including DDT, chlordane, toxaphene, aldrin, dieldrin, and heptachlor) have been used extensively to control termites, ants, cockroaches, and other insects. Studies have established that these compounds are pro-inflammatory. Though they are still used in some countries, organochlorine pesticides have been banned in the United States.

Organochlorines were replaced by organophosphate compounds (such as malathion, chlorpyrifos, and diazinon), which are safer for people. They are biodegradable in the outdoors, but some have been shown to persist for months in poorly ventilated buildings without sunlight. With repeated sprayings, pesticide levels may remain high because they don't have a chance to disperse or deteriorate.

And at high levels, they cause inflammation. Malathion, used in aerial spraying for the medfly in Florida and California, has been shown to stimulate a type of inflammatory cell called a macrophage.

Toxic exposures to organophosphates can cause damage to nerves. A possibly related effect was reported in 2002, when scientists found that farmers who had been exposed to organophosphate pesticides had nearly six times the risk of developing depressive symptoms. In addition, the allergic and irritant effects of these pesticides can cause inflammation of the skin, respiratory system, and eyes. Recently their use in dwellings has been restricted, though they are still on the market for outdoor use.

The safest pesticides for indoor use are the pyrethrums, made of compounds that occur naturally in the chrysanthemum plant. The biggest hazards of these compounds are allergic reactions and asthma attacks. There have been a few deaths, typically in individuals with asthma who shampooed their dogs with flea shampoos containing pyrethrums. In these susceptible people, pyrethrums kill by producing massive airway inflammation and constriction of the bronchial tubes. There is cross-reactivity between ragweed pollen and chrysanthemum allergens, so if you have ragweed allergy (hay fever) you are more likely to also be allergic to pyrethrums.

A fine line has to be walked between protecting ourselves from insects—termites that eat homes, cockroaches that cause asthma attacks, mosquitoes that carry viruses—and protecting ourselves from pesticides.

Inflammation Fighters

• Routine or maintenance sprayings, particularly in poorly ventilated buildings, should be avoided. Integrated pest management (IPM) is a program for replacing routine spraying with surveillance and spot applications when needed. IPM greatly reduces human exposures to pesticides while reducing the evolution of resistant insects. Money is saved on pesticide purchases, but personnel costs (from extra maintenance) may go up.

• Nonvolatile solid pesticides, such as roach traps and boric acid pellets, should be used whenever possible.

• If spraying becomes necessary, nonpersistent pesticides should be used in a well-ventilated area. Humans and pets should be restricted from the area until it has been adequately ventilated to remove irritant solvents and pesticides from the air. In addition, food, dishes, and cookware should all be protected from exposure.

• If your neighborhood is sprayed for pests, remain inside for several hours after the spraying.

• Although we don't think of them as pesticides, insect repellents, flea and tick sprays (including pet collars), weed killers, and kitchen and bath disinfectants are all considered pesticides. All must be handled with caution.

• If you use a lawn service that puts down weed killer, or if you use such a product yourself, remove your shoes before going inside for the first two days after application to avoid tracking the pesticide into your house. Make sure pets and children stay off the lawn during that time. Wipe pet's paws before allowing them back in the house.

• Always store pesticides in their original containers so that you know what you have and so you always have access to the safety information on the label.

• If you must use a pesticide on your pet or on indoor houseplants, apply the pesticide outside to avoid contaminating your home.

• When using insect repellents, never apply to broken or irritated skin. Apply sparingly. Never spray insect repellents near food or indoors.

• If you have any questions about the safety of a pesticide product in your home, contact the National Pesticide Information Center (800-858-7378; http://npic.orst .edu).

Outdoor Air Pollution

Studies have shown that, for most of us, indoor air pollution is worse than outdoor air pollution. But in many large or industrial cities, outdoor air pollution is a serious concern. Bumper-to-bumper traffic, diesel truck fumes, and pollutants from oil refineries and other chemical plants can create a toxic landscape. Although there are ways to control our indoor air, we have very little control over the air we breathe once we step out of our homes. People who live near thruways, oil refineries, chemical plants, power plants, diesel truck depots, and plastic factories have significant exposures to a horde of inflammatory pollutants in the outdoor air.

Research shows that exposure to diesel exhaust is related to a higher level of prostate cancer and lung cancer among men. Environmental factors have been linked with autoimmune disorders, including lupus, scleroderma, and autoimmune thyroid disease. Outdoor air pollution has also been linked with increased risks of heart attacks. Emergency visits and hospitalization for asthma and chronic bronchitis increase significantly on "bad air" days. These are not minor concerns; they have life-altering consequences. And those are just the obvious links. The pollution also has more subtle effects that can lead to long-term problems. For example, researchers found that breathing typical polluted air even for just two hours caused blood vessels to narrow, and narrower blood vessels means greater risk of heart attack and stroke.

Inflammation Fighters

• If at all possible, move away from highly polluted cities and switch to a job that does not expose you to diesel emissions.

• If you must work around diesels or live in a city with high pollution levels, don't smoke. Smoking will make all risks worse.

• Support programs, organizations, industries, and politicians that work for clean outdoor air. Make personal transportation choices that limit air pollution.

WHAT WE DO

LIFESTYLE SOLUTIONS

◉

People generally don't like to hear that they have to change the way they live. Over time, our daily habits become part of who we are, making change difficult and sometimes painful. And yet, these types of changes are some of the most powerful health tools we have. Of all the changes anyone can make, the single biggest health improvement comes from quitting smoking. For people who don't smoke, it's starting a regular program of exercise.

SMOKING

When it comes to smoking, I have to be blunt. Tobacco smoke kills. It kills the people who smoke. It kills the people who breathe in the secondhand smoke from people smoking around them. A large-scale analysis has shown that passive smokers have a 24 percent greater risk of lung cancer and a 30 percent greater risk of heart disease compared with those who don't breathe in others' smoke. Studies have shown, over and over again, that smoking causes cancer of the lungs, mouth, esophagus, pancreas, kidney, and bladder. Smoking is also associated with an increased risk of heart disease, obstructive lung disease, and stroke. Smoking causes inflammation, and its effects are felt throughout the body. The more cigarettes one smokes, the more years one smokes, the worse the inflammation and the worse the health risks.

That smoking increases inflammation is seen in its effects on inflammatory markers. Smoking raises levels of C-reactive protein (CRP). Animal studies have shown that simply breathing secondhand smoke raises levels of damaging free radicals (also known as reactive oxygen species) and increases the pro-inflammatory cytokines interleukin-6 (IL-6), IL-1 beta, and tumor necrosis factor-alpha.

The good news is that stopping smoking really does help, no matter what age you stop. You can reduce your risk of lung cancer if you stop smoking at age forty, fifty, sixty, or older. That's because tobacco smoke causes cancerous cellular mutations and also turns the potential cancer into real cancer. There are several points, then, at which the development of cancer can be halted simply by stopping smoking. Stopping smoking also reduces the risk of heart disease, stroke, and severe gum disease (periodontitis) usually seen in smokers. (Smokers who smoke half a pack of cigarettes a day are three times more likely than nonsmokers to get periodontitis; the more you smoke, the greater the risk.)

It's important for you to understand that you can quit. However many times you've tried before, you still have another shot at it. Don't think of those earlier attempts as failures; think of them as practice sessions. Millions of people have quit, and you can be one of them. Never give up trying. Your life is too important. Remember that although you think that smoking calms your nerves, irritability is actually a major component of nicotine withdrawal. The sensation of being calmed by smoking is false; what is actually happening is you are blunting withdrawal symptoms.

Inflammation Fighters

• Many experts suggest setting a date to quit. Write it on the calendar, tell everyone you know, make it a day to celebrate your new commitment to health. When choosing a date, try to plan for a nonstressful time. Stress increases the desire to smoke, so quitting will be much harder if you try to stop near the holidays or during a stressful work time.

• Know what symptoms to expect. That way you won't be taken by surprise and can ride them out. For the first few weeks you may experience insomnia or excessive sleeping, fatigue, unusual hunger, gastrointestinal upset, and the familiar irritability. You also may cough more and have a sore throat as your body tries to rid itself of the accumulation of mucus. Most of these symptoms will go away within a month. Not everybody gets the same set of symptoms, so it isn't helpful to try to compare your experience with someone else's experience.

• When you quit smoking, the two challenges are living through the cravings and breaking the smoking habit. Although some people can successfully go "cold turkey," many people need additional help to conquer one or both of the challenges. Nicotine replacements—available as patches, gum, inhalers, or nasal sprays—deliver nicotine to the blood to reduce or eliminate cravings.

   • Patches are available over the counter and are worn on the skin somewhere on the upper body, usually only during the day. They deliver a steady amount of nicotine absorbed through the skin throughout the day. Treatments last six to eight weeks, and the patches are graduated so that the amount of nicotine is gradually diminished. By the end of the treatment phase, you should no longer feel cravings.

   • Nicotine-containing gum is also available over the counter. These products are more flexible than the patches in that you can use them only when needed, whenever a craving hits. They are not chewed like normal gum. Instead, you chew the gum for a few minutes until it tastes peppery, then let it sit near your cheek without chewing. After about twenty to thirty minutes, you'll need to chew it a little more, and then let it sit again. Chewing releases the nicotine, which is then absorbed through the membranes in your mouth. Nicotine gum is usually used for about three to six months.

   • Nicotine inhalers and nasal sprays are only available by prescription. Inhalers are plastic tubes with nicotine inserts that are inhaled through the mouth. Nasal sprays deliver nicotine quickly to the bloodstream through the nose. They can be used whenever cravings hit.

   • **Important Notes:** For all nicotine replacements, follow package or physician instructions precisely to make sure they work properly and to avoid side effects. You must not smoke while using a nicotine replacement. The added dose of nicotine could be toxic. Symptoms of overdose include dizziness, vomiting, bad headache, blurred vision, weakness, or fainting. If you experience any of these symptoms, call your doctor immediately. Also, tell your doctor about your intent to use nicotine replacements because they can interfere with the way certain other drugs work. It's especially important to tell your doctor if you have chest pain, diabetes, thyroid disease, stomach ulcers, skin rashes, high blood pressure, kidney disease, or liver disease.

• Behavioral treatment groups can help you work through the process of breaking the smoking habit. Combining behavioral therapy with nicotine replacement is much more likely to be successful than nicotine replacement alone. Many local hospitals have smoking cessation groups; call to see what is available in your area. Other good programs of note include the following:

- The American Lung Association's Freedom from Smoking program offers group meetings, guidebooks, audiotapes, and videotapes. There is also a special online support program at ffsonline.org. Contact the American Lung Association for more information at 800-LUNG-USA (800-586-4872).

- Another free online support program is QuitNet, at quitnet.com. This site offers information on devising your own quitting program, online experts to answer questions, a support community, and written information.

- Telephone Quit Lines are available in many U.S. states. These lines offer information and support for people trying to quit smoking. To find out about a Quit Line in your area, call the American Cancer Society at 800-ACS-2345 (800-227-2345).

- The Centers for Disease Control and Prevention (CDC) and the National Cancer Institute (NCI) offer a lot of information about smoking and quitting. Visit their websites for more information. For the CDC, go to cdc.gov/tobacco. For the NCI, go to cancer.gov.

- Nicotine Anonymous is an international twelve-step program to help smokers quit, the same way Alcoholics Anonymous helps people to stop drinking alcohol. You can find the location of a group near you by searching the website at nicotine-anonymous.org or by calling the California office at 415-750-0328.

• Bupropion (Zyban) is an antidepressant that also seems to help people quit smoking. It moderates brain chemistry to dampen cravings. It is only available by prescription and cannot be taken by everyone. Talk with your doctor to see if this medication might be appropriate for you.

• Smoking cessation can be especially difficult for people who suffer from anxiety or depression. Getting treated for these psychological disorders will greatly increase your chances of quitting successfully. Ask your doctor about medications or other treatments for these disorders.

• Exercise will give you energy, distract you from cravings, raise levels of endorphins (the "feel good" chemicals), and help keep you from gaining weight. Any kind of exercise will do, so choose something you find enjoyable.

• Hypnosis (or hypnotherapy) is a relaxation tool that allows people to enter a state of restful alertness. This combination of relaxation plus alertness allows people to block out environmental distractions and focus on a single thought or message. For smoking cessation, a person would be put into this very pleasant, relaxing state and then be given instructions about how to stop smoking and ways to go back to the relaxing state whenever the craving for a cigarette hits. Hypnosis has comparable success rates to other methods and can be very effective for some people. If you think hypnotherapy might be helpful for you, give it a try. It can be difficult to locate a good hypnotherapist. Ask your doctor for a referral, or contact your local hospital. Once you find a hypnotherapist, ask about his or her credentials. Ideally, the hypnotherapist should also hold an advanced degree in medicine or psychology. You can contact the American Psychological Association to find a psychologist who practices hypnotherapy in your area at 800-964-2000 (also see the website, apa.org).

• Give up alcohol, too. At least temporarily. Drinking alcohol raises the chances of giving in and smoking.

• Although it may be tempting to comfort yourself with sweet or rich foods, try to maintain a healthy diet. Quitting smoking is likely to make you feel terrible for a few weeks, physically and emotionally. Eating candy, cookies, and other goodies may help you feel better for ten minutes, but they will only make you feel worse for days later, making quitting smoking more difficult.

• Clear your environment of all tobacco and tobacco-related products. Throw away the extra cigarettes and ashtrays. Go into this knowing that you will never smoke again, so there is no reason to save these things. If other people in your household are smoking, ask them to quit with you or at least to smoke outside.

• If you are married to or living with someone who smokes, it can be very difficult to quit smoking. It is best for couples to quit together and give each other mutual support. Also try to avoid friends and coworkers who smoke during the critical withdrawal period.

Exercise

If we could bottle the benefits of exercise, it would be the most potent medication in history. Holding all other things equal, people who exercise live about two years longer than people who don't exercise, they have fewer physical disabilities, and they seem to delay aging disability by about fifteen years. A recent thirteen-year study of runners aged fifty to seventy-two years, indicates that people who were not runners had a death rate more than triple the death rate of runners *from all causes*. A host of studies prove that exercise protects against chronic disease, extends life, and leads to a better quality of life as we age.

Exercise—any kind of exercise—can lower the risk of heart disease by more than 50 percent. A study published in the *Journal of the American Medical Association* reported that walking, running, rowing, and weight training are all protective. Men who walked as little as a half hour every day reduced their risk of heart attack by nearly 20 percent. Running for an hour or more per week reduced the risk by 42 percent, and training with weights for only a half hour or more per week reduced the risk by 19 percent. Another study showed that women who walked a half hour each day reduced their risk of heart disease by 30 percent—and walking gave the same benefit as more vigorous exercise. Basically, you can reduce your risk of heart disease every time you get up off the couch and take a walk. For men, some research shows that the more intense the exercise (short of painful, strenuous training or overtraining), the greater the risk reduction. So brisk walking beats strolling and running beats brisk walking for heart protection. Strenuous exercise, on the other hand, can be harmful, suppressing immune functions.

Exercise seems to benefit anyone with an inflammation-related illness. People with diabetes, obesity, arthritis, osteoporosis, depression, fatigue, and many other disorders all feel better and have better illness control with exercise. High levels of physical activity—either leisure or work activity—have been shown to decrease the risk of developing type 2 diabetes by as much as 50 percent.

Why does exercise work so well? There are a number of benefits to exercise, including improvements in heart function and an increased ability to defend against free radical damage. But the latest discovery is that exercise lowers levels of the inflammation marker CRP in the blood. This means that exercise reduces inflammation in the body. Studies have shown that everyone benefits. Even moderately fit people can lower their CRP levels by more than half compared with unfit people.

There is no age limit to the benefits of exercise. People can start exercising at any age and can continue exercising throughout life. The earlier you start, the better off you'll be, but people who do not begin exercising until age 75 still can expect to see some increases in life expectancy. In fact, at least one study found that people who started exercising late in life had lower death rates compared with people who exercised in their youth but stopped exercising as they got older.

Over the long term, exercise also can reduce cognitive decline as we age by improving our memories, reaction times, and other brain functions. Recent research has found, quite surprisingly, that adult brains can still grow new brain cells and blood vessels and that exercise seems to help this process along.

Inflammation Fighters

• See your doctor before starting on any exercise program. Although just about everyone can safely walk for half an hour each day, you should have your doctor's approval before starting any intense regimen.

• Both aerobic and strengthening exercises have been shown to decrease levels of inflammation in the body. Ideally, both should be a part of your weekly routine.

  • Aerobic exercise is the active type of activity we typically think of as "exercise"—anything that makes your heart beat faster. Walking, running, skiing, swimming, bicycling, and jumping rope are all examples of aerobic activity. This type of exercise is strongly linked to improved immune function and decrease in inflammation. Thirty minutes of any type of aerobic exercise five to seven days each week should be every beginner's goal.

  • Strengthening exercises, sometimes called resistance training, strengthen muscles. These exercises require using different muscles of the body to lift, pull, or push some weight. It is especially important for beginners to start slowly, and I recommend getting the advice of an exercise physiologist or a certified trainer at a fitness center before starting a strengthening routine. It is far too easy to do harm to the body by performing exercises incorrectly. The goal should be to do a strengthening program one to three times per week. Call your local YMCA/YWCA, community college, or fitness center to find out if they have licensed fitness trainers on staff and programs for beginners.

• Wear loose, comfortable clothing. If it is cold, dress in layers to provide greater warmth and to allow easy removal if necessary as you warm up during exercise. Make sure your shoes fit well, with good arch support and flexible soles.

• Moderate fitness can be attained simply by walking for thirty minutes a day, five to seven days per week. Start slowly at a pace that is comfortable for you, and for just ten minutes. As the exercise gets easier, pick up the pace a little and then walk for a little longer. Keep upping the pace and time until you are walking briskly for thirty minutes every day. If you find yourself unable to talk while walking due to shortness of breath, slow down. Don't push yourself beyond your comfort level.

• Many people think of exercise as something they do only when they want to lose weight, but research shows that the heart is helped by exercise even when there is no weight loss. If weight loss is a goal, many people give up exercising when they lose the weight or when they get frustrated at not being able to lose the weight. Keep fitness and inflammation control as your goal—weight will come off eventually with continued exercise.

• If you have difficulty walking or if your movements are limited because of joint problems, try tai chi. This slow, gentle exercise helps build strength and flexibility through fluid movements and graceful poses. Many hospitals, colleges, and fitness centers have classes in tai chi for people of all fitness levels.

• Integrate other, smaller amounts of exercise into your daily routine. For example, instead of trolling the parking lot for a spot closest to the building, park farther away and use the opportunity to walk an additional few steps. Take the stairs instead of the elevator. Walk the dog twice as far as usual. The trick is to look for reasons to move, instead of looking for reasons to sit down.

- Take music with you while you walk. In a study that looked at patients with chronic obstructive pulmonary disease, those who listened to music through headphones while exercising walked farther than those who didn't listen to music. It could be that the music was distracting, or soothing, or uplifting, but the effect was an increase in stamina and a decrease in the amount of reported discomfort. If it worked for these patients, there's no reason why it shouldn't work for everybody.

- If you live in an area where you feel uncomfortable walking outside, either for safety or weather concerns, consider purchasing a treadmill for your home. There are a variety of models available, including some that fold down for easy storage under a bed. Prices can range from under $200 to several thousand dollars, depending on how many extras you want to pay for. The best way to find the right treadmill for you is to visit a fitness or sporting goods store and test out all the models. Don't be afraid to ask questions. Once you know the price and brand you want, you can purchase one there (it will usually come with a service warranty) or look for the same model on sale in the want ads of your local newspaper.

- Call your doctor if you experience chest pain or extreme muscle aches while exercising. In fact, talk with your doctor if you have any concerns at all about exercise. Your doctor wants you to exercise and will likely jump at the chance to answer your questions.

A Few Other Helpful Changes

Drinking a moderate amount of wine, avoiding marijuana and cocaine, and enjoying safe sex can all be helpful inflammation fighters.

Alcohol

An occasional glass of wine can reduce inflammation. White wine contains two of the same substances that make olive oil so healthy: tyrosol and caffeic acid. These compounds modulate the pro-inflammatory cytokines IL-1 beta, IL-6, and tumor necrosis factor-alpha. Red wine contains certain nutritional phytochemicals called flavonoids, which can reduce inflammatory cytokines and help prevent atherosclerosis. Drinking alcohol (particularly wine) in moderation can be helpful for some people. Moderation is defined as about one drink per day for women and two drinks per day for men. People who have a history of alcohol abuse, however, should avoid alcohol entirely. Excess alcohol (more than about two drinks per day) increases the risk of heart problems.

Cocaine and Marijuana

Heart attacks can occur in cocaine users with no other risk factors for heart disease, even in young women whose heart attack risk is otherwise virtually zero. Cocaine causes heart attacks and strokes by causing vasospasm and making platelets sticky—two quick inflammation reactions. Chronic use causes accelerated atherosclerosis related to inflammation. The tragic story of Len Bias, the University of Maryland basketball star who celebrated his multimillion dollar contract with the Boston Celtics with a cocaine binge and suffered sudden cardiac death, is all too familiar. One study found a person's risk of a heart attack increases 23.7 times after using cocaine. To a much lesser extent, heart attacks can also occur after marijuana use, raising risk 4.8 times.

Sex

Though the benefits of being sexually active have not been studied to the extent that exercise, diet, supplements, and smoking cessation have, there are both theoretical reasons and animal data to support that safe sex is a great benefit to health and may be associated with reduced inflammation. The biological imperative for all species, including humans, is reproduction. People who are sexually active are in a reproductive mode, and the biological response will be to maintain health and vigor. Wholesome sex, while being great fun, can also greatly increase well-being. Sexual activity increases levels of hormones that tend to decrease with age and is also associated with increased activity of the neurotransmitter dopamine. Research suggests that dopamine may have anti-inflammatory properties and has been shown to suppress the production of the pro-inflammatory cytokine IL-12 while stimulating the production of the anti-inflammatory cytokine IL-10. Animal studies have shown that rats with a high level of sexual activity have longer life spans than rats with a low level of sexual activity. Frequent safe sex with one partner is highly recommended. Unsafe sex should be avoided at all times.

12

How We Think

Mind-Body Solutions

◉

It's intuitively easy to make the link between our health and environmental toxins, food, smoking, or alcohol consumption. These are outside forces corrupting our previously "pure" bodies, so that we become less pure with each whiff of polluted air, doughnut, cigarette, or martini. What many people don't realize, however, is that these "pure" and natural bodies of ours can create inflammation problems on their own, with no outside influence at all. Our thoughts, stress levels, moods, and even social lives can trigger a cascade of inflammatory reactions in our bodies that could lead to heart disease, asthma, or other health problems.

Every time you engage your brain—every time you speak, move, read, ponder, plan, or daydream—the nerves in your brain communicate with each other by chemical messengers called neurotransmitters. So with every thought, the brain releases body chemicals that have effects beyond that original thought. We know, for example, that neurotransmitters are intimately tied to moods. The neurotransmitter serotonin is sometimes called the "feel good" chemical because it is responsible for feelings of calm and happiness. People who don't produce enough serotonin or who break down serotonin too quickly tend to be depressed and/or anxious. That's why medications that increase the amount of serotonin available in the brain—such as Prozac, Paxil, and Zoloft—are used as antidepressants and mood stabilizers.

The relationship between neurotransmitters and mood have been known for decades. What's new is that scientists have discovered that being depressed, anxious, hostile, or stressed also has an effect on inflammation-related chemicals. When we have extreme emotions, the body chemicals associated with those emotional states can change how our immune, cardiovascular, and endocrine systems function. Certain inflammation-related chemicals are thrown out of balance. For example, production of interleukin-6 (IL-6), one of the major pro-inflammatory cytokines, is increased during certain emotional states. This means that the delicate balance of inflammation and anti-inflammation is lost, and our bodies become at risk for all the interconnected inflammation-related diseases.

DEPRESSION, ANXIETY, AND HOSTILITY

Depression, anxiety, and anger or hostility have all been shown to have serious health consequences, but depression has generated the bulk of scientific studies.

Depression

We all feel sad or blue once in a while. Clinical depression is different, both more severe and of longer duration. A person is defined as depressed if he or she has feelings of sadness that last two weeks or longer, along with loss of interest or pleasure in usual activities, irritability, changes in sleep patterns, weight gain or loss, inability to concentrate, fatigue or loss of energy, feelings of hopelessness, or thoughts of suicide.

Studies have shown that depression is associated with increases in pro-inflammatory cytokines, such as IL-6. These relationships, however, can be confusing. Which occurs first? Does having high levels of IL-6 (which might occur due to simple aging or as a result of other inflammatory disorders) cause depression? Or does having depression cause high levels of IL-6? Several studies have attempted to answer these questions, but the answer is still unclear. Here's what we know:

- People who are depressed have elevated levels of inflammatory cytokines, higher than people who are not depressed.

- Giving cytokines to people, as might be done to battle hepatitis C or other diseases, can bring on symptoms of depression.

- In animals, giving cytokines experimentally can cause many of the same behavior patterns associated with depression: lower food intake, less activity, and an inability to feel pleasure.

- People with other inflammation-related diseases, such as diabetes, heart disease, or autoimmune diseases, tend to have higher rates of depression than healthy people.

- Giving antidepressant medications reduces depression and also reduces levels of certain cytokines in the blood.

One theory of how emotions might increase inflammation is that depression (and anxiety) causes hyperactivity of the body system known as the hypothalamic-pituitary-adrenal (HPA) axis. The HPA axis is a neuroendocrine system, meaning that it connects brain structures (*neuro-*) to hormone production and secretion (*endocrine*). When the HPA axis is activated, certain hormones—including epinephrine, growth hormone, and cortisol—are produced in higher than normal levels. In the long term, these hormones can cause changes to the immune system that upset the inflammation balance in the body, causing higher levels of pro-inflammatory cytokines. In turn, inflammation can sometimes cause similar increases in hormone production, which increases inflammation, which again causes more hormones, and so on.

For example, we know that depression is associated with increased levels of IL-6, especially in older adults. IL-6 is known to stimulate production of a hormone called corticotrophin-releasing hormone, which leads to greater HPA axis activity, which leads to more cortisol production, which further upsets the immune system and inflammation balance, leading to greater production of IL-6. The whole system feeds on itself to create larger and larger inflammation imbalances in the body.

But what does this mean for health? Because depression so influences inflammatory and immune system functions, it is likely that the risk for many inflammation-related illnesses increases. We know that feeling depressed or hopeless increases the risk of heart disease and death. Healthy people who are depressed are more likely to develop heart disease, and people who have heart disease are more likely to be depressed than the rest of the population. People with heart disease who are also depressed are about four times more likely to die within six months of a heart attack than those who are not also depressed. Researchers are still trying to figure out why depression should have such a strong association with heart disease. It is likely that increases in inflammatory substances damage blood vessels, starting the process of atherosclerosis. If depression remains untreated, inflammatory cytokines and other proteins—including the infamous C-reactive protein, which has been shown to be a better predictor of heart disease than cholesterol levels (see Chapter 13 for more information)—continue to circulate, creating an environment where plaque in the arteries can continue to grow.

Anxiety

Although there have been fewer studies of the effects of anxiety on inflammation-related disorders, there is evidence that these emotions also affect how our bodies function. People who tend to get cold sores or who have herpes know that outbreaks often occur just after a period of intense stress or anxiety, likely due to a blunting of certain immune responses that normally keep those viruses under control. Studies have found that people experiencing anxiety had higher levels of the pro-inflammatory cytokine interferon-gamma, lower levels of the anti-inflammatory cytokines interleukin-10 (IL-10) and IL-4, lower levels of the immune system protein immunoglobulin A, and lower lymphocyte responses—all of which mean increased inflammation and an unbalance in the immune system.

High levels of anxiety have also been shown to be related to a higher risk of heart disease and can double or even triple the risk of dying of a heart attack. Not all studies have been consistent, however. Although chronic anxiety seems to make us more susceptible to pathogens, short-term anxiety may actually enhance immunity. More research will be needed before we can say when anxiety turns dangerous.

Anger and Hostility

Anger and hostility are always dangerous. Remember all those studies from the 1970s and 1980s that claimed that people who had hard-driving type A personalities were more likely to develop heart disease? It turned out that when all the personality factors that went into making a type A person were looked at individually, only hostility was found to be related to heart disease.

Hostility seems to increase blood pressure, even in response to minor stressors, such as doing a mental task. One study asked people who rated high or low on levels of hostility to choose a memory of a time they got angry and then "relive" the event in their minds. During this mind exercise, hostile people had their blood pressure rise higher and for longer duration than nonhostile people. Other studies have shown that hostility is also correlated with an increase in blood levels of the hormone cortisol and a decrease in some immune functions.

Of course, these changes affect health. One study found that men who scored high on measures of hostility were more than twice as likely to die of anything (including heart disease) than men who scored low for hostility. Hostile people also tend to have higher cholesterol levels, have higher blood pressure, and be more overweight than nonhostile people. In another study, men who scored high on measure of anger were found to have triple the risk of heart attack compared with men who showed low propensity for anger. Even a single episode of anger can double the immediate risk of heart attack.

Anger and hostility are so toxic that in 2002 researchers found that having high hostility levels predicted future heart disease better than all the traditional risk factors, including having high cholesterol, smoking, and being overweight. If a person has heart disease and undergoes angioplasty to clear the arteries, having a high level of hostility puts that person at higher risk of "restenosis" (when the arteries become blocked up again) and causes the disease to progress faster than someone with low levels of hostility. And the more hostile the person, the greater the health risk.

Inflammation Fighters

• If you think you might be depressed, see your doctor. There are many different types of treatment available, including highly effective antidepressant medications. Along with their known mechanisms of action—increasing the availability of neurotransmitters in the brain—some antidepressant medications also have been shown to reduce the production of pro-inflammatory cytokines and increase the production of anti-inflammatory cytokines. If antidepressants work in part by modifying the inflammation processes in the body, then being treated medically for depression may also help reduce your risk of many other inflammation-related diseases.

• If you feel nervous or anxious much of the time, you may be suffering from an anxiety disorder. Make an appointment to discuss your concerns with your doctor. Anxiety disorders can also be effectively treated with medications, which may also reduce inflammation. Animal studies have demonstrated that some antianxiety medications (benzodiazepines, such as Valium) can reduce inflammation, perhaps by reducing the production of pro-inflammatory cytokines.

• Consider seeing a psychologist for therapy to help treat depression or anxiety. In 2001 two separate groups of researchers discovered that interpersonal psychotherapy—sitting and talking with a therapist one on one—was able to change brain chemistry in people with depression. Because every thought we have changes our brain chemistry, it is not earth-shattering news that therapy might also create changes. What was astounding was that therapy seemed to create changes in brain chemistry on par with the changes created by antidepressant medication. (The changes measured were blood flow to specific parts of the brain and alterations in brain metabolism.) Look for a qualified and licensed psychologist, with a Ph.D. or Psy.D. degree. Ask your health care provider for a referral, or call the American Psychological Association (800-964-2000) for a list of psychologists near you.

• Cognitive behavioral therapy can help get all these emotions under control. This type of therapy is active, is structured, and keeps the focus on changing the pattern of destructive behaviors. In cognitive behavioral therapy, the person seeking treatment learns to recognize what types of stimuli generally provoke a hostile response and then learns alternate ways of responding. The person practices these new, less hostile responses in a therapeutic setting until the responses are automatic. Ask your health care provider for a referral, or call the American Psychological Association (800-964-2000) for a list of psychologists near you who are skilled at cognitive behavioral therapy.

• Exercise is one of the single best remedies for most forms of depression and anxiety. Regular exercise, done at an intensity level that is comfortable, has anti-inflammatory actions in the body. Beta-endorphins and other "feel good" chemicals are released in response to exercise, so most people feel better within about twenty minutes of starting their exercising. Just about any type of exercise is helpful, so choose an activity that you like. (For more information about exercise, see Chapter 11.)

• The proper balance of medication, psychotherapy, environmental or situation factors, and exercise for treating anxiety and depression varies from individual to individual. It may take some time, and a little trial-and-error testing, to find the best combination for you. Be patient. Stay in touch with your physician or psychologist to get the proper guidance and to report on your progress.

PSYCHOLOGICAL STRESS

The known risk factors for heart disease—including smoking, lack of exercise, high blood pressure, and high cholesterol—seem to account for only about half the risk. That means that if everyone in the world had about the same physiologic makeup, doctors would only be able to predict who would die of heart disease about half of the time. About 40 percent of people who have heart disease have none of the typical risk factors at all. Some scientists believe that stress alone may cause enough physical changes to account for a good portion of that unexplained disease risk.

Psychological stress can cause temporary increases in pro-inflammatory cytokines, including tumor necrosis factor-alpha, interferon-gamma, and interleukin-6 (IL-6). Our stress-jangled nerves can produce potent inflammation-related chemicals, including prostaglandins, neuropeptide Y, and corticotropin-releasing factor. Corticosteroids, such as cortisol, can be produced in large quantities. In fact, a high level of cortisol in the bloodstream is one of the main markers of stress. The stress reaction is thought to be present—and have health effects—throughout the body.

Many scientists believe that the inflammatory changes brought about by long-term stress or repeated episodes of short-term stress can either begin the process of atherosclerosis or accelerate the process in someone already suffering from the disease. With stress, there are changes in blood pressure and blood flow and an increase in homocysteine, which can cause the initial damage to the linings of the blood vessels. The stress-related hormones and cytokines allow monocytes to move to the artery wall and start the process—becoming foam cells, then fatty streaks in the arteries, and finally fragile plaque capable of bursting and causing a heart attack.

Some of the most influential studies of stress were conducted by the researchers T. Holmes and R. Rahe. They created a scale called the Recent Life Change Questionnaire. It listed the most common sources of stress in life, with each item being assigned a particular weight that denoted its severity. Death of a spouse, loss of a job, and divorce were among the most severe stressors, whereas minor events, such as taking a vacation, were rated as mild stressors. Increases in life stress (as measured by higher overall scores on the questionnaire) were found to be related to an increased risk of heart attacks within six months. This suggests that the stress-related changes in body physiology continue to wreak havoc on the body long after the stress itself has disappeared.

Sudden or acute stress can also have serious health effects. Studies have shown that death of a spouse increases the risk of death for the surviving spouse twofold for men and threefold for women within one month after the death. Tragedies—such as earthquakes, initiation of war, and terrorist activities—also have been shown to cause an increase in heart attacks and other health problems on the day the tragedy strikes and for the next few days after the tragedy.

Although heart disease and death are the most serious of the stress outcomes, they are not the only health risks. Chronic stress has been shown to cause flare-ups of many inflammation-related diseases, including gum disease, some autoimmune diseases, arthritis, irritable bowel syndrome, migraine headaches, and asthma. Remember the stress of taking tests in school? Even that level of stress has been shown to increase airway inflammation in students with asthma, which could lead to a full-blown asthma attack. Nasal allergy symptoms—the runny nose and stuffed-up sinuses caused by allergies to pollen, cat dander, dust mites, and other sources—can also be worsened by stress.

Psychological stress can also affect blood sugar control in people with type 2 diabetes. The hormones produced and released in the body during stress often cause more glucose to flood into the bloodstream. In the distant past, this would have been a good thing because it would mean that energy (in the form of glucose) would be available to the body so it could deal with the stressful situation—such as having to escape from a hungry tiger. However, in today's world, where the vast majority of stress is mental stress, this excess blood sugar serves no purpose and only harms the health of people with diabetes.

One unique aspect of stress, depression, and anxiety is that these distressing emotions often lead to even more health-destructive behaviors. People who are depressed or stressed often eat more (and more sugary and fatty foods), smoke more, and drink more alcohol. They are also more likely to take drugs, exercise less, sleep erratically, and ignore their social lives. So on top of all the inflammation-related problems, distressed people chip away at the very foundation of their health. Plus, smoking, lack of exercise, and obesity all increase inflammation in the body, so all negative effects of emotional turmoil are increased exponentially.

As we age, our ability to balance inflammation factors becomes more precarious as more pro-inflammatory chemicals and fewer anti-inflammatory chemicals are produced. It isn't surprising, therefore, that stress creates more health problems as we age. And this comes at a time when stress is more likely as health fails, financial issues become more of a strain, and our support systems weaken and collapse. It becomes critical, then, to take steps to gain control over stress.

Inflammation Fighters

• As with depression and anxiety, exercise is one of the single best ways people can deal with psychological stress. Exercise can reduce inflammation and seems to help rid the body of damaging body chemicals that are produced during stressful episodes (such as cortisol). (For more information about exercise, see Chapter 11.)

• Take a stress management class. In a study conducted at Duke University, people with diabetes who were given stress management classes had a significant reduction in blood glucose, with better control, than people who did not receive instruction. These classes are typically offered at hospitals, universities, and wellness centers. Ask your health care provider to recommend a program near you, or call your local hospital for a referral. These programs teach all facets of stress management, including progressive muscle relaxation training, how to recognize sources of stress, guided imagery, thought stopping, and deep breathing. (See Box 12-1 for more information about these techniques.)

• Learn to meditate. A number of meditation practices are widely available today. The zazen meditation of Zen Buddhism and the meditation of Tibetan Buddhism are highly refined and tied to religious beliefs and practices. Transcendental Meditation is the most studied, and studies have shown that three months of practicing Transcendental Meditation can reduce blood pressure in older people. Any other type of meditation should also work. The best results come from practicing meditation every day, twice a day—fifteen minutes in the morning and fifteen minutes in the evening. Transcendental Meditation is a specific technique taught by trained instructors around the world. To learn more about Transcendental Meditation, visit the official website at tm.org. There you can also find an instruction center near you, or call 888-532-7686 from the United States or Canada. (See Box 12-1 for more information about general meditation.)

• Stress increases the risk for other unhealthy habits, such as eating poorly (or not at all), smoking more, drinking more alcohol, and skipping exercise. It is human nature to want to nurture ourselves during times of stress. After the World Trade

Center tragedy of September 11, 2001, sales of comfort foods, such as high-fat brands of ice cream, increased markedly. But all these unhealthy behaviors only create additional inflammation, so all the health problems are compounded. In stressful times it is doubly important to maintain healthful habits. Although we would all be better off eating right and exercising every day, the realities of daily life don't always fit with our plans. Do what you can. If time constraints mean no time for exercise, be more diligent about your diet. If you find yourself eating poorly in times of stress, walk an extra mile or two for exercise. Although we can't "make up" for these health slips, we can try to balance out the damage until we are less stressed and can get back to a normal, healthier routine.

• Eat more fish, or take omega-3 fatty acid supplements. As discussed in Chapter 9, omega-3 fatty acids in the diet are important for maintaining an anti-inflammatory balance in the body. There are two types of polyunsaturated fats we eat in foods: omega-6s (which cause inflammation) and omega-3s (which are anti-inflammatory). The ideal is to eat equal amounts of both types of fatty acids, a 1:1 ratio. One study looked at the levels of inflammation-related changes in the blood of college students during academic examinations. The researchers found that students who had an unbalance in the omega-6:omega-3 ratio had greater stress-related changes, including increases in the pro-inflammatory chemicals tumor necrosis factor-alpha and interferon-gamma. This means that it is possible that simply adding omega-3s to our diets might help protect us against some stress-related physical reactions. Because most people don't get enough omega-3s in their diets, I recommend taking fish oil or flaxseed oil supplements. Although there are no definite dosage recommendations, these supplements are safe. I typically recommend about 1,000 milligrams of fish oil supplements daily, or 1 teaspoon of flaxseed oil daily. (See Chapter 9 for more information about omega-3s.)

• Get a massage. We know it feels relaxing, but now the benefits of getting a massage to relieve stress have been verified by science. Researchers have discovered that massage not only relaxes muscles, it increases blood circulation, reduces anxiety, and shows signs of being able to increase immune function by increasing the activity of natural killer cells in the body.

• If job stress is extreme, consider your options. Do you find yourself developing headaches or fatigue at work? Is your morale low? Do you constantly feel "on edge" or pushed to an uncomfortable limit? According to at least one study, it's not how hard you work that puts you at risk for stress; instead, the key factors are the perceived imbalance between work and payoff (either financial or psychological) and the lack of job control. Working eleven hours a day or more also may increase the risk of heart disease. But really, stress is in the eye of the beholder. A job that is stressful to one person may be merely stimulating to another. Ask yourself: How mentally straining do you consider your work? How great is the strain due to deadlines or pace of work required? Do you consider your job relatively secure, or do you fear being laid off? Do you come home from work feeling uncomfortably drained and fatigued and irritable and angry, or does your work complement your life? The only solutions to work stress are to learn to manage your stress or switch jobs. Check with your human resources department to see if your company holds stress management classes or if there is any other forum for talking about job stress. Some companies have a referral service for stress counseling for their employees. If you decide you need a change in your job, or if you want advice on dealing with job stress, consider contacting a career counselor. These trained professionals can help you figure out what job might better match your skills and interests, guide you on the path to finding the right job, and provide advice about dealing with stress on the job. The National Career Development Association Web site (ncda.org) has a consumer section that provides information about choosing a career counselor, as well as a list of certified counselors throughout the United States. Another organization that can help you find a career development counselor near you is the National Board of Certified Counselors and Affiliates (nbcc.org), through its CounselorFind search feature.

• Consider seeing a psychologist. Life can become overwhelming at times. Many people don't realize that short-term counseling from a professional can help them through the most trying episodes of their lives. Psychologists can help you deal with stress, especially stress due to bereavement, job strain, divorce and marital issues, or any other life change. Contact the American Psychological Association (800-964-2000) for a referral to a qualified psychologist near you, or ask your health care provider for a recommendation.

POSITIVE EMOTIONS

When it comes to research, negative emotions get all the attention. With few exceptions, when positive emotions are discussed in the medical literature, it is almost as

RELAXATION TECHNIQUES

There is nothing magical about relaxation. We all intuitively know what to do, it's just that we tend to be so stressed and busy that we forget how to do it naturally. These days, most of us need to schedule time for relaxation, and we need reminders about how to let go of stress. You can become as involved with relaxation as you would like. For each of the popular (and effective!) techniques listed below, you have a choice of trying the do-it-yourself approach, or you can take classes or training sessions from professionals.

There are several ways to find relaxation classes near you. Many local hospitals now conduct relaxation classes or can provide referrals. Check the bulletin board or newsletter of your local health food store. You don't have to be a fan of health food to try relaxation, but that's the best place for relaxation instructors to advertise because people who visit health food stores tend to want to improve all aspects of their health. If you live in a large city, you can also search the Internet by typing the keywords for your chosen relaxation technique (such as *meditation* or *guided imagery*) plus the name of your city. Colleges and universities also often offer relaxation classes at night that are open to the community—contact the adult learning center there.

Here are the basics of the four major relaxation techniques:

• **Progressive muscle relaxation.** When we are mentally tense, we tend to create tension in our muscles, as well. We do this without realizing how tense we are becoming until we find ourselves clenching a fist or frowning or grinding our teeth. Progressive muscle relaxation involves tensing and then relaxing individual muscle groups in the body. The tension allows us to concentrate on those muscles and really feel the muscles, which allows for total relaxation. Sit in a comfortable position or lie down on your back. Concentrate on your toes, and tense all the muscles in your toes. Hold that for a count of three, then totally relax those muscles so that your toes are completely relaxed. Then move up to your ankles and repeat the process—first tense, then relax. Do this for all major muscle groups, moving up your body from your feet right up to the muscles in your forehead. You can practice this technique whenever your body feels stiff and tense.

• **Meditation.** The basics of meditation are simple, but it is amazingly difficult to perfect. The goal of meditation is to stop all thoughts, to quiet the incessant chatter in our heads. In the beginning, you might experience flashes of absolute quiet—split seconds of a calm mind. With practice, these moments can be extended for the entire length of the meditation. There are many different forms of meditation, each with a slightly different method. For the basic method, sit in a comfortable position and close your eyes. Inhale through your nose, and silently say the word *one*. Just focus lightly on your breath. Then exhale, and silently say the word *one*. The word will always be *one*, regardless of how many breaths you take. If you find your mind wandering, gently guide your attention back to your breath. Allow your mind to relax. During the meditation, relinquish all thoughts, all planning, all worries. There is no way to meditate wrong—just sit quietly with eyes closed and observe your breath. Do this for fifteen minutes twice a day.

- **Guided imagery.** If you have ever just closed your eyes and imagined yourself on a tropical island or in a grassy meadow, you've already practiced part of guided imagery. The basic form of guided imagery can start with a brief meditation (see above). Allow yourself to become relaxed. This technique differs from meditation in that the end point is not to clear your mind, but to fill your mind with calming, restful images. Imagine a place that is special to you. It can be a real location or a make-believe vision. Then allow your mind to fill in as many details about the place as possible. If your image is of a tropical beach, try to feel the warmth and texture of the sand under your feet, the warm breeze, the sound of the ocean, the smell of tropical flowers and ocean air. Allow yourself to fully be in that place. Feel the calm of relaxing in your chosen location. You can do this whenever you feel the need to unwind or escape from stress. Many people play tapes or CDs of nature sounds to enhance their experience. There are also tapes of special guided image "tours" in which the narrator will walk you through exotic locations or other helpful images. These are usually available any place that sells CDs, including Amazon.com (amazon.com), or from guided imagery Web sites, such as Academy for Guided Imagery (interactiveimagery.com).

- **Deep breathing.** Although we breathe constantly, most of us breathe ineffectively, in shallow sips from the tops of our lungs. Deep breathing for relaxation requires breathing deeply and fully, from the diaphragm—that band of muscle that lies over your stomach and under your ribs. Put a hand on your stomach just below your ribs, then take a deep breath so that it feels like your stomach is pushing your hand away. That is deep breathing. For relaxation, sit in a comfortable position with your back straight, or lie down on your back. Put your hand below your ribs again so you can feel the movement of your diaphragm. Breathe in to a slow count of four, making sure you can feel your hand rise and fall with the movement of your diaphragm. Then try to fully empty your lungs as you exhale to a slow count of four. After a while, you won't need to put your hand on your stomach to recognize when you are breathing correctly, and you can practice this technique anywhere anytime stress feels overwhelming.

an afterthought. In some ways, this focus seems logical. We *feel* bad when we have negative emotions, therefore there must be bad things happening in the body. Feeling good has typically been thought to be the absence of feeling bad. What this meant for research was that scientists focused their efforts on learning how to fix the "feeling bad" part, assuming that the result would be "feeling good." But positive emotions are not merely the absence of negative emotions; they are in a class of their own. Researchers are finally beginning to take humor, optimism, and other positive emotions seriously as we discover that they are critical for health and can provide a balance to the inflammatory and other physiologic reactions of depression, stress, anxiety, and hostility.

All clichés aside, laughter really is pretty good medicine. Way back in the 1970s, Norman Cousins wrote about his personal discovery that laughing for a minimum of ten minutes per day was enough to help reduce the pain he felt from a form of arthritis called ankylosing spondylitis. Since then, a few researchers have been trying to discover if there is scientific merit to laughter and, if so, how it works. The research is tricky—after all, not everyone thinks the same things are funny, so it becomes nearly impossible to do controlled research.

A few published studies have shown that laughter does seem to change our physiology in a way that reverses the effects of stress and depression and increases immune and anti-inflammatory chemicals. For example, studies have shown that when people with rheumatoid arthritis watched a humorous video for an hour, their levels of the pro-inflammatory cytokine IL-6 decreased and they reported less pain. In healthy people, watching a humorous video decreased blood levels of cortisol and increased natural killer cell activity—which means that their immune systems temporarily got a boost.

Another fascinating study looked at people with allergies to dust mites. When people who are allergic to dust mites have a little bit of that allergen scratched onto their skin, they will develop a wheal (a large, inflamed red bump) at the scratched place. In this study, everyone had an allergen scratch test before and after watching a humorous video, and then before and after watching a (nonhumorous) video about weather. After each test scratch, the size of the wheal was measured. The wheal sizes before and after watching the weather video were the same. But the average size of wheals changed from 11 millimeters to 5 millimeters after watching the humorous video. This means that watching a humorous video reduced the allergic inflammation reaction by more than half. How? Nobody knows for certain, but other studies that have measured blood levels found that laughter seems to reduce cortisol and other stress-related hormones. Laughter also increases markers of immunity, including natural killer cell activity, immunoglobulin G (IgG), IgA, and IgM. Some of these physiologic changes lasted for as long as twelve hours after just a few minutes of laughter.

Inflammation Fighters

• Laugh whenever you can. Seek out joyful friends, watch humorous movies, bring laughter into your life as often as possible.

• Try one of the relaxation therapies. Even if you don't feel stressed, relaxation techniques (see Box 12-1) can help you develop a sense of calm and contentment.

• Get out into nature. Being in natural settings—in the woods, by water, in a park, or even just sitting under a tree in your backyard—has been shown to be relaxing and calming and can create a sense of joy in many people.

• Put a smile on your face, whether you feel happy or not. Studies have shown that by adopting a particular expression, the "muscle memory" can trigger the associated emotion. So if you smile, your muscles communicate with your mind and send a signal that if you're smiling, you must be happy. According to studies, this works about two-thirds of the time.

• Amuse yourself with active or creative play. Given a choice of mindless entertainment (such as watching television) or mindful entertainment (such as doing artwork, playing a sport, or meeting with friends), choose mindful entertainment. These types of activities allow for feelings of accomplishment and expand the sense of joy and playfulness that is inside all of us. Some scientists who study happiness believe that the more we expand our minds, the more creative and playful we are, and the greater the opportunity for happiness and an escalating sense of joy.

• Find positive meaning in life. It is easy to get stuck in a rut of pessimism and boredom. Studies have shown that over the course of a lifetime, people who are optimistic have better physical health and mental functioning and live longer than people who adopt a pessimistic way of thinking. Most researchers in this area believe that we are born with a personality that makes us tend to be more optimistic or more pessimistic. But at least part of that propensity is learned, and it can become automatic over time. Every time you start to think pessimistically about a situation, try to find a way to reframe events in a positive light or to imagine the best possible outcome. This will be difficult in the beginning, and it will probably sound forced and false if you are not used to it, but over time your mind will automatically start looking for the bright side to any situation.

• Be useful to others. If ever there was an example of why it is better to give than to receive, this is it. Researchers at the University of Michigan reported that older people who were followed for five years reduced their risk of dying 60 percent by providing help to friends, neighbors, or relatives. People who received help had no survival benefit. In other words, that friend in need may indeed help prolong your life. No one knows why this should be true, but it could be that people who help are generally more active, or they benefit from social contacts, or they receive a sense of happiness from helping others. The lesson is that requests for help may sometimes feel like a burden, but they may be another opportunity for improved health.

13

WHAT MEDICINE CAN DO

TESTS AND MEDICATIONS

◉

It is always easier to prevent disease than to treat it. Diseases of inflammation are especially tricky to treat because inflammation has such far-reaching effects, and because the diseases often escalate. If chronic inflammation goes untreated, risks of additional diseases increase dramatically. A person who is overweight is more likely to develop diabetes, a person with diabetes is more likely to develop heart disease, a person with heart disease is more likely to develop depression, and all are more likely to be fatigued.

The common link to these and other disorders is inflammation. Anything that upsets the balance of pro-inflammatory and anti-inflammatory factors in the body can make the difference between wellness and illness. We don't yet know everything that affects inflammation, but we know that the balance is tipped in favor of inflammation as we grow older. Aging and inflammation are so closely related that inflammation may be a built-in biological method to cause aging. So as we age, it becomes even more important to monitor what is going on in our bodies and to treat inflammation promptly and aggressively. Diet, exercise, environmental factors, lifestyle choices, and emotional stress are all part of the inflammation balancing equation. But when inflammation gets out of control, treatment may be necessary.

When it comes to medical tests and medications, no one can make a blanket recommendation that suits every individual. Everyone needs to talk with his or her physician to determine the best medical treatment. The medications mentioned here should not be taken without first consulting a physician.

MEDICAL TESTS

There is no direct test for inflammation in the body. We cannot use x-rays to see inflammation, and there is no blood test that can confirm specific cases or causes of inflammation. The best we can do is measure certain substances in the blood that signal that a problem may be developing. Right now, the two best indicators that problems related to inflammation may be developing are cholesterol and C-reactive protein.

Cholesterol

Cholesterol is a naturally occurring substance in the body. Our bodies manufacture cholesterol on their own, and we also get cholesterol from foods made from animal products, such as meats, eggs, and cheese. We need cholesterol because it is used to make the steroid hormones, including sex hormones and the inflammation-related corticosteroids.

The body has mechanisms to control production, transport, and delivery of cholesterol. Cholesterol is transported on two different proteins in the blood: the high-density lipoproteins (HDLs) and the low-density lipoproteins (LDLs). Studies have shown that high levels of LDL cholesterol increase the risk of heart disease and stroke, but high levels of HDL cholesterol actually have a protective effect. That's because the role of LDL cholesterol is to transport excess cholesterol in the body for storage. If there is excess cholesterol, it gets deposited in the arteries, and cholesterol in the arteries is part of the disease process of atherosclerosis. HDL cholesterol's role is to pick up cholesterol and bring it to the liver for processing, so it helps keep cholesterol out of the arteries.

Understanding cholesterol allowed scientists to create a blood test that could measure the amounts of different types of cholesterol in the blood, and then use those numbers to estimate a person's risk of having a heart attack or stroke. The general cholesterol guidelines are:

desirable total cholesterol: < 200 milligrams per deciliter (mg/dL)
desirable HDL cholesterol: > 45 mg/dL

desirable LDL cholesterol: < 130 mg/dL
borderline total cholesterol: 200 to 240 mg/dL
borderline HDL cholesterol: 35 to 45 mg/dL
borderline LDL cholesterol: 130 to 160 mg/dL
dangerous total cholesterol: > 240 mg/dL
dangerous HDL cholesterol: < 35 mg/dL
dangerous LDL cholesterol::   > 160 mg/dL

Because we know that HDLs are protective, high levels of HDLs are good. But that also will raise the total amount of cholesterol in your blood. In order to account for good versus bad cholesterol, many physicians now rely on the ratio of total cholesterol to HDL cholesterol as a measure of heart risk. To calculate this ratio, divide your total cholesterol number by your HDL cholesterol number. If your ratio is less than 3, that is desirable, regardless of your total cholesterol number. If your ratio is greater than 4, that signifies a dangerous level of harmful cholesterol in your blood.

Of course, cholesterol isn't the only factor that goes into calculating risk of heart disease. Other factors include smoking, high blood pressure, family history of early onset atherosclerosis, age, sex, and diabetes. But your cholesterol numbers are an important marker of overall health and risk, and high cholesterol should be taken as a warning of future disease. By lowering your cholesterol, you can lower the risk of having a heart attack or stroke. The best ways to lower cholesterol are with diet (see Chapter 9), weight loss (if necessary), and exercise (see Chapter 11). People with very high cholesterol may be given a prescription for one of the statin drugs (refer to the statin discussion later in this chapter), which can lower the risk by reducing cholesterol and inflammation.

C-Reactive Protein

Although there are no direct tests of inflammation in the body, we can test indirectly by looking for markers of inflammation. When there is inflammation anywhere in the body, no matter what the cause, a number of inflammation-related proteins are found in higher amounts in the bloodstream. These proteins are called acute phase reactants and include proteins named alpha-1 antitrypsin, ceruloplasmin, fibrinogen, haptoglobin, and C-reactive protein. We can measure the levels of these chemicals, and if they are higher than what is typically found in a healthy person, then we assume that inflammation is present.

C-reactive protein (CRP) appears in the blood whenever there is acute inflammation or tissue destruction. (Its name comes from the fact that it reacts with a protein called C-polysaccharide, which is a cell wall constituent of the pneumococcal bacteria.) CRP levels rise about four to six hours after inflammation begins. If CRP is elevated in the blood, we can be pretty sure that there is inflammation somewhere in the body. A number of studies have shown that high levels of CRP are related to an increased risk of heart attack, stroke, sudden death from heart disease, and peripheral vascular disease. A study by Dr. Paul Ridker and his collaborators at Harvard Medical School directly compared CRP and LDL cholesterol levels to see which was a better predictor of heart problems. After studying nearly twenty-eight thousand women, the researchers found that high CRP levels predicted future cardiovascular events (such as heart attack) better than high LDL cholesterol levels. (The combination of CRP and LDL cholesterol provided a better screen than either alone.) This means that CRP is a valuable tool for assessing risk of cardiovascular disease. Some physicians are so convinced of its power that they recommend statin medication for their patients with high CRP levels.

Inflammation Fighters

• Have your cholesterol and CRP levels checked yearly. If your doctor does not routinely order CRP testing, discuss adding this test to your profile. Although most health insurance plans do not yet cover CRP testing, the test is relatively inexpensive (usually less than $20) and can provide you and your doctor with valuable information about your health.

• If your LDL cholesterol or CRP levels are high, consider it a serious warning and recognize that it is time to take steps to prevent cardiovascular disease. Start with the diet, exercise, lifestyle, and mind-body solutions recommended in Chapters 9 through 12.

• Talk with your physician about the possibility of taking one of the statin medications to lower cholesterol and CRP levels.

• If you see a steep increase in cholesterol or CRP, talk with your physician about the possibility of getting a cardiovascular evaluation—including a stress test and stress echocardiogram—to make sure your coronary arteries are not blocked.

MEDICATIONS

As our understanding of inflammation at the cellular and molecular levels evolved over the last half of the twentieth century, new drugs were developed to help us control the pain and suffering of inflammation. The main inflammation fighters, used for a broad spectrum of diseases, are nonsteroidal anti-inflammatory drugs (NSAIDs) and corticosteroids. Other medications—such as antihistamines, ACE (angiotensin converting enzyme) inhibitors, and hormone replacement therapy— are useful in controlling diseases related to inflammation. The newest of the anti-inflammatory medications is a class of drugs known as statins. They were originally introduced to prevent atherosclerosis by lowering cholesterol, but now scientists realize that their ability to prevent heart disease is due to their anti-inflammatory effects more than their cholesterol-lowering effects.

As this book is being written, researchers are continuing to unlock the secrets of the biological processes involved in inflammation and aging, and this research is driving the development of new medications. For example, there is great promise that Alzheimer's disease will soon be treatable and preventable, and new anti-inflammatory medications are being tested to treat depression, arthritis, cancer, and aging itself. Right now, medicine's best options are included in this chapter.

Nonsteroidal Anti-Inflammatory Drugs (NSAIDs)

Nonsteroidal anti-inflammatory drugs (NSAIDs, pronounced "en-seds") are very potent at reducing inflammation, relieving pain, and lowering fever. Some, such as aspirin, naproxen, and ibuprofen, are available over the counter. Others can only be purchased with a doctor's prescription. Box 13-1 lists generic and brand names for NSAIDs.

Aspirin

The most famous NSAID of all time is aspirin, a synthetic chemical inspired by willow tree bark. Since ancient times, people throughout the world have discovered that the bitter brew of willow bark reduces pain, swelling, and heat of inflammation. No matter what the cause, willow bark medicines lower fever, relieve pain, reduce tenderness, and alleviate heat and redness. As chemistry developed, scientists identified and purified the active ingredient of willow bark—salicin.

Nonsteroidal Anti-Inflammatory Drugs (NSAIDs)

GENERIC NAME	BRAND NAMES
aspirin*	ASA, Asaphen, Bayer, Ecotrin, Empirin
celecoxib	Celebrex
diclofenac	Cataflam, Voltaren, Voltaren XR
diflunisal	Dolobid
etodolac	Lodine, Lodine XL
flurbiprofen	Ansaid, Frobin
ibuprofen*	Advil, Motrin, Nuprin, Rufin
indomethacin	Indocin, Indocin XR, Indocid, Indotec
ketoprofen	Actron, Orafen, Orudis, Oruvail
ketorolac	Toradol
meclofenamate	Meclodium, Meclomen
meloxacam	Mobic
nabumetone	Relafen
naproxen*	Aleve, Anaprox, EC-Naprosyn, Naprelan, Naprosyn, Naxen, Synflex
oxaprocin	Daypro
piroxicam	Feldene, Fexicam
rofecoxib	Vioxx
salsalate	Disalcid, Saliflex
sulindac	Clinoril
tolmetin	Tolectin

*denotes availability without a prescription

As helpful as willow bark tea and salicin were, they were also expensive and very rough on the stomach, causing stomach erosion and bleeding. Synthetic chemistry came to the rescue. By 1875 chemists developed a compound related to salicin called sodium salicylate, which was used to treat fever and inflammatory conditions, including arthritis. A short time later, the chemical acetylsalicylic acid, commonly known as aspirin, was synthesized at the Bayer Company in Germany and introduced to combat inflammation in arthritis, rheumatic fever, and other disorders. Eventually, other synthetic NSAIDs were developed.

COX Inhibitors

NSAIDs combat inflammation in part by blocking the action of an enzyme named cyclooxygenase, or COX. The enzyme COX produces a class of chemicals known as prostaglandins, which are part of the complex chain of events leading to inflammation. NSAIDs block COX, which means that prostaglandins aren't produced and inflammation is blunted. But the pro-inflammatory prostaglandins are part of the process of repair in the stomach, so when we stop prostaglandin production, small irritations are not repaired. This increases the chances of getting gastritis, peptic ulcers, and gastrointestinal bleeding—all common side effects of aspirin, ibuprofen, and other NSAIDs. In the recent past, people who had diseases with chronic painful inflammation, such as arthritis, needed to balance their need for inflammation control with possibly serious stomach side effects.

Scientists later discovered that there are actually two types of COX enzymes, predictably named COX-1 and COX-2. COX-1 is mainly involved in the normal repair processes in the stomach, and COX-2 is involved in producing inflammation. In the 1990s researchers developed drugs that singled out and blocked the production of only COX-2. These selective COX-2 inhibitors (brand names Celebrex and Vioxx) still control the pain, heat, and inflammation of arthritis and a number of other conditions, but with much less gastrointestinal irritation. Still, there are drawbacks to their widespread use. Selective COX-2 inhibitors are very expensive, and many prescription plan companies are reluctant to reimburse for their cost. Rofecoxib (Vioxx) was found in one study to raise blood pressure. Another study found that people taking Vioxx for inflammation were about four times as likely to have a heart attack as people taking another NSAID, naproxen. No one knows whether this difference is due to some wonderful preventive effect of naproxen or a harmful effect of rofecoxib, but researchers are studying both possibilities.

Anti-Inflammatory Action

NSAIDs are used to reduce fever and pain no matter what the cause. Athletes take NSAIDs both before and after workouts and competitive events to reduce muscle pain and inflammation that can result from vigorous exercise. NSAIDs are a mainstay of therapy for a number of chronic diseases associated with inflammation, such as rheumatoid arthritis, lupus, rheumatic fever, and gout. Unfortunately, NSAIDs only provide temporary relief from inflammation and do not prevent progression of diseases. While NSAIDs are in the body, pain and inflammation are reduced. Once the drugs are eliminated from the body by the liver or kidneys, pain and inflammation return.

Over time, inflammation will still damage the body, even if NSAIDs are taken continuously. For example, the inflammation of rheumatoid arthritis will destroy joints and produce deformities even when the level of aspirin or another NSAID in the blood is maintained at all times. So although NSAIDs are valuable for pain relief and temporary treatment of inflammation, the best strategy is to fight the inflammation at its root cause. If factors can be identified that trigger or exacerbate inflammation, these must be eliminated (see Chapters 9 through 12). If lifestyle modifications and substance eliminations are not successful, other drugs can be added that prevent the chronic damage.

NSAIDs are not always helpful for inflammation-related diseases. For airway inflammation, NSAIDs have had mixed results. Some patients with asthma and rhinitis benefit from NSAIDs, while others experience asthma attacks after taking NSAIDs. For that reason, aspirin is a very dangerous drug for about 5 percent of people with asthma, and allergy-like reactions to aspirin are quite common.

(*Note:* Not all pain relievers are NSAIDs. Acetaminophen, such as Tylenol and other nonaspirin pain relievers, reduces pain and fever, but it has only a mild effect on inflammation.)

NSAIDs and Heart Disease

A number of studies have shown that taking a single aspirin each day can reduce the risk of heart attack and stroke. That's because aspirin has a powerful anti-inflammatory effect in the body, plus it acts like a blood thinner, making blood clots less likely. Aspirin is even used to treat heart attacks once they occur. At the onset of a heart attack, taking just one aspirin prevents death about as well as high-tech recombinant clot-busting drugs that can cost more than $2,000 per dose. (Of course, the combination of aspirin plus a clot buster is better than one alone.) Other NSAIDs also reduce heart attack risk to variable degrees, but they haven't been studied as extensively as aspirin.

Should everyone take an aspirin a day to prevent heart attacks and strokes? Unfortunately, no, which makes individual recommendations more difficult. Researchers studied a large group of physicians to determine the preventive effects of aspirin. Half the physicians took an aspirin each day, and the other half took a sugar pill that looked like aspirin. The study was stopped early because a preliminary analysis showed that, as expected, the physicians who took aspirin had fewer heart attacks—but the number of deaths in the two groups was the same! People who took an aspirin a day were more likely to die from a hemorrhagic stroke (caused by bleeding in the brain due to aspirin's blood-thinning properties), while those not on aspirin were more likely to die from a heart attack. Taking an aspirin a day did not reduce the total number of deaths, it just changed the percentages of deaths from different causes.

Of course, some people have a greater risk of dying of a heart attack than others. For example, people with high blood pressure or high cholesterol, smokers, and those with a family history of heart disease all have a higher risk of heart disease than the average person. For these individuals, taking aspirin may be worth the gamble because the potential for death by heart attack may be greater than the potential for death by hemorrhagic stroke. For this group of people, taking an aspirin each day can cut their risk of heart attack in half.

NSAIDs and Alzheimer's Disease

Scientists trying to find causes of Alzheimer's disease accidentally discovered that people who take NSAIDs have a decreased risk of developing the disease. A study in the Netherlands found that people who used NSAIDs for two or more years over the six- to eight-year period of study had a dramatic reduction in Alzheimer's disease relative to those who did not take NSAIDs. People who never took NSAIDs were five times more likely to develop Alzheimer's disease than those who used them heavily. Even short-term use reduced the risk by 5 percent. This study did not look at which NSAIDs were used, so we don't yet know which NSAIDs may be better than others at reducing risk.

Once Alzheimer's has set in, NSAIDs are of no benefit. Physicians now believe that if people want to prevent Alzheimer's disease, they need to take NSAIDs for many years, starting well before the onset of dementia. At this writing, large-scale clinical trials are under way to determine just how good NSAIDs are and the relative benefits of the various NSAIDs.

Inflammation Fighters

• Do not start taking aspirin or other NSAIDs without the advice of your physician or cardiologist. Every individual is different, with different sets of risk factors for heart attack, stroke, allergies, or other disorders. Although many people tend to think of aspirin as a harmless over-the-counter medication, it is really a very powerful drug that is able to help or to harm.

• Talk with your physician about whether or not you should take an aspirin a day to prevent heart attack, especially if you are a smoker, have high cholesterol, high blood pressure, or are over age forty-four.

• If Alzheimer's disease runs in your family, talk with your doctor about whether you could be enrolled in one of the ongoing studies investigating the preventive effects of NSAIDs, or if you should start taking NSAIDs as part of your personal prevention strategy.

• If you and your doctor decide that aspirin or another NSAID therapy is right for you, watch for possible side effects. Discontinue the medication and call your doctor if you experience severe stomach pain, blood in your stool, fast heart rate, difficulty breathing, weakness, or fatigue.

• Although selective COX-2 inhibitors are easier on the stomach, they may still cause gastrointestinal problems for some people. Discontinue the medication and call your doctor if you experience stomach pain after taking these medications.

Corticosteroids

Corticosteroids are drugs based on the hormone cortisone and its relatives. Produced by the adrenal glands located at the tops of the kidneys, these hormones regulate metabolism and are essential for life. Corticosteroid medications suppress inflammation, which make them valuable for treating many different diseases. But they also suppress the immune system, which makes the people who use them vulnerable to germs. (See "Common Corticosteroid Medications" for common corticosteroid medications.)

Corticosteroids reduce inflammation by suppressing the production of many types of inflammation-related cells, including most white blood cells. With steroid therapy, a person's levels of circulating basophils, eosinophils, and monocytes fall to only 20 percent of their normal amounts. T-helper cells, a type of lymphocyte that controls the inflammatory process by secreting cytokines, decrease in number.

COMMON CORTICOSTEROID MEDICATIONS

GENERIC DRUG	BRAND NAMES
beclomethasone	Beclovent, Vancenase, Vanceril
betamethasone	Celestone, Diprosone
cortisone	Coriftone
dexamethasone	Decadron
flunisolide	Aerobid
fluticasone	Flonase, Flovent
hydrocortisone	Cortef
methylprednisolone	Solu-Medrol
prednisolone	Prelone
prednisone	Deltasone
triamcinolone	Aristocort, Azmacort, Kenalog

The effect of corticosteroids on suppressing lymphocytes is so profound that these medications are used to treat lymphomas and acute lymphocytic leukemia.

The anti-inflammatory effect of these medications is so powerful that when these drugs first came to market in the 1950s, physicians thought that a cure had been found for every inflammation-related disease, from asthma to rheumatoid arthritis. In fact, when these drugs came to market, asthma death rates fell 50 percent.

It did not take long for the euphoria surrounding the new wonder drugs to dissipate. The drugs proved to be too dangerous for casual use. When a person takes corticosteroids, virtually every tissue in the body is affected by their action. Long-term use at high doses profoundly changes a person's physiology and even changes the body's appearance. People who take high doses of corticosteroids for long periods of time find that their faces get as round as a full moon (moon facies). They gain weight through their torso (trunkal obesity), while their arms and legs become skinny and wasted (extremity wasting). Their skin gets thin and discolored, and their muscles become weak. With continued use, bones become thin, osteoporosis sets in, and fractures occur. A person's blood sugar, blood pressure, cholesterol, and lipids all rise, leading to accelerated atherosclerosis. Psychosis and depression can also occur in some patients. Wound healing is delayed, and serious infections can take hold.

In order to use these drugs safely, a number of strategies have been developed. Short-term use is usually safe and well tolerated, so a quick burst of steroids is used to bring a number of inflammation-related diseases under control, including asthma, many types of skin rashes, Crohn's disease, rheumatoid arthritis, rhinitis and sinusitis, lupus, and ulcerative colitis. After the disease is brought under control, the dose is gradually lowered to the lowest dose that controls the inflammation. Sometimes patients are given a steroid every other day, which minimizes bad side effects. Another strategy is to just deliver the steroid drugs to the diseased part of the body. Inhaled steroids for asthma, steroid nasal sprays for rhinosinusitis, and creams for the skin can be used safely, with a great reduction in systemic side effects. Steroids can also be injected into inflamed joint spaces so that only the joint gets a big dose.

The development of inhaled corticosteroids for asthma revolutionized treatment. Drugs called bronchodilators are inhaled to relax the smooth muscles of the airways and open constricted breathing passages. But these drugs do nothing to reduce inflammation, and asthma can appear to get better when in fact it is getting worse. In some settings use of bronchodilators have actually been shown to increase the death rate from asthma. In a hospital emergency department, giving a person with severe asthma a shot of the potent corticosteroid methylprednisolone reduces their chance of having to be admitted to the hospital by half. Inhaled corticosteroids (such as Azmacort, Flovent, and Vanceril) deliver the drug to the lining of the airway while sparing the rest of the body from the ravaging side effects seen with systemic steroid use.

Corticosteroids also revolutionized treatment of some infections. Damage from infections is often caused by the inflammation produced by the body to fight off germs, rather than by the germs themselves. For example, bacterial meningitis is a devastating disease, with a high death rate, and those who survive often are left with permanent brain damage. A recent European study found that giving the corticosteroid dexamethasone to adults with bacterial meningitis early, before the inflammation did its damage, more than doubled the chance of survival. Patients who received the dexamethasone also were much less likely to have permanent nerve damage. (Of course, antibiotics have to be given at the same time to kill the germs that cause the inflammation.)

Inflammation Fighter

• Corticosteroids can be life saving for people with specific conditions, but they have potentially devastating side effects. Their use should be reserved for specific conditions, under close medical supervision. They have absolutely no role as preventive agents against inflammation-related diseases.

Antihistamines

Antihistamines are drugs that block the action of histamine in the body. Histamine, a naturally occurring immune chemical, binds to tailor-made receptors on certain body cells. Once histamine binds to its target cell, it triggers inflammatory effects. Sometimes these effects are appropriate and help us fight off germs and parasites and heal damaged tissues. Other times, such as when allergic people breathe in harmless grains of ragweed pollen, the histamine causes misery without beneficial effects.

With nasal allergies, histamine causes runny nose and sneezing. With allergic anaphylactic reactions to bee stings, massive releases of histamine cause increased heart rate and low blood pressure, sometimes leading to shock or death. In the intestines, histamine release causes bloating of the abdomen, nausea, vomiting, and diarrhea. In the skin, hives and other itchy or swollen rashes occur. In such cases, we want to block the nastiness by taking antihistamines, which bind to the histamine receptors so histamine is blocked and the inflammatory effects aren't triggered.

Histamine is found in many places in the body. It is a neurotransmitter in the central nervous system; it is found in cells in the intestines and signals the release of stomach acid; and it plays a role in tissue repair and wound healing. Fortunately, the various roles of histamine involve distinct receptors, so that antihistamines that block one effect do not always block the others. The H1 histamine receptor is found in the blood vessels and on smooth muscles in the gut and airway. The H2 histamine is found in the stomach lining and is involved in acid secretion. H1 antihistamines are useful in treating hives, while H2 antihistamines are useful in treating gastrointestinal ulcers from acid secretion. In general, antihistamines block just one of the many complex steps leading to inflammation. While their role is very limited, there is great relief of suffering from those symptoms mediated by histamine.

One long-standing problem with antihistamines used to treat allergic symptoms has been sleepiness. The problem is so severe that the antihistamine diphenhydramine (brand name Benadryl) is also marketed as a sleeping pill (brand name Sominex). Most antihistamines readily pass into the brain and block histamine there to cause sleepiness. This side effect has been engineered away with the design of antihistamines that cannot get into the brain. The nonsedating antihistamines, fexofenadine (Allegra), loratadine (Claritin), cetirizine (Zyrtec), and desloratidine (Clarinex), allow relief of runny noses and sneezing without drowsiness. Claritin and the older, sleep-enhancing antihistamines are available over the counter, without a prescription.

Inflammation Fighters

• There is no reason to suffer with allergy symptoms. Talk with your doctor about what type of antihistamine might be right for you.

• If you are trying a new antihistamine, if possible, take the first dose at some time when you will not be required to drive or operate heavy machinery. Different people react differently to different antihistamines. A medication that one person can take without problem may cause another person to fall asleep or become too dizzy to function normally. In fact, about 1 percent of people who take the "nondrowsy" antihistamines actually get drowsy. Once you know how you react to a particular medication, you'll know the best times to take it.

Statins

Statins form a group of drugs that came to prominence for their ability to reduce the total amount of cholesterol in the blood, reduce the bad LDL cholesterol, and (to a lesser extent) raise the good HDL cholesterol. A number of studies have shown that as cholesterol levels fall, for whatever the reason, so does the risk of heart attack and stroke. For people with high cholesterol, the first line of therapy is to change to a healthier diet and do more exercise. Simply following a diet high in fruits and vegetables and low in calories can lower cholesterol, sometimes dramatically. Adding a program of exercise has further benefits. (See Chapters 9 and 11 for more information about diet and exercise.)

For those who cannot lower their cholesterol by diet and exercise alone, one of the statin drugs is often prescribed. Statins work by inhibiting the enzyme HMG-CoA reductase, which regulates cholesterol production, and by enhancing removal of LDL cholesterol from the blood. Scientific studies have shown that taking statins reduces the risk of heart attack and stroke, even in people who do not have high cholesterol. Statins have been shown to reduce cholesterol levels by between 15 and 60 percent and to reduce the risk of heart attacks and other cardiac events by about one-third. As of this writing, the commonly prescribed statins are atorvastatin (Lipitor), cerivastatin (Baycol), fluvastatin (Lescol), lovastatin (Mevacor), pravastatin (Pravachol), and simvastatin (Zocor).

We now know that although cholesterol is an important factor in causing heart disease, inflammation is even more important and is directly linked to atherosclerosis, heart attacks, and strokes. It is now recognized that statins block inflammation and inhibit several steps involved in the formation of an atherosclerotic plaque. One of the early steps in forming a plaque is the activation of endothelial cells—the layer of cells lining blood vessels. No matter what the cause of activation—cigarette smoke, particulate air pollution, or other irritant—statins can block that activation effect.

Statins also lower the levels of C-reactive protein in a person's blood. CRP is a marker of inflammation and is known to be elevated in patients with unstable coronary artery disease. People with high levels of CRP have an increased risk of developing heart disease. Among those with heart disease, high CRP is a potent predictor of mortality. But taking statins reduces CRP, reduces inflammation, and reduces death from heart disease.

Medical scientists are also studying statins to see if they might be helpful in reducing inflammation in other diseases. Dr. Scott Zamvil at the University of California at San Francisco and his colleagues have shown that statin treatment can help in a mouse model of multiple sclerosis, the autoimmune disease of the central nervous system in which inflammation destroys the myelin sheaths of nerve cells. In these mice, treatment with the statin Lipitor prevented or reversed paralysis. Although it is not known whether people will respond the same way, studies are being proposed.

Scientists at the University of Milan have used the inflammation connection to argue for using statins to treat lupus and rheumatoid arthritis. Patients with these diseases have an increased risk of coronary artery disease that cannot be explained by smoking, high cholesterol, or treatment with corticosteroids. The increased risk is thought to be due to the inflammatory nature of these diseases spilling over into the coronary arteries. Since statins block inflammation in the coronary arteries, perhaps they can help with the arthritis and other inflammatory manifestations of rheumatoid arthritis. With time, clinical research will establish the value of statins in treating a broader class of inflammatory disorders.

Nothing in life is without risk—taking statins can cause some side effects. Toxicity to muscles is seen in a small percentage of people taking statins. People who take statins should watch for muscle aches, pains, weakness, or tenderness and see their physician immediately if these symptoms develop. Dark urine can also be a sign of muscle damage, caused when myoglobin, an iron-carrying molecule, is secreted from damaged muscle and eliminated in the urine. Statins can also elevate the liver enzymes, though liver damage is rare. Less common side effects of statins include headache, rash, and upset stomach.

Inflammation Fighters

• People with elevated LDL cholesterol and/or high CRP levels should do everything they can to lower those markers with diet and exercise (see Chapters 9 and 11).

• If diet and exercise are not enough to bring cholesterol and CRP levels within the normal range, consider taking statins. Although many people avoid taking medications, statins are saving lives daily. Take them if you and your doctor decide you need them.

• Although some practitioners recommend that everyone start taking statins as a general prevention medication, especially once they reach age forty-five, there is no data to justify their casual use. Don't start taking medications "just in case" if your cholesterol and CRP levels are within normal range.

• Some people experience unpleasant side effects taking statin medications. See your doctor immediately if you take statins and experience muscle pain, weakness, or tenderness. These often occur in the thigh muscles, but may be experienced anywhere in the body. Also see your doctor if your urine looks red or pink while taking statins.

Ace Inhibitors

Angiotensins are molecules produced by the kidneys that can raise blood pressure by narrowing blood vessels. One of the key elements is an enzyme called angiotensin converting enzyme (ACE), which takes the mild form of angiotensin and converts it to the harmful form. ACE inhibitors block that enzyme, thereby blocking the production of this harmful form of angiotensin, so blood pressure doesn't rise. The ACE inhibitor ramipril (Altace) has been shown to significantly reduce the rate of death, heart attacks, and strokes in patients without heart failure. Along with their effects on blood pressure, ACE inhibitors can also improve heart function in patients with heart failure and can reduce the incidence of kidney disease in people with diabetes.

The same angiotensin that causes high blood pressure also affects many other body functions, including inflammation, cell growth and death, and blood clotting. That is why ACE inhibitors have a protective effect against atherosclerosis. A related class of drugs, the angiotensin receptor blockers, work by blocking the action of angiotensin, rather than blocking its production. These drugs also lower blood pressure and may have a much broader benefit than lowering blood pressure with fewer side effects than ACE inhibitors.

Inflammation Fighters

• ACE inhibitors are generally prescribed for blood pressure control. They are a good medication choice for control of blood pressure in people with heart failure, diabetes, coronary artery disease, a recent heart attack, or risk factors for cardiovascular disease.

• ACE inhibitors can cause a harsh cough that can make it hard to talk. Swelling of the lips, tongue, and other tissues can occur. Other side effects can include diarrhea, loss of taste, weakness or fatigue, dizziness, or sexual dysfunction (in men). Talk with your doctor if you experience any of these side effects while taking the medication.

Hormone Replacement Therapy

In women of reproductive age, the ovaries manufacture the sex hormones estrogen, progesterone, and, to a lesser extent, testosterone. The pituitary gland in the brain regulates the production of these hormones by excreting luteinizing hormone (LH) and follicle-stimulating hormone (FSH), and the pituitary in turn is regulated by hormones secreted by another brain structure, the hypothalamus. Female sex hormones give rise to secondary sexual characteristics, including body shape, voice pitch, and body hair distribution. These hormones regulate monthly periods and changes associated with pregnancy and give rise to sexual appetite and drive. Female sex hormones protect against degenerative diseases, including osteoporosis and atherosclerosis.

Women undergo menopause when their ovaries quit producing estrogen and progesterone, usually between ages forty-five and fifty-five. A number of adverse changes take place in their bodies due to the loss of hormones. Bones become thin, skin loses tone, and the body begins a metamorphosis, changing its shape and profile. Hot flashes, mood swings, and sleep disturbances with frequent nocturnal awakenings can torment. Most significant for our discussion of inflammation is the fact that when hormone levels decline, they no longer provide protection for the heart. Women's risk of cardiovascular disease rises dramatically after menopause, approaching the same high level experienced by men.

Naturally occurring estrogen seems to have an anti-inflammatory action in the body. So when women's hormone levels drop during menopause, they lose their advantage in the inflammation balance. The promise of hormonal replacement therapy (HRT) was that some, if not all, of the postmenopausal changes in women's bodies could be reduced or delayed by taking pills that replaced the estrogen and progesterone lost during menopause.

It had been assumed for years that HRT could reduce the risk of heart disease, which typically increases after menopause. The information coming from the research has been confusing, to say the least. Studies have shown that HRT can improve the health of blood vessels by keeping them flexible and may be moderately helpful in reducing cholesterol. However, recent studies have shown that HRT raises blood levels of C-reactive protein, the marker of inflammation. And the first major long-term study of HRT was terminated in July 2002 because the risk of several diseases—including heart disease—actually increased with HRT treatment. The risk of developing coronary heart disease was increased by nearly 30 percent in women taking hormones, breast cancer risk was increased by about 25 percent, stroke risk was increased by about 40 percent, and the risk of blood clots in the lung more than doubled. This was surprising news to most physicians and researchers, as well as to women across the world.

The same study found that there were also benefits to taking hormones. Cancers of the colon and rectum were actually decreased by 63 percent in those taking hormones. Hip fractures were reduced by 34 percent. Death from all causes was not different between the two groups, but people taking hormones were 22 percent less likely to have any of a variety of health problems.

The investigators concluded that overall health risks exceeded the benefits for women using combined estrogen plus progestin HRT and that HRT should not be considered to be a good preventive treatment for heart disease. The women in the study were followed for an average of five years, but because the study was ended early, we will never know what would have happened after ten years or twenty years. There was a trend that looked as though longer lengths of time on HRT might lead to higher rates of death, but that question will remain unanswered for now. It's important to understand that this study considered only one regimen, at one dosage, with the synthetic progestin rather than natural progesterone.

My hope is that this issue is not closed. I firmly believe that safe regimens can be developed that will combine the benefits of hormonal replacement while reducing the negative effects. For example, what would happen if women took hormonal replacement therapy to protect against osteoporosis and colon cancer, and also took an aspirin a day or statins to reduce risk of cardiovascular disease? These types of studies have not been done, so no physician can make this type of recommendation. Clearly more work is needed to sort out the risks and benefits of HRT.

Inflammation Fighter

• Hormonal replacement therapy has both risks and benefits. Every woman has to make a personal decision, weighing the potential benefits against risks. For example, a woman with osteoporosis, a strong family history of colon cancer but not breast cancer, no risk factors for coronary heart disease, and severe menopausal disturbances might benefit from HRT. On the other hand, a woman with multiple risk factors for cardiovascular disease and a strong family history of breast cancer might be wise to avoid HRT. Stay tuned, because this is an evolving area of knowledge.

14

THE ANTI-
INFLAMMATION
PRESCRIPTION

◉

So when all is said and done, what's a person to do? We are bombarded with health books, diet aids, prescription drug ads, public service messages, vitamin and supplement ads, dire health warnings, herbal medicine claims, and all manner of propaganda about health and longevity. It's nearly at the point where some people are blamed if they get sick, as if the disease were due to their negligence. When people have a heart attack, they get blame instead of sympathy. If they had quit smoking, eaten more vegetables, gotten more exercise, taken blood pressure medicine and Lipitor, or done a host of other things it would never have happened. Right? Wrong.

People who don't smoke but eat right and get exercise still die, most commonly of heart attacks. My grandfather smoked unfiltered cigarettes and ate a diet high in saturated fats until his death at age eighty-nine. He was lucky and perhaps had some fortunate genes. His brother who didn't smoke was healthy and well until he died as a passenger in a car crash when he was ninety-six years old. Some people who never smoke die in their twenties and thirties. When it comes to health and disease, John F. Kennedy was correct when he stated that *it's just not fair*.

What we are dealing with is risk. There are no guarantees in matters of life and death and health. But there are definite risks, as there are also ways to reduce those risks. Of the things that can be done to reduce one's risks, many are specific to a given individual, particularly when it comes to inflammation. Some things are bad for everyone, some things are good for everyone. But some good things can be very damaging to some people.

GOOD THINGS FOR EVERYONE

Let's start with the recommendations that are good for everyone. First, *avoid cigarettes and other tobacco products.* Don't use them yourself, and don't be around the smoke from these products. A study in California found a dramatic reduction in chronic respiratory problems in nonsmoking bartenders after smoking was banned in bars. But that's just the start of it. Tobacco smoke contains carcinogens and is pro-inflammatory. It causes heart disease and strokes.

There's nothing unique about tobacco smoke. All smoke is bad, whether from cigarettes, wood stoves, fireplaces, furnaces, or automobile exhaust. Avoid the products of combustion, no matter what the source. The highest incidence of lung cancer in the world is found in a region of Mexico where the women cook all day over smoky fires. City dwellers who do not smoke have higher rates of lung cancer and heart attacks than people in less polluted areas. Fight for clean air. Fight for automakers to increase the gasoline mileage of their vehicles. Support new technologies that reduce air pollution in cities, such as hybrid cars and hydrogen fuel cell cars.

Exercise is the single most positive thing one can do for health. "Use it or lose it" is more than a catchphrase. Exercise reduces the risk of just about everything bad that can happen to one's health, from heart attacks and strokes to Alzheimer's disease. Exercise pushes back the deterioration of joints and muscle and bones that occurs with age. It improves mood and sense of well-being. And it is fun—once you give yourself time to get used to moving your body.

Eating a healthy diet does not mean eating bland or unappealing foods. Our grocery stores are filled with delectable fresh fruits and vegetables from all over the world that are seemingly never out of season. They can be prepared in many appealing dishes. And they are loaded with all sorts of health-promoting substances: flavonoids and antioxidants and fibers and vitamins and minerals. Fish is good for you, and fish oil supplements are available in pharmacies and grocery stores everywhere. Risk of sudden cardiac death, a plague that threatens everyone's life and loved ones, is cut in half by fish oil supplements. Just three servings of fish a week can greatly increase one's well-being.

Aristotle taught us the great golden mean: *moderation in all things*. Alcohol can be enjoyed in moderation by most people with definite health benefits, but excessive drinking carries great risks to health. A wholesome sex life is of benefit. But sex, like alcohol, carries great risks to health if not controlled and safe. Excessive weight is a drag on health and should be controlled through diet and exercise. A positive mental attitude, control of stress, and good social relationships and support should be cultivated.

GOOD THINGS FOR SOME

Some people face very difficult health problems related to inflammation, even when they do everything right. Some of us suffer from chronic nagging problems with inflammation, whether in the airway (asthma and rhinosinusitis), joints (arthritis), muscles (myositis), head (migraine), skin (dermatitis), or virtually any other part of the body. The natural tendency of the body is not to be inflamed, and if there is chronic inflammation, there is a cause. Finding the cause can be difficult, time-consuming, and frustrating because we are exposed to literally thousands of things that can inappropriately induce inflammation in some people. The air is filled with biological materials and chemicals of all sorts. Every food that we eat contains hundreds of proteins and chemicals, some natural and some added. Drinking water can contain a host of chemicals, though at small levels.

The inflammation triggers that we can detect well are allergic (immunoglobulin E–mediated) reactions to proteins. *Allergy skin testing* is effective in establishing allergy to things like pollens, molds, dust mites, cockroaches, venoms, and animals. A combination of avoidance of the allergens and allergy shots can effectively abolish inflammatory reactions to allergens.

For other forms of food intolerance and for chemicals, the only method available is the tedious trial and error through *elimination testing*. Take something away and see if you get better. Avoid a food for a week or more and see if there is an improvement. Take a holiday from a potentially sick building and see if symptoms improve. The greatest challenge is when people are sick from more than one thing. For example, a person with a food intolerance who also works in a sick building can have difficulty sorting out the two. Still, it may be possible to feel much, much better simply by discovering and eliminating one inflammation-causing factor.

For those lucky enough to find a cause for their chronic inflammation, the benefit of fixing a health problem is well worth the effort. Not everyone is so lucky, and there is very little professional help available in this area. At one time there were environmental control units in this country, where every aspect of one's diet was controlled, as well as the air and water. Changes in the financing and structure of health care delivery in this country forced these units out of business. A solid research database never existed to define the indications for these units. At this writing, the government of Japan has funded a research environmental control unit that may generate data that may one day lead to these facilities being available in the United States again.

Chronic infections can cause chronic inflammation. *Inflammation-causing infections should never be ignored.* Lyme disease, an infection with an organism transmitted by ticks, can cause arthritis and other forms of inflammation that persist until the cause is determined and the germ is eliminated with antibiotics. Peptic ulcers can be caused by chronic infection of the stomach lining. In some cases of chronic inflammation, colonization with a bacteria or fungus may incite the inflammation, but cases with a particular pattern of inflammation linked to a specific germ are limited. As strange as it sounds, these are the easy diseases. They have cures. They may be difficult to diagnose at first, but with proper medication, the diseases will go away. For other diseases, no cure is possible. In these cases, eliminating some inflammation may mean the difference between being merely sick and being disabled.

NEVER TOO LATE TO FIGHT

The good news about inflammation is that it is seldom too late to start looking for causes. An example is people with inflamed coronary arteries in their hearts. After angioplasty and even bypass surgery, if the inciting factors are eliminated, there can still be great benefits with great improvements in quality of life. Cigarette smokers who develop blockages in their arteries and then have bypass surgery will continue to have progression of the disease if they don't stop smoking. They can even develop blockages in their bypass grafts. Those who quit smoking, start exercising, control their blood pressure, take anticholesterol agents that also squelch inflammation, and eat lots of fruits and vegetables can find that their disease has stopped.

Once inflammation progresses to permanent organ damage, however, such as joint destruction (in the case of rheumatoid arthritis) or kidney failure (in the case of inflammatory diseases of the kidneys), there is no turning back. It is important to learn what's triggering the inflammation earlier rather than later, before permanent damage is done. But even then, eliminating other sources of inflammation can improve quality of life and may reduce pain for some people.

We need to rejoice about the great things that are happening in medicine. Our knowledge about inflammation and its role in many diseases is expanding. and will surely lead to new therapies and interventions to relieve suffering, prolong life, and improve the quality of life as we age. Recent research has demonstrated the interplay between the nervous system and immune system in producing inflammation and is revealing the mechanisms by which environmental chemicals lead to inflammation. The biotech industry offers hope of a host of new therapies to modify the inflammatory response in diseases ranging from multiple sclerosis to rheumatoid arthritis. The pharmaceutical industry offers hope of finding new treatments for generative diseases and therapies to slow or halt the aging process. The importance of environmental factors cannot be stressed enough, and much research is currently being conducted to ferret out possible environmental causes of many diseases.

The outlook for preventing and treating diseases of inflammation is very bright, indeed. This is not the last you'll hear on the subject.

THE PATH TO MEDICAL KNOWLEDGE

◉

The author of a book claiming to tell people how they should eat appeared on network television to discuss her book and stated that she thought carrots are the most dangerous food a person can eat! Most of us think carrots are safe and healthy and do not feel in great danger when eating them. How did this author know that carrots are the most dangerous food that we can eat? Was there evidence to support her claim? Had she collected data on the health status and life expectancy of carrot eaters compared to people who don't eat carrots? The answer is no! She had a theory about carbohydrates and proteins and fats that allowed her to deduce the great danger of eating carrots. She had not done a double-blinded prospective randomized controlled study comparing people who eat carrots with those who do not, which would be the way to prove her belief.

Authors of health books ask us to buy their books and live by their guidelines after assembling a hodgepodge of theory, data, and opinion. In all fairness to the carrot lady, it would be very difficult to study every point and to collect data on every possibility. As the author of this book, I do not claim to have scientific proof of every point contained here. In this section, I want to explain to the reader how people arrive at medical knowledge, the uncertainties of that knowledge, and the lack of predictability in medicine.

The scientific method can be used to answer questions that confront both patients and their physicians. The scientific method can be simply stated in two words: *test assumptions*. Hypotheses are generated from observations and experience. These hypotheses are tested in experiments. The results are then used to modify or reformulate one's assumptions. Physicians now strive to practice evidence-based medicine. Research is constantly modifying our assumptions about various procedures and therapies embraced by physicians.

There are serious limitations to evidence-based medicine. There will never be a research database large enough to give a rational answer to the multiple situations encountered in matters of health and disease. The evidence-based medicine database will always lag behind new approaches, new discoveries, and new therapies. Further, medical data is always given in percentages so that in their decision making, physicians must play the odds.

Case reports and then case series are at the bottom of the ladder of medical knowledge. A retrospective study that enrolls patients after the fact is only a little better. A prospective study is one that enrolls patients before the outcome is known; it has more validity. The highest level of validity is a double-blinded case-controlled randomized study, but very few questions and recommendations achieve that level of proof.

Perhaps the greatest intellectual debate of the twentieth century was between the atomic physicist and Nobel laureate Niels Bohr and the founder of relativity and Nobel laureate Albert Einstein. Einstein succinctly expressed his side of the debate with his famous proclamation that God does not throw dice. Bohr argued that nature is innately probabilistic, that God does throw dice.

Einstein proved that quantum physics leads to absurdities, but lost the debate anyway when experiments demonstrated that the absurdities predicted by quantum mechanics do happen. If Einstein had studied medicine, he would have had to face the role of chance in nature every day.

PROBABILITY AND CHANCE IN MEDICINE

Why bring up the Einstein-Bohr debate in a health book? Because biology and medicine are part of the natural world, and the probability and chance formulated by Bohr extend to biology and medicine. One of the theories to explain why life arises, the biological homing theory, holds that biological molecules exist in complementary pairs that have a lock-and-key, or hand-in-glove, relationship. There is a high quantum mechanical probability these complementary pairs of molecules will join. The world is driven toward living systems because life is the most probable thing that can happen.

If biology is a probabilistic system, then certainly medicine will be probabilistic, for medicine is the study of deviations from good health in biological systems, whether animal (veterinary medicine) or human. One does not have to look far to find evidence of the probabilistic nature of medicine.

The most striking evidence of probability and chance in medicine is found in toxicology. A simple question like what dose of a poison like cyanide is needed to kill a person can only be answered as a probability. As the dose of the poison is increased, the likelihood that a person will be killed by that dose increases. An LD_{50} is the lethal dose that kills 50 percent of those who receive it.

It is hard to accept that the only difference between the half who survive and the half who die of an LD_{50} is the luck of the draw, but that is the way of nature. People argue that those who died must have been more susceptible. However, if ten mice of an inbred strain, with the same genes, same sex, same cage, and same food, are given an LD_{50} dose of a poison, half will be dead and half will be running around as if nothing happened.

Every paper in medicine is couched in probabilities. The percentage of patients who respond to a therapy, the percentage of patients with a serious side effect, and the percentage of patients with a given disease who present in a particular way are all examples.

RISK AND CAUSATION

There is a difference between risk and causation. A risk factor is something that increases one's risk for a disease or premature death. A cause is something that directly produces the disease or premature death. For example, AIDS is caused by the human immunodeficiency virus (HIV). Unprotected sex, blood transfusion in countries with poor screening of blood supplies, and sharing needles for IV drugs are all risk factors to get AIDS, but in themselves they do not cause AIDS. Having a high blood cholesterol level increases one's risk for coronary artery disease and heart attacks, but the majority of people who get coronary artery disease do not have high blood cholesterol levels.

Taking an aspirin a day does not prevent heart attacks, but it does cut the risk of having a heart attack by about one-half. At the same time, it increases the risk of having a cerebral hemorrhage. The bottom line is that medicine is about playing the odds. Lifestyle modifications can reduce one's risk of a disease and increase one's odds of delaying the aging process. There are no guarantees in medicine, and there is no guarantee that the recommendations in this book will let any person avoid anything. We do know that the recommendations herein, some with greater certainty than others, will decrease the probability of getting a disease and increase the probability of a long and healthy life.

Medical knowledge is fragmentary and incomplete. Recommendations for treatment and prevention are based on a combination of current knowledge, clinical judgment, common sense, and plain old hunch. Outcomes are probabilistic in nature, and no one can predict what will happen in an individual case. Nonetheless, we play the odds as best we can and win some while losing some. In this book, I've done my best to integrate all of the data in order to give the reader a sense of what is solidly known, what is belief, and what should be avoided.

Selected References

◉

Introduction and Chapter 1

Afshari NA, Afshari MA, Foster CS. Inflammatory conditions of the eye associated with rheumatic diseases. *Curr Rheumatol Rep.* 2001;3(5):453–458.

Bascom R, Meggs WJ, Frampton M, et al. Neurogenic inflammation: with additional discussion of central and perceptual integration of nonneurogenic inflammation. *Environmental Health Perspectives.* 1997;105(suppl 2):531–537.

Brod SA. Unregulated inflammation shortens human functional longevity. *Inflamm Res.* 2000;49:561–570.

DeMaria AN. Relative risk of cardiovascular events in patients with rheumatoid arthritis. *Am J Cardiol.* March 21, 2002;89(6A):33D–38D.

Franceschi C, Bonafe M, Valensin S, et al. Inflamm-aging: an evolutionary perspective on immunosenescence. *Ann N Y Acad Sci.* 2000;908:244–254.

Freeman DJ, Norrie J, Caslake MJ, et al. C-reactive protein is an independent predictor of risk for the development of diabetes in the West of Scotland Coronary Prevention Study. *Diabetes.* May 2002;51(5):1596–1600.

Goodson N. Coronary artery disease and rheumatoid arthritis. *Curr Opin Rheumatol.* 2002;14(2):115–120.

Kiecolt-Glaser JK, McGuire L, Robles TF, Glaser R. Emotions, morbidity, and mortality: new perspectives from psychoneuroimmunology. *Annu Rev Psychol.* 2002;53:83–107.

Kroot EJ, van Gestel AM, Swinkels HL, et al. Chronic comorbidity in patients with early rheumatoid arthritis: a descriptive study. *J Rheumatol.* July 2001; 28(7):1511–1517.

Lavelle C. Is periodontal disease a risk factor for coronary artery disease (CAD)? *J Can Dental Assoc.* March 2002;68(3):176–180.

Matthews DC. The relationship between diabetes and periodontal disease. *J Can Dental Assoc.* March 2002;68(3):161–164.

McGaw T. Periodontal disease and preterm delivery of low-birth-weight infants. *J Can Dental Assoc.* March 2002;68(3):165–169.

Meggs WJ. Neurogenic switching: a hypothesis for a mechanism for shifting the site of inflammation in allergy and chemical sensitivity. *Environmental Health Perspectives.* January 1995;103(1):54–56.

Park DJ, Cho CS, Lee SH, et al. Thyroid disorders in Korean patients with systemic lupus erythematosus. *Scand J Rheumatol.* 1995;24(1):13–17.

Schmidt MI, Duncan BB, Sharrett AR, et al. Markers of inflammation and prediction of diabetes mellitus in adults (Atherosclerosis Risk in Communities study): a cohort study. *Lancet.* 1999;356(9165):1649–1652.

Smith GC, Pell JP, Walsh D. Pregnancy complications and maternal risk of ischaemic heart disease: a retrospective cohort study of 129,290 births. *Lancet.* June 23, 2001;357(9273):2002–2006.

CHAPTER 4

Abbasi F, Brown BW Jr, Lamendola C, et al. Relationship between obesity, insulin resistance, and coronary heart disease risk. *J Am Coll Cardiol.* 2002;40(5):937–943.

Blake GJ, Ridker PM. Inflammatory bio-markers and cardiovascular risk prediction. *J Intern Med.* 2002;252(4):283–294.

Buffon A, Biascucci LM, Liuzzo G, et al. Widespread coronary inflammation in unstable angina. *N Engl J Med.* 2002;347:5–12.

Danesh J, Whincup P, Walker M, et al. Low grade inflammation and coronary heart disease: prospective study and updated meta-analyses. *BMJ.* 2000;321:199–204.

Gustavsson P, Plato N, Hallqvist J, et al. A population-based case-referent study of myocardial infarction and occupational exposure to motor exhaust, other combustion products, organic solvents, lead, and dynamite. *Epidemiology.* 2001;12:222–228.

Jialal I, Devaraj S. Inflammation and atherosclerosis: the value of the high-sensitivity C-reactive protein assay as a risk marker. *Am J Clin Pathol.* 2001;116 (suppl):S108–S115.

Kannel WB, Wolf PA, Castelli WP, D'Agostino RB. Fibrinogen and risk of cardiovascular disease: the Framingham study. *JAMA*. 1987;258:1183–1186.

Libby P, Ridker PM, Maseri A. Inflammation and atherosclerosis. *Circulation*. 2002;105:1135–1143.

Lowe GD. The relationship between infection, inflammation, and cardiovascular disease: an overview. *Ann Periodontol*. 2001;6(1):1–8.

Ludewig B, Zinkernagel RM, Hengartner H. Arterial inflammation and atherosclerosis. *Trends Cardiovasc Med*. 2002;12:154–159.

Peters A, Dockery DW, Muller JE, Mittleman MA. Increased particulate air pollution and the triggering of myocardial infarction. *Circulation*. 2001;103: 2810–2815.

Poloniecki JD, Atkinson RW, de Leon AP, Anderson HR. Daily time series for cardiovascular hospital admissions and previous day's air pollution in London, UK. *Occup Environ Med*. 1997;54:535–540.

Resnick HE, Howard BV. Diabetes and cardiovascular risk. *Annu Rev Med*. 2002;53:245–267.

Rosenlund M, Berglind N, Gustavsson A, et al. Environmental tobacco smoke and myocardial infarction among never-smokers in the Stockholm Heart Epidemiology Program (SHEEP). *Epidemiology*. September 2001;12(5):558–564.

Sakkinen P, Abbott RD, Curb JD, et al. C-reactive protein and myocardial infarction. *J Clin Epidemiol*. 2002;55(5):445–451.

Servoss SJ, Januzzi JL, Muller JE. Triggers of acute coronary syndromes. *Prog Cardiovasc Dis*. 2002;44:369–380.

Zebrack JS, Anderson AJ. The role of inflammation and infection in the pathogenesis and evolution of coronary artery disease. *Curr Cardiol Rep*. 2002;4(4): 278–288.

CHAPTER 5

Akhmedkhanov A, Toniolo P, Zeleniuch-Jacquotte A, et al. Aspirin and lung cancer in women. *Br J Cancer*. 2002;87(1):49–53.

Akre K, Ekstrom AM, Signorello, et al. Aspirin and risk for gastric cancer: a population-based case-control study in Sweden. *Br J Cancer*. 2001;84(7):965–968.

Baron JA, Sandler RS. Nonsteroidal anti-inflammatory drugs and cancer prevention. *Annu Rev Med*. 2000;51:511–523.

Carroll KK. Obesity as a risk factor for certain types of cancer. *Lipids*. 1998;33(11): 1055–1059.

Collet J-P, Sharpe C, Belzile E, et al. Colorectal cancer prevention by non-steroidal anti-inflammatory drugs: effects of dosage and timing. *Br J Cancer.* 1999;81(1): 62–68.

Dang CT, Shapiro CL, Hudis CA. Potential role of selective COX-2 inhibitors in cancer management. *Oncology.* 2002;16(suppl 4):30–36.

Eaden J, Abrams K, Ekbom A, et al. Colorectal cancer prevention in ulcerative colitis: a case-control study. *Aliment Pharmacol Ther.* 2000;14(2):145–153.

Gridley G, McLaughlin JK, Ekbom A, et al. Incidence of cancer among patients with rheumatoid arthritis. *J Natl Cancer Inst.* 1993;85:307–311.

Helicobacter and Cancer Collaborative Group. Gastric cancer and Helicobacter pylori: a combined analysis of 12 case control studies nested within prospective cohorts. *Gut.* 2001;49:347–353.

Kantor AF, Hartge P, Hoover RN, et al. Urinary tract infection and risk of bladder cancer. *Am J Epidemiol.* 1984;119(4):510–515.

Khuder SA, Mutgi AB. Breast cancer and NSAID use: a meta-analysis. *Br J Cancer.* 2001;84(9):1188–1192.

Lu C, Sheehan C, Rak JW, et al. Endogenous interleukin 6 can function as an in vivo growth-stimulatory factor for advanced-stage human melanoma cells. *Clin Cancer Res.* 1996;2(8):1417–1425.

Ngoan LT, Mizoue T, Fujino Y, et al. Dietary factors and stomach cancer mortality. *Br J Cancer.* 2002;87(1):37–42.

Parsonnet J. Bacterial infection as a cause of cancer. *Environ Health Perspect.* 1995; 103(suppl 8):263–268.

Phillips RK, Wallace MH, Lynch PM, et al. A randomized, double blind, placebo controlled study of celecoxib, a selective cyclooxygenase 2 inhibitor, on duodenal polyposis in familial ademomatous polyposis. *Gut.* 2002;50(6):857–860.

Shacter E, Weitzman SA. Chronic inflammation and cancer. *Oncology.* 2002;16(2): 217–232.

Stoll BA. Association between breast and colorectal cancers. *Br J Surg.* 1998;85: 1468–1472.

CHAPTER 6

Arnold MC, Papanicolaou DA, O'Grady JA, et al. Using an interleukin-6 challenge to evaluate neuropsychological performance in chronic fatigue syndrome. *Psychol Med.* 2002;32(6):1075–1089.

Baraniuk JN, Clauw DJ, Gaumond E. Rhinitis symptoms in chronic fatigue syndrome. *Ann Allergy Asthma Immunol.* 1998;81(4):359–365.

Bell IR, Jasnoski ML, Katgan J, King DS. Depression and allergies: survey of a nonclinical population. *Psychother Psychosom.* 1991;55:24–31.

Black D, Rathe A, Goldstein RB. Environmental illness: a controlled study of 26 subjects with 20th century disease. *JAMA.* 1990;264:3166–3170.

Blazer DG, Moody-Ayers S, Craft-Morgan J, Burchett B. Depression in diabetes and obesity: racial/ethnic/gender issues in older adults. *J Psychosom Res.* 2002; 53(4):913–916.

Borish L, Schmaling K, DiClementi JD, et al. Chronic fatigue syndrome: identification of distinct subgroups on the basis of allergy and psychologic variables. *J Allergy Clin Immunol.* 1998;102(2):222–230.

Buchwald D, Wener MH, Pearlman T, Kith P. Markers of inflammation and immune activation in chronic fatigue and chronic fatigue syndrome. *J Rheumatol.* 1997;24(2):372–376.

Davi G, Guagnano MT, Ciabattoni G, et al. Platelet activation in obese women: role of inflammation and oxidant stress. *JAMA.* 2002;288(16):2008–2014.

Faith MS, Matz PE, Jorge MA. Obesity-depression associations in the population. *J Psychosom Res.* 2002;53(4):935–942.

Flegal KM, Carroll MD, Ogden CL, Johnson CL. Prevalence and trends in obesity among US adults, 1999–2000. *JAMA.* 2002;288(14):1723–1727.

Grimble RF. Inflammatory status and insulin resistance. *Curr Opin Clin Nutr Metab Care.* 2002;5(5):551–559.

Heilbronn LK, Noakes M, Clifton PM. Energy restriction and weight loss on very-low-fat diets reduce C-reactive protein concentrations in obese, healthy women. *Arterioscler Thromb Vasc Biol.* 2001;21(6):968–970.

Marshall PS. Allergy and depression: a neurochemical threshold model of the relation between the illnesses. *Psychol Bull.* 1993;113:23–43.

Marshall PS, O'Hara C, Steinberg P. Effects of seasonal allergic rhinitis on fatigue levels and mood. *Psychosom Med.* 2002;64(4):684–691.

Mullington JM, Hinze-Selch D, Pollmacher T. Mediators of inflammation and their interaction with sleep: relevance for chronic fatigue syndrome and related conditions. *Ann N Y Acad Sci.* 2001;933:201–210.

Peres M, Zukerman E, Young W, Silberstein S. Fatigue in chronic migraine patients. *Cephalalgia.* 2002;22(9):720–724.

Pradhan AD, Ridker PM. Do atherosclerosis and type 2 diabetes share a common inflammatory basis? *Eur Heart J.* 2002;23:831–834.

Simic BS, Jorga J, Dimitrijevic D, et al. Android and gynecoid types of obesity as factors in the onset of certain related diseases. *Acta Med Iugosl.* 1989;43(2): 95–102. Abstract.

Straczkowski M, Dzienis-Straczkowska S, Stepien A, et al. Plasma interleukin-8 concentrations are increased in obese subjects and related to fat mass and tumor necrosis factor-alpha system. *J Clin Endocrinol Metab.* 2002;87(10):4602–4606.

Von Behren J, Kreutzer R, Hernandez A. Self-reported asthma prevalence in adults in California. *J Asthma.* 2002;39(5):429–440.

CHAPTER 7

Bardana EJ Jr, Malinow MR, Houghton DC, et al. Diet-induced systemic lupus erythematosus (SLE) in primates. *Am J Kidney Dis.* 1982;1(6):345–352.

Belongia EA, Hedberg CW, Gleich GJ, et al. An investigation of the cause of the eosinophilia-myalgia syndrome associated with tryptophan use. *N Engl J Med.* 1990;323:357–365.

Braun-Fahrlander C, Riedler J, Herz U, et al. Environmental exposure to endotoxin and its relation to asthma in school-age children. *N Engl J Med.* 2002;347: 869–877.

DeMaria AN. Relative risk of cardiovascular events in patients with rheumatoid arthritis. *Am J Cardiol.* March 21, 2002;89(6A):33D–38D.

Diaz-Sanchez D, Garcia MP, Wang M, et al. Nasal challenge with diesel exhaust particles can induce sensitization to a neoallergen in the human mucosa. *J Allergy Clin Immunol.* 1999;104:1183–1188.

Dooms-Gossens A, Deleu H. Airborne contact dermatitis: an update. *Contact Dermatitis.* 1991;25:211–217.

Folkerts G, Busse WW, Nijkam FP, et al. Virus-induced airway hyperresponsiveness and asthma. *Am J Respir Crit Care Med.* 1998;157:1708–1720.

Goodson N. Coronary artery disease and rheumatoid arthritis. *Curr Opin Rheumatol.* 2002;14(2):115–120.

Hafstrom I, Ringertz B, Spangberg A, et al. A vegan diet free of gluten improves the signs and symptoms of rheumatoid arthritis: the effects on arthritis correlate with a reduction in antibodies to food antigens. *Rheumatology.* October 2001;40(10):1175–1179.

Haugen MA, Kjeldsen-Kragh J, Forre O. A pilot study of the effect of an elemental diet in the management of rheumatoid arthritis. *Clin Exp Rheumatol.* May–June 1994;12(3):275–279.

Huang S-L, Lin K-C, Pan W-H. Dietary factors associated with physician-diagnosed asthma and allergic rhinitis in teenagers: analyses of the first Nutrition and Health Survey in Taiwan. *Clin Exp Allergy*. 2001;31:259–264.

Kardestuncer T, Frumkin H. Systemic lupus erythematosus in relation to environmental pollution: an investigation in an African-American community in North Georgia. *Arch Environ Health*. 1997;52(2):85–90.

Kimyai-Asadi A, Usman A. The role of psychological stress in skin disease. *J Cutan Med Surg*. 2001;5(2):140–145.

Kjeldsen-Kragh J, Haugen M, Borchgrevink CF, et al. Controlled trial of fasting and one-year vegetarian diet in rheumatoid arthritis. *Lancet*. 1991;338(8772): 899–902.

Kroker GF, Stroud RM, Marshall R, et al. Fasting and rheumatoid arthritis: a multicenter study. *Clin Ecology*. 1984;11:137–144.

Malinow MR, Bardana EJ Jr, Pirofsky B, et al. Systemic lupus erythematosus-like syndrome in monkeys fed alfalfa sprouts: role of a nonprotein amino acid. *Science*. 1982;216(4544):415–417.

Mangione S, Yuen EJ, Balsley C. Asthma prevalence in children: a survey of 57 Philadelphia middle schools. Abstract, scientific meeting of the American College of Chest Physicians; San Diego, Calif.; November 4, 2002.

Marshall R, Stroud RM, Kroker GF, et al. Food challenge effects on fasted rheumatoid arthritis patients: a multicenter study. *Clin Ecology*. 1984;11:181–190.

Park DJ, Cho CS, Lee SH, et al. Thyroid disorders in Korean patients with systemic lupus erythematosus. *Scand J Rheumatol*. 1995;24(1):13–17.

Redd SC. Asthma in the United States: burden and current theories. *Environ Health Perspect*. 2002;110(suppl 4):557–560.

Rodgers KE. Effects of oral administration of malathion on the course of disease in MRL-lpr mice. *J Autoimmun*. 1997;10(4):367–373.

Stalnikowicz R, Tsafrir A. Acute psychosocial stress and cardiovascular events. *Am J Emerg Med*. 2002;20(5):488–491.

Steen VD. Occupational scleroderma. *Curr Opin Rheumatol*. 1999;11:490–494.

Urowitz M, Gladman D, Bruce I. Atherosclerosis and systemic lupus erythematosus. *Curr Rheumatol Rep*. 2000;2(1):19–23.

van de Laar MA, van der Korst JK. Rheumatoid arthritis, food, and allergy. *Semin Arthritis Rheum*. August 1991;21(1):12–23.

von Kries R, Hermann M, Grunert VP, von Mutius E. Is obesity a risk factor for childhood asthma? *Allergy*. 2001;56:318–322.

Wertman E, Zilber N, Abramsky O. An association between multiple sclerosis and type 1 diabetes mellitus. *J Neurol.* 1992;239(1):43–45.

CHAPTER 8

Anderson DH, Mullins RF, Hageman GS, Johnson LV. A role for local inflammation in the formation of drusen in the aging eye. *Am J Ophthalmol.* 2002;134(3): 411–431.

Bonaiuti D, Shea B, Iovine R, et al. Exercise for preventing and treating osteoporosis in postmenopausal women. *Cochrane Database Syst Rev.* 2002;(3):CD 000333.

Brod SA. Unregulated inflammation shortens human functional longevity. *Inflamm Res.* 2000;49:561–570.

Chung HY, Kim HJ, Kim JW, Yu BP. The inflammation hypothesis of aging. *Ann N Y Acad Sci.* 2001;928:327–335.

Clyman B. Exercise in the treatment of osteoarthritis. *Curr Rheumatol Rep.* 2001; 3(6):520–523.

Crisby M, Carlson LA, Winblad B. Statins in the prevention and treatment of Alzheimer disease. *Alzheimer Dis Assoc Disord.* 2002;16(3):131–136.

Curtis CL, Rees SG, Little CB, et al. Pathologic indicators of degradation and inflammation in human osteoarthritic cartilage are abrogated by exposure to n-3 fatty acids. *Arthritis Rheumatism.* 2002;46(6):1544–1553.

Engelhart MJ, Geerlings MI, Ruitenberg A, et al. Dietary intake of antioxidants and risk of Alzheimer disease. *JAMA.* 2002;287(24):3223–3229.

Ershler WB. Interleukin-6: a cytokine for gerontologists. *J Am Geriatr Soc.* 1993;41 (2):176–181.

Evans JR. Antioxidant vitamin and mineral supplements for age-related macular degeneration. *Cochrane Database Syst Rev.* 2002;(2):CD000254.

Feskanich D, Willett W, Colditz G. Walking and leisure-time activity and risk of hip fracture in postmenopausal women. *JAMA.* 2002;288(18):2300–2306.

Fillit HM. The role of hormone replacement therapy in the prevention of Alzheimer disease. *Arch Intern Med.* 2002;162(17):1934–1942.

Fossel M. Cell senescence in human aging and disease. *Ann N Y Acad Sci.* 2002;959: 14–23.

Franceschi C, Valensin S, Bonafe M, et al. The network and the remodeling theories of aging: historical background and new perspectives. *Exp Gerontol.* 2000; 35:879–896.

Gonos ES. Genetics of aging: lessons from centenarians. *Exp Gerontol.* 2000; 35:15–21.

Honorati M, Bovara M, Cattini L, et al. Contribution of interleukin 17 to human cartilage degradation and synovial inflammation in osteoarthritis. *Osteoarthritis Cartilage.* 2002;10(10):799.

Lindsay J, Laurin D, Verreault R, et al. Risk factors for Alzheimer's disease: a prospective analysis from the Canadian Study of Health and Aging. *Am J Epidemiol.* 2002;156(5):445–453.

Maia L, de Mendonca A. Does caffeine intake protect from Alzheimer's disease? *Eur J Neurol.* 2002;9:377–382.

Marriott LK, Hauss-Wegrzyniak B, Benton RS, et al. Long-term estrogen therapy worsens the behavioral and neuropathological consequences of chronic brain inflammation. *Behav Neurosci.* 2002;116(5):902–911.

McGeer PL, McGeer EG. Inflammation autotoxicity and Alzheimer disease. *Neurobiol Aging.* 2001;22:799–809.

Morris MC, Evans DA, Bienias JL, et al. Dietary intake of antioxidant nutrients and the risk of incident Alzheimer disease in a biracial community study. *JAMA.* 2002;287(24):3230–3237.

Nelson HD, Rizzo J, Harris E, et al. Osteoporosis and fractures in postmenopausal women using estrogen. *Arch Intern Med.* 2002;162(20):2278–2284.

Neuroinflammation Working Group: Akiyama H, Barger S, Barnum S, et al. Inflammation and Alzheimer's disease. *Neurobiol Aging.* 2000;21:383–421.

Pasco JA, Kotowicz MA, Henry MJ, et al. Statin use, bone mineral density, and fracture risk. Geelong osteoporosis study. *Arch Intern Med.* 2002;162(5):537–540.

Pavelka K, Gatterova J, Olejarova M, et al. Glucosamine sulfate use and delay of progression of knee osteoarthritis. *Arch Intern Med.* 2002;162(18):2113–2123.

Perry EK, Pickering AT, Wang WW, et al. Medicinal plants and Alzheimer's disease: from ethnobotany to phytotherapy. *J Pharm Pharmacol.* 1999;51(5):527–534.

Polisson R. Innovative therapies in osteoarthritis. *Curr Rheumatol Rep.* 2001; 3(6):489–495.

Qin L, Au S, Choy W, et al. Regular Tai Chi Chuan exercise may retard bone loss in postmenopausal women: a case-control study. *Arch Phys Med Rehabil.* 2002; 83(10):1355–1359.

Sano M, Ernesto C, Thomas RG, et al. A controlled trial of selegiline, alpha-tocopherol, or both as treatment for Alzheimer's disease. The Alzheimer's Disease Cooperative Study. *N Engl J Med.* 1997;336(17):1216–1222.

Schmidt R, Schmidt H, Curb JD, et al. Early inflammation and dementia: a 25-year follow-up of the Honolulu-Asia Aging Study. *Ann Neurol.* 2002; 52(2):168–174.

Sowers M. Epidemiology of risk factors for osteoarthritis: systemic factors. *Curr Opin Rheumatol.* 2001;13(5):447–451.

Taaffe DR, Harris TB, Ferrucci L, et al. Cross-sectional and prospective relationships of interleukin-6 and C-reactive protein with physical performance in elderly persons: MacArthur studies of successful aging. *J Gerontol A Biol Sci Med Sci.* 2000;55(12):M709–M715.

Tucker KL, Hannan MT, Chen H, et al. Potassium, magnesium, and fruit and vegetable intakes are associated with greater bone mineral density in elderly men and women. *Am J Clin Nutr.* 1999;69:727–736.

Visser M, Pahor M, Taaffe DR, et al. Relationship of interleukin-6 and tumor necrosis factor-alpha with muscle mass and muscle strength in elderly men and women: the Health ABC study. *J Gerontol A Biol Sci Med Sci.* 2002;57(5): M326–M332.

Volpato S, Guralnik JM, Ferrucci L, et al. Cardiovascular disease, interleukin-6, and risk of mortality in older women: the women's health and aging study. *Circulation.* 2001;103(7):947–953.

Walson J, McBurnie MA, Newman A, et al. Frailty and activation of the inflammation and coagulation systems with and without clinical comorbidities. *Arch Intern Med.* 2002;162(20):2333–2341.

Weaver JD, Huang MH, Albert M, et al. Interleukin-6 and risk of cognitive decline: MacArthur studies of successful aging. *Neurology.* 2002;59(3):371–378.

Zandi PP, Breitner JCS. Do NSAIDs prevent Alzheimer's disease? And, if so, why? The epidemiological evidence. *Neurobiol Aging.* 22:811–817.

CHAPTER 9

Adom KK, Liu RH. Antioxidant activity of grains. *J Agric Food Chem.* 2002; 50(21):6182–6187.

Barberger-Gateau P, Letenneur L, Deschamps V, et al. Fish, meat, and risk of dementia: cohort study. *BJM.* 2002;325:932–933.

Berrigan D, Perkins SN, Haines DC, Hursting SD. Adult-onset calorie restriction and fasting delay spontaneous tumorigenesis in p53-deficient mice. *Carcinogenesis.* 2002;23(5):817–822.

Bickford PC, Gould T, Briederick L, et al. Antioxidant-rich diets improve cerebellar physiology and motor learning in aged rats. *Brain Res.* 2000;866 (1–2):211–217.

Birks J, Grimley Evans J, Van Dongen M. Ginkgo biloba for cognitive impairment and dementia (Cochrane Review). In: *The Cochrane Library*, issue 4 2002. Oxford:Update Software.

Brigelius-Flohe R, Kelly FJ, Salonen JT, et al. The European perspective on vitamin E: current knowledge and future research. *Am J Clin Nutr.* 2002;76 (4):703–716.

Craig W. Phytochemicals: guardians of our health. *J Am Diet Assoc.* 1997;97 (suppl 2):S199–S204.

Devaraj S, Jialal I. Alpha tocopherol supplementation decreases serum C-reactive protein and monocyte interleukin-6 levels in normal volunteers and type 2 diabetic patients. *Free Radic Biol Med.* 2000;29(8):790–792.

Eastwood MA. Interaction of dietary antioxidants in vivo: how fruit and vegetables prevent disease. *QJM* 1000;92(9):527–530.

Engelhart MJ, Geerlings MI, Ruitenberg A, et al. Dietary intake of antioxidants and risk of Alzheimer disease. *JAMA.* 2002;287(24):3223–3229.

Fung TT, Hu FB, Pereira MA, et al. Whole-grain intake and the risk of type 2 diabetes: a prospective study in men. *Am J Clin Nutr.* September 2002;76 (3):535–540.

Grant W. Dietary links to Alzheimer's disease. *Alz Dis Rev.* 1997;2:42–55.

Guo Z, Mitchell-Raymundo F, Yang H, et al. Dietary restriction reduces atherosclerosis and oxidative stress in the aorta of apolipoprotein E-deficient mice. *Mech Ageing Dev.* 2002;123(8):1121–1131.

Hakim IA, Harris RB, Weisgerber UM. Tea intake and squamous cell carcinoma of the skin: influence of type of tea beverages. Cancer *Epidemiol Biomarkers Prev.* 2000;9(7):727–731.

Hidaka H, Ishiko T, Furuhashi T, et al. Curcumin inhibits interleukin 8 production and enhances interleukin 8 receptor expression on the cell surface: impact on human pancreatic carcinoma cell growth by autocrine regulation. *Cancer.* 2002;95(6):1206–1214.

Holick CN, Michaud DS, Stolzenberg-Solomon R, et al. Dietary carotenoids, serum beta-carotene, and retinol and risk of lung cancer in the alpha-tocopherol, beta-carotene cohort study. *Am J Epidemiol.* 2002;156(6):536–547.

Ingram DK, Weindruch R, Spanger EL, et al. Dietary restriction benefits learning and motor performance of aged mice. *J Gerontol.* 1987;42:78–81.

Jenkins DJ, Kendal CW, Connelly PW, et al. Effects of high- and low-isoflavone (phytoestrogen) soy foods on inflammatory biomarkers and proinflammatory cytokines in middle-aged men and women. *Metabolism.* 2002;51(7):919–924.

John JH, Ziebland S, Yudkin P, et al. Effects of fruit and vegetable consumption on plasma antioxidant concentrations and blood pressure: a randomized controlled trial. *Lancet.* 2002;359(9322):1969–1974.

Kremer JM. n-3 fatty acid supplements in rheumatoid arthritis. *Am J Clin Nutr.* 2000;71(suppl 1):348S–351S.

Le Marchand L. Cancer preventive effects of flavonoids—a review. *Biomed Pharmacother.* 2002;56:296–301.

Lin CL, Fang TC, Gueng MK. Vascular dilatory functions of ovo-lactovegetarians compared with omnivores. *Atherosclerosis.* 2001;158(1):247–251.

Mahaffey KR. Methylmercury: a new look at the risks. *Public Health Rep.* 1999;114(5):396–399,402–413.

Maislos M, Abow-Rabiah Y, Zuili I, et al. Gorging and plasma HDL-cholesterol—the Ramadan model. *Eur J Clin Nutr.* 1998;52:127–130.

Marchioli R, Schweiger C, Tavazzi L, Valagussa F. Efficacy of n-3 polyunsaturated fatty acids after myocardial infarction: results of GISSI-Prevenzione trial. Gruppo Italiano per lo Studio della Sopravvivenza nell'Infarto Miocardico. *Lipids.* 2001;36(suppl):S119–S126.

Mayeux R, Costa R, Bell K, et al. Reduced risk of Alzheimer's disease among individuals with low calorie intake. *Neurology.* 1999;59:S296–S297.

McDougall J, Bruce B, Spiller G, et al. Effects of a very low-fat, vegan diet in subjects with rheumatoid arthritis. *J Altern Complement Med.* 2002;8(1):71–75.

Meydani M, Meydani M. Nutrition interventions in aging and age-associated disease. *Proc Nutr Soc.* 2002;61(2):165–171.

Nakachi K, Matsuyama S, Miyake S, et al. Preventive effects of drinking green tea on cancer and cardiovascular disease: epidemiological evidence for multiple targeting prevention. *Biofactors.* 2000;13:49–54.

Paisley JA. Beta-carotene and lung cancer: a review of randomized clinical trials. *Can J Diet Pract Res.* 1999;60(3):160–165.

Rissanen TH, Voutilainen S, Nyyssonen K, et al. Low serum lycopene concentration is associated with an excess incidence of acute coronary events and stroke: the Kuopio Ischaemic Heart Disease Risk Factor study. *Br J Nutr.* 2001;85(6):749–754.

Seaman DR. The diet-induced proinflammatory state: a cause of chronic pain and other degenerative diseases? *J Manipulative Physiol Ther.* 2002;25(3):168–179.

Sinclair H. The relative importance of essential fatty acids of the linoleic and linolenic families: studies with an Eskimo diet. *Prog Lipid Res.* 1981;20:897–899.

Stark AH, Madar Z. Olive oil as a functional food: epidemiology and nutritional approaches. *Nutr Rev.* 2002;60(6):170–176.

Thompson B, Demark-Wahnefried W, Taylor G, et al. Baseline fruit and vegetable intake among adults in seven 5 a day study centers located in diverse geographic areas. *J Am Diet Assoc.* 1999;99(10):1241–1248.

Walford RL, Mock D, Verdery R, MacCallum T. Calorie restriction in biosphere 2: alterations in physiologic, hematologic, hormonal, and biochemical parameters in humans restricted for a 2-year period. *J Gerontol A Biol Sci Med Sci.* 2002; 57(6):B211–B224.

Wooltorton E. Facts on mercury and fish consumption. *CMAJ.* 2002;167(8):897.

Youdim KA, Joseph JA. A possible emerging role of phytochemicals in improving age-related neurological dysfunctions: a multiplicity of effects. *Free Radic Biol Med.* 2001;30(6):583–594.

CHAPTER 10

Blondell J. Epidemiology of pesticide poisonings in the United States, with special reference to occupational cases. *Occup Med.* 1997;12:209–220.

Boffetta P, Dosemeci M, Gridley G, et al. Occupational exposure to diesel engine emissions and risk of cancer in Swedish men and women. *Cancer Causes Control.* 2001;12(4):365–374.

Book SA, Jackson RJ, Fan AM, et al. Health risk assessment of aerial application of malathion-bait. Berkeley, Calif.: California Department of Health Services, 1991.

Brook RD, Brook JR, Urch B, et al. Inhalation of fine particulate air pollution and ozone causes acute arterial vasoconstriction in healthy adults. *Circulation.* 2002; 105(13):1534–1536.

Buckley DA, Rycroft RJ, White IR, McFadden JP. Fragrance as an occupational allergen. *Occup Med.* 2002;52(1):13–16.

Eggleston PA, Bush RK. Environmental allergen avoidance: an overview. *J Allergy Clin Immunol.* 2001;107(3 suppl):S403–S405.

Hoffman RE, Wood RC, Kreiss K. Building-related asthma in Denver office workers. *Am J Public Health.* 1993;83:89–93.

Jarvis D, Chinn S, Luczynska C, Burney P. Association of respiratory symptoms and lung function in young adults with use of domestic gas appliances. *Lancet.* 1996;347(8999):426–431.

Kreutzer R, Harmon L, Hoshiko S. Citizen illness reports following February–May 1994 aerial malathion applications in Corona and Norco, Riverside County, California. Emeryville, California: California Department of Health Services, 1996.

Kumar P, Caradonna-Graham VM, Gupta S, et al. Inhalation challenge effects of perfume scent strips in patients with asthma. *Ann Allergy Asthma Immunol.* 1995; 75(5):429–433.

Menconi S, Clark JM, Langenberg P, Hryhorczuk D. A preliminary study of potential human health effects in private residences following chlordane applications for termite control. *Arch Environ Health.* 1988;43(5):349–352.

Robertson AS, Burge PS, Hedge A, et al. Comparison of health problems related to work and environmental measurements in two office buildings with different ventilation systems. *BMJ Clin Res Ed.* 1985;291:373–376.

Schanker HM, Rachelefsky G, Siegel S, et al. Immediate and delayed type hypersensitivity to malathion. *Ann Allergy.* 1992;69:526–528.

Scheinman PL. Prevalence of fragrance allergy. *Dermatology.* 2002;205(1):98–102.

Shafey O, Sekereke HJ Jr, Hughes BJ, et al. Surveillance for acute pesticide-related illness during the medfly eradication program—Florida, 1998. *MMWR Morb Mortal Wkly Rep.* 1999;48(44):1015–1018,1027.

Stallones L, Beseler C. Pesticide poisoning and depressive symptoms among farm residents. *Ann Epidemiol.* 2002;12(6):389–394.

Ziem G, McTamney J. Profile of patients with chemical injury and sensitivity. *Environ Health Perspect.* 1997;105(suppl 2):417–436.

CHAPTER 11

Abbot NC, Stead LF, White AR, et al. Hypnotherapy for smoking cessation. *Cochrane Database Syst Rev.* 2000;(2):CD001008.

Ahijevych K, Yerardi R, Nedilsky N. Descriptive outcomes of the American Lung Association of Ohio hypnotherapy smoking cessation program. *Int J Clin Exp Hypn.* 2000;48(4):374–387.

Bauldoff GS, Hoffman LA, Zullo TG, Sciurba FC. Exercise maintenance following pulmonary rehabilitation: effect of distractive stimuli. *Chest.* 2002;122 (3):948–954.

Bermudez EA, Rifai N, Burning J, et al. Interrelationships among circulating inter-leukin-6, C-reactive protein, and traditional cardiovascular risk factors in women. *Arterioscler Thromb Vasc Biol.* 2002;22(10):1668–1673.

Bertelli A, Migliori M, Bertelli AA, et al. Effect of some white wine phenols in pre-venting inflammatory cytokine release. *Drugs Exp Clin Res.* 2002;28(1):11–15.

Bertelli AA, Migliori M, Panichi V, et al. Oxidative stress and inflammatory reac-tion modulation by white wine. *Ann N Y Acad Sci.* 2002;957:295–301.

Church TS, Barlow CE, Earnest CP, et al. Associations between cardiorespiratory fitness and C-reactive protein in men. *Arterioscler Thromb Vasc Biol.* 2002;22 (11):1869–1876.

Churchill JD, Galvez R, Colcombe S, et al. Exercise, experience and the aging brain. *Neurobiol Aging.* 2002;23:941–955.

daLuz PL, Coimbra SR. Alcohol and atherosclerosis. *An Acad Bras Cienc.* 2001;73 (1):51–55. Abstract.

Ford ES. Does exercise reduce inflammation? Physical activity and C-reactive pro-tein among U.S. adults. *Epidemiology.* 2002;13(5):561–568.

Fries JF. Physical activity, the compression of morbidity, and the health of the eld-erly. *J R Soc Med.* 1996;89:64–68.

Fulton-Kehoe D, Hamman RF, Baxter J, Marshall J. A case-control study of phys-ical activity and non-insulin dependent diabetes mellitus (NIDDM). The San Luis Valley Diabetes Study. *Ann Epidemiol.* 2001;11(5):320–327.

Hasko G, Szabo C, Nemeth ZH, Deitch EA. Dopamine suppresses IL-12 p40 production by lipopolysaccharide-stimulated macrophages via a beta-adreno-ceptor-mediated mechanism. *J Neuroimmunol.* 2002;122(1–2):34–39.

Hennekens CH. Brisk walking and vigorous exercise provide similar cardiovascu-lar disease benefits. *Eur Heart J.* 2000;21:1559.

Ji LL. Exercise at old age: does it increase or alleviate oxidative stress? *Ann N Y Acad.* 2001;928:236–247.

Knoll J. Sexual performance and longevity. *Exp Gerontol.* 1997;32(4–5):539–552.

Kraus WE, Houmard JA, Duscha BD, et al. Effects of the amount and intensity of exercise on plasma lipoproteins. *N Engl J Med.* 2002;347(19):1483–1492.

Manson JE, Greenland P, LaCroix AZ, et al. Walking compared with vigorous exer-cise for the prevention of cardiovascular events in women. *N Engl J Med.* 2002; 347(10):716–725.

Nied RJ, Franklin B. Promoting and prescribing exercise for the elderly. *Am Fam Physician.* 2002;65(3):419–426.

Paffenbarger RS Jr, Hyde RT, Wing AL, Hsieh CC. Physical activity, all-cause mortality, and longevity of college alumni. *N Engl J Med.* 1986;314:605–613.

Rienzo A. The impact of aging on human sexuality. *J School Health.* 1985;55 (2):66–68.

Tanasescu M, Leitzmann MF, Rimm EB, et al. Exercise type and intensity in relation to coronary heart disease in men. *JAMA.* 2002;288(16):1994–2000.

Wang BWE, Ramey DR, Schettler JD, et al. Postponed development of disability in elderly runners: a 13-year longitudinal study. *Arch Intern Med.* 2002; 162:2285–2294.

White JR, Case DA, McWhirter D, Mattison AM. Enhanced sexual behavior in exercising men. *Arch Sex Behav.* 1990;19(3):193–209.

Woods JA, Lowder TW, Keylock KT. Can exercise training improve immune function in the aged? *Ann N Y Acad Sci.* 2002;959:117–127.

Zhang J, Liu Y, Shi J, et al. Side-stream cigarette smoke induces dose-response in systemic inflammatory cytokine production and oxidative stress. *Exp Biol Med* (Maywood) 2002;227(9):823–829.

CHAPTER 12

Appels A, Bar FW, Bar J, et al. Inflammation, depressive symptomatology, and coronary artery disease. *Psychosom Med.* 2000;62:601–605.

Barnes VA, Treiber FA, Davis H. Impact of Transcendental Meditation on cardiovascular function at rest and during acute stress in adolescents with high normal blood pressure. *J Psychosom Res.* 2001;51:597–605.

Barrick CB. Sad, glad, or mad hearts? Epidemiological evidence for a causal relationship between mood disorders and coronary artery disease. *J Affect Dis.* 1999; 53:193–201.

Berk LS, Felten DL, Tan SA, et al. Modulation of neuroimmune parameters during the eustress of humor-associated mirthful laughter. *Altern Ther Health Med.* 2001;7(2):62–72,74–76.

Berk LS, Tan SA, Fry WF, et al. Neuroendocrine and stress hormone changes during mirthful laughter. *Am J Med Sci.* 1989;298(6):390–396.

Berkman LF, Syme SL. Social networks, host resistance, and mortality: a nine-year follow-up study of Alameda County residents. *Am J Epidemiol.* 1979;109 (2):186–204.

Black PH, Garbutt LD. Stress, inflammation and cardiovascular disease. *J Psychosom Res.* 2002;52:1–23.

Brody AL, Saxena S, Stoessel P, et al. Regional brain metabolic changes in patients with major depression treated with either paroxetine or interpersonal therapy: preliminary findings. *Arch Gen Psychiatry.* 2001;58(7):631–640.

Carney RM, Freedland KE, Miller GE, Jaffe AS. Depression as a risk factor for cardiac mortality and morbidity. A review of potential mechanisms. *J Psychosom Res.* 2002;53:897–902.

Castanon N, Leonard BE, Neveu PJ, Yirmiya R. Effects of antidepressants on cytokine production and actions. *Brain Behav Immun.* 2002;16:569–574.

Chrousos GP. Stress, chronic inflammation, and emotional and physical well-being: concurrent effects and chronic sequelae. *J Allergy Clin Immunol.* 2000;106 (5):S275–S291.

Cousins N. Anatomy of an illness (as perceived by the patient). *N Engl J Med.* 1976; 295(26):1458–1463.

Dentino AN, Pieper CF, Rao KMK, et al. Association of interleukin-6 and other biologic variables with depression in older people living in the community. *J Am Geriatr Soc.* 1999;47:6–11.

Everson SA, Kauhanen J, Kaplan GA, et al. Hostility and increased risk of mortality and acute myocardial infarction: the mediating role of behavioral risk factors. *Am J Epidemiol.* 1997;146:142–152.

Fredrickson BL, Maynard KE, Helms MJ, et al. Hostility predicts magnitude and duration of blood pressure response to anger. *J Behav Med.* 2000;23(3):229–243.

Goebel MU, Mills PJ. Acute psychological stress and exercise and changes in peripheral leukocyte adhesion molecule expression and density. *Psychosom Med.* 2000;62:664–670.

Haines AP, Imeson JD, Meade TW. Phobic anxiety and ischemic heart disease. *BMJ Clin Res Educ.* 1987;295:297–299.

Holmes T, Rahe R. The social readjustment rating scale. *J Psychosom Res.* 1967; 11:213–218.

House JS, Landis KR, Umberson D. Social relationships and health. *Science.* 1988; 241:540–545.

Kawachi I, Sparrow D, Spiro A III, et al. A prospective study of anger and coronary heart disease. The Normative Aging Study. *Circulation.* 1996;94(9): 2090–2095.

Kawachi I, Sparrow D, Vokonas PS, Weiss ST. Symptoms of anxiety and risk of coronary heart disease. The Normative Aging Study. *Circulation.* 1994;90: 2225–2229.

Kiecolt-Glaser JK, McGuire L, Robles TF, Glaser R. Emotions, morbidity, and mortality: new perspectives from psychoneuroimmunology. *Annu Rev Psychol.* 2002;53:83–107.

Kimata H. Effect of humor on allergen-induced wheal reactions. *JAMA.* 2001; 285(6):738.

Kivimaki M, Leino-Arjas P, Luukkonen R, et al. Work stress and risk of cardio-vascular mortality: prospective cohort study of industrial employees. *BJM.* 2002; 325:857–861.

Koh KB. Emotion and immunity. *J Psychosom Res.* 1998;45(2):107–115.

Levenson RW, Ekman P, Friesen WV. Voluntary facial action generates emotion-specific autonomic nervous system activity. *Psychophysiology.* 1990;27:363–384.

Levy BR, Slade MD, Kasl SV. Longitudinal benefit of positive self-perceptions of aging on functional health. *J Gerontol B Psychol Sci Soc Sci.* 2002;57(5): P409–P417.

Liu LY, Coe Cl, Swenson CA, et al. School examinations enhance airway inflam-mation to antigen challenge. *Am J Respir Crit Care Med.* 2002;165(8):1062–1067.

Maes M, Bosmans E, De Jongh R, et al. Increased serum IL-6 and IL-1 receptor antagonist concentrations in major depression and treatment resistant depres-sion. *Cytokine.* 1997;9(11):853–858.

Maes M, Christophe A, Bosmans E, et al. In humans, serum polyunsaturated fatty acid levels predict the response of proinflammatory cytokines to psychologic stress. *Biol Psychiatry.* 2000;47:910–920.

Maes M, Song C, Lin A, et al. The effects of psychological stress on humans: increased production of pro-inflammatory cytokines and a Th1-like response in stress-induced anxiety. *Cytokine.* 1998;10(4):313–318.

Martin SD, Martin E, Rai SS, et al. Brain blood flow changes in depressed patients treated with interpersonal psychotherapy or venlafaxine hydrochloride: prelim-inary findings. *Arch Gen Psychiatry.* 2001;58(7):641–648.

Maruta T, Colligan RC, Malinchoc M, Offord KP. Optimism-pessimism assessed in the 1960s and self-reported health status 30 years later. *Mayo Clin Proc.* 2002; 77(8):748–753.

Mix C, Bergmann S, Muhlpfordt S, et al. Influence of psychosocial resources on the relationship between lifestyle and cardiovascular or mental health. *Clin Lab.* 2001;47(9–10):493–495.

Niaura R, Todaro JF, Stroud, et al. Hostility, the metabolic syndrome, and incident coronary heart disease. *Health Psychol.* 2002;21(6):588–593.

Rahe RH, Romo M, Bennett L, Siltanen P. Recent life changes, myocardial infarction, and abrupt coronary death. *Arch Intern Med.* 1974;133:221–228.

Rozanski A, Blumenthal JA, Kaplan J. Impact of psychological factors on the pathogenesis of cardiovascular disease and implications for therapy. *Circulation.* 1999; 99(16):2192–2217.

Schneider RH, Staggers F, Alexander CN, et al. A randomized controlled trial of stress reduction for hypertension in older African Americans. *Hypertension.* 1995; 26:820–827.

Sluzewska A, Rybakowski JK, Laciak M, et al. Interleukin-6 serum levels in depressed patients before and after treatment with fluoxetine. *Ann N Y Acad Sci.* 1995;762:474–476.

Surwit RS, van Tilburg MAL, Zucker N, et al. Stress management improves long-term glycemic control in type 2 diabetes. *Diabetes Care.* 2002;25:30–34.

Torres SR, Frode TS, Nardi GM, et al. Anti-inflammatory effects of peripheral benzodiazepine receptor ligands in two mouse models of inflammation. *Eur J Pharmacol.* 2000;408(2):199–211.

Uchino BN, Cacioppo JT, Kiecolt-Glaser JK. The relationship between social support and physiological processes: a review with emphasis on underlying mechanisms and implications for health. *Psychol Bull.* 1996;119(3):488–531.

Weber-Hamann B, Hentschel F, Kniest A, et al. Hypercortisolemic depression is associated with increased intra-abdominal fat. *Psychosom Med.* 2002;64 (2):274–277.

Zeitlin D, Keller SE, Shiflett SC, et al. Immunological effects of massage therapy during academic stress. *Psychosom Med.* 2000;62:83–84.

CHAPTER 13

Blake GJ, Ridker PM. Inflammatory bio-markers and cardiovascular risk prediction. *J Intern Med.* 2002;252(4):283–294.

Crea F, Monaco C, Lanza GA, et al. Inflammatory predictors of mortality in the Scandinavian Simvastatin Survival Study. *Clin Cardiol.* 2002;25(10):461–466.

De Denus S, Spinler SA. Early statin therapy for acute coronary syndromes. *Ann Pharmacother.* 2002;36(11):1749–1758.

in t' Veld BA, Ruitenberg A, Hofman A, et al. Nonsteroidal antiinflammatory drugs and the risk of Alzheimer's disease. *N Engl J Med.* 2001;345(21):1515–1521.

Kiel DP, Felson DT, Anderson JJ, et al. Hip fracture and the use of estrogens in postmenopausal women: the Framingham Study. *N Engl J Med.* 1987;317 (19):1169–1174.

Koh KK. Effects of estrogen on the vascular wall: vasomotor function and inflammation. *Cardiovasc Res.* 2002;55(4):714–726.

Lauer MS. Clinical practice. Aspirin for primary prevention of coronary events. *N Engl J Med.* 2002;346(19):1468–1474.

Meroni PL, Luzzana C, Ventura D. Anti-inflammatory and immunomodulating properties of statins. An additional tool for the therapeutic approach of systemic autoimmune diseases? *Clin Rev Allergy Immunol.* 2002;23(3):263–277.

Pradhan AD, Manson JE, Rossouw JE, et al. Inflammatory biomarkers, hormone replacement therapy, and incident coronary heart disease. *JAMA.* 2002;288 (8):980–987.

Ridker PM, Rifai N, Rose L, et al. Comparison of C-reactive protein and low-density lipoprotein cholesterol levels in the prediction of first cardiovascular events. *N Engl J Med.* 2002;347(20):1557–1565.

Schiffrin EL. Vascular and cardiac benefits of angiotensin receptor blockers. *Am J Med.* 2002;113(5):409–418.

Writing Group for the Women's Health Initiative Investigators. Risks and benefits of estrogen plus progestin in healthy postmenopausal women: principal results from the Women's Health Initiative randomized controlled trial. *JAMA.* 2002; 288(3):321–333.

Youssef S, Stuve O, Patarroyo JC, et al. The HMG-CoA reductase inhibitor, atorvastatin, promotes a Th2 bias and reverses paralysis in central nervous system autoimmune disease. *Nature.* 2002;420(6911):78–84.

Yusuf S, Sleight P, Pogue J, et al. Effects of an angiotensin-converting-enzyme inhibitor, ramipril, on cardiovascular events in high-risk patients. The Heart Outcomes Prevention Evaluation Study Investigators. *N Engl J Med.* 2000; 342(3):145–153.

Zamvil SS, Steinman L. Cholesterol-lowering statins possess anti-inflammatory activity that might be useful for treatment of MS. *Neurology.* 2002;59 (7):970–971.

Zandi PP, Anthony JC, Hayden KM, et al. Reduced incidence of AD with NSAID but not H2 receptor antagonists: the Cache County Study. *Neurology.* 2002;59 (6):880–886.

APPENDIX

Meggs WJ. Biological homing: hypothesis for a quantum effect that leads to the existence of life. *Med Hypotheses.* 1998;51:503–506.

Whitaker A. *Einstein, Bohr, and the quantum dilemma.* Cambridge: Cambridge University Press; 1996.

INDEX

◉